List of Contents

CENSORSHIP IN PUBLIC LIBRARIES

in the United Kingdom during the Twentieth Century

ANTHONY HUGH THOMPSON

BOWKER
1975

First published in 1975 by the Bowker Publishing Company, Epping, Essex, England

Printed and bound in Great Britain by
Redwood Burn Limited, Trowbridge & Esher
Photoset by Amos Typesetters, Hockley, Essex

Censorship in
Public Libraries
in the United Kingdom during the
Twentieth Century

"Blessed are the pure, for they shall inhibit the earth"
—H. Caen, *San Francisco Chronicle,* January 1969

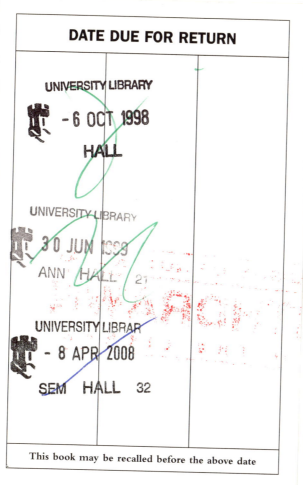

List of Illustrations

Acknowledgements

Firstly, I must express my thanks to all those who have contributed to the production of this book: to the Librarian and Information Officer of the Library Association and his staff, and the Librarian of the College of Librarianship, Wales, and his staff, for supplying me with information and answering my queries; to my colleagues at the College, particularly Michael Wise and Peter Wright, to Robert Phillips for his graphics, and my typists, Wendy Reader, Wendy Stoddart and Briggitte Heller. My gratitude is also due to those librarians who so kindly answered my questions, supplied me with additional information and encouraged me in the task, particularly John Bebbington, John Allen and Kenneth Stockham. A particular acknowledgement is due to Margaret R. Whiteman, Librarian of the Welsh Agricultural College, who compiled the comprehensive index which forms a valuable contribution to this book. Especial thanks to my friends Philip Whiteman, Head of the Department of Social and Management Studies at the College of Librarianship, Wales, for his constant advice and encouragement, and to my wife, Kathryn, for her interest, patience and considerable help.

Secondly, I wish to thank ALL those whose work is quoted and used in this book, for wherever possible material has been reproduced in its original form. Full bibliographical citations of all material used in the text are given in the Bibliography. I am grateful to the following for permission to reproduce material from their publications:

An Leabharlann
Association of Assistant
   Librarians
Banbury Guardian
Baptist Times
Belfast Telegraph
Birmingham Post and Mail Ltd

Blackburn Evening Telegraph
Blackburn Times
The Bookseller
Bridgnorth Journal
Brighton and Hove Gazette
Burnley Express
Caernarvon Herald

Cambrian News
Chester Chronicle
Chronicle and Echo, Northampton
Croydon Advertiser Group of Newspapers
Cumberland and Westmorland Herald
Daily Mail
Daily Telegraph
Denbighshire Free Press
Dimbleby Newspaper Group
Dudley Herald
Ealing Public Library Service
East Anglian Daily Times Co. Ltd
East Kent Gazette
Edinburgh Corporation
Essex and Chelmsford Weekly News
Evening Express (Aberdeen Journals Ltd)
Evening Gazette, Teesside
Evening Post, Hemel Hempstead
T. Bailey Foreman, Ltd
Gay News
Gazette Series, Middlesex County Press Group
Glasgow Herald
Greenock Telegraph
The Guardian
Hanson Books
Heart of England Newspapers Ltd
Her Majesty's Stationery Office
Herts Advertiser
Hertfordshire County Library Service
Hertfordshire Mercury Series
Highland News Group
Huddersfield Examiner
Henry Hughes Newspapers Ltd
Hull Daily Mail
Keswick Reminder
Lancaster Guardian Series
Liaison

The Library Association
Library Review
Liverpool Daily Post
Llandudno Advertiser
London and Essex Guardian Newspapers Ltd
London Express News and Feature Services
London Evening News
Luton Evening Post
Manchester Evening News
Manchester Public Libraries
Morning Telegraph, Sheffield
Municipal and Public Services Journal
National Book League
Nelson Leader and Colne Times Ltd
The News and Advertiser Group, West Cheshire Newspapers Ltd
New Statesman
Newbury Weekly News
Newcastle Evening Chronicle
Newsagent and Bookshop
North Eastern Evening Gazette Ltd
North London Press
North Western Evening Mail
Northamptonshire Evening Telegraph
Northern Echo
The Observer
Oldham Chronicle
Oldham Evening Chronicle
Paisley Daily Express
The Press Association
Richmond Herald
Rochdale Observer Series
Salop County Library Service
The Scotsman
Scottish Library Association News
Sevenoaks Chronicle
Shropshire Star Ltd
South East London Mercury

South Lancashire Newspapers Ltd
Southport Visiter Group of
  Newspapers
W. H. Smith and Son Ltd
Staffordshire Sentinel
  Newspapers Ltd
The Star, Sheffield
The Sun
Sunday Express
Sunday Mail
Surrey and South London
  Newspapers
Surrey Herald Newspapers
Surveyor
Syndication International
Telegraph and Argus, Bradford
Time and Tide
Tonbridge Free Press
Tribune
Weekly News Group on
  Merseyside
Welwyn Times and *Hatfield
  Advertiser*
West Lancashire Evening Gazette
West London Observer
West Suffolk Newspapers Ltd
Western Daily Press
Western Mail and Echo Ltd
Western Telegraph
Weston Mercury
Wiltshire Newspapers
Worthing Gazette
Yarmouth Mercury
Yorkshire Post Newspapers Ltd

Craig, Alec. *The Banned Books of England.* George Allen and Unwin
  Ltd.
Neville Spearman Ltd, for the reproduction of the illustration on the
  Hertfordshire County Library Service Booklist: "Sex and Marriage",
  taken from I and S Hegler, *An ABZ of Love.*
Material from *The Sunday Times, The Times* and *The Times Literary
  Supplement* reproduced by permission of Times Newspapers Ltd.
Blishen, Edward. "Who's afraid of Enid Blyton?", reprinted from
  Where, the education magazine for parents, published by the
  Advisory Centre for Education, Cambridge.
Tucker, Nicholas. "All things Blyton beautiful" printed in *The Times
  Literary Supplement,* reproduced by permission of the author.

Notes

1. Bibliographical citations are in the form prescribed in British
   Standard for *Bibliographical References* (B.S. 1629:1950).
2. Periodical and newspaper titles in the text are given in the form used
   in the *Newspaper Press Directory,* London, Benn Brothers.

Introduction

This work began as a thesis presented to the Queens University of Belfast for the degree of Master of Arts in 1972. To present it as a book has necessitated some considerable editing, and over a third of the original work has been removed. The style of the thesis has been retained to avoid excessive verbosity (!) and to allow the reader to reach his own conclusions. The cases which remain present a complete cross section of the many cases that have occurred over the last seventy-five years. They are usually presented in the language of the original, for any attempt to paraphrase would have clouded the facts and the emotions involved and destroyed the considerable element of humour found in many of them.

Censorship in public libraries is a fascinating and significant aspect of the total area of censorship, and hitherto there has been little collection and examination of material relating specifically to British libraries. Censorship in some form is known to exist in libraries in the non-public sector, but on a far smaller scale than in the public sector, and often for different reasons. Nor is public library censorship confined to the United Kingdom—all countries with public library services have or have had to face this problem. Much has been written on the subject in the United States, for instance.

Although public libraries have been in existence in the United Kingdom for over 100 years, this book is confined to censorship in them during this century. This period was chosen because it offered the possibility of access to full reports of events and to first hand accounts from some of the people involved. Furthermore, it is a period which has seen considerable changes in standards of acceptability.

Source material is of three main types: 1. press cuttings, mostly from local newspapers; 2. papers, notes and comment in the leading professional journals; 3. information supplied to the author by librarians. While the authenticity of material from sources 2 and 3 can usually be relied upon, some newspaper reports may be biased, inaccurate and/or distorted, and this fact made it necessary in certain instances to interpret such reports to maintain a proper perspective.

Some definition of terms is necessary. The Oxford English Dictionary defines *censorship* and *censor* as follows:

censorship. The office or function of a censor . . .

(a) *censor*. One who exercises official or officious supervision over morals and conduct.

(to) *censor*. Official licensing, or suppressing as immoral, seditious, or inopportune, books, plays, news, . . .

In the United Kingdom there are only two sources of "official supervision" for the arts: the State, which exercises certain controls on a variety of art forms through the law of the land; and the British Board of Film Censors, established by the film industry to operate a self-imposed system of control in respect of films shown to the public. State control is not a significant factor in most of the cases discussed in this book, since they mainly concern attempts to restrict access to literature which has not been the subject of action by the State.

The object then is to examine 'officious supervision'. The Oxford English Dictionary provides further definitions:

officious. Unduly forward in proffering services or taking business upon oneself; doing, or prone to do, more than is asked or required; interfering with what is not one's concern; pragmatical, meddlesome.

officiousness. Over-forwardness in proffering services or taking anything upon one as a duty; well-intentioned meddlesomeness.

The last term "well intentioned meddlesomeness" is an expressive phrase, but are the facts of censorship in public libraries as simple as that? I hope some of the cases here presented will enable readers to come to their own conclusions.

Local government reorganisation took place in 1974 during the preparation of this book. The names of library services and their librarians are given in their correct form before reorganisation, when many of these library authorities were amalgamated to produce the present network of fewer, larger public library systems.

CHAPTER 1

Censorship 1900–1939

Censorship in public libraries is as old as the public library movement itself; and from its beginnings in the 1850's, control has been exercised over the subject matter of the material purchased. In many cases the censorship was more blatant at this time than in later years, due mainly to the constraints on literary freedom imposed by the attitudes of the Victorian era.

Before examining the situation in the rate supported public library, reference must be made to one of its predecessors, the commercial circulating library. These libraries were at their most popular in the mid-nineteenth century; and despite the development of the rate supported public libraries, they lingered on until the middle of this century. They exercised a considerable influence over the literature of the nineteenth century in that reputable authors wrote only what they knew would be acceptable to the circulating libraries and also to the booksellers, who would not countenance anything which could not safely be read aloud in the family circle. Thus authors adopted a self-imposed censorship.

During this time Mudie's Circulating Library was the most important single distributor of fiction in England; and Mudie and his rival W. H. Smith exerted such a profound influence over publishers, critics, and readers that they became virtual dictators of the literary world; and neither escaped the deserved epithet of "censor".

George Moore, in his *Literature at Nurse, or Circulating Morals* published in 1885,[1] attacked Mudie and Smith for their censorial selection policy and appealed to readers to withdraw their support of the libraries for failing to supply the books they wanted. George Moore's attack was but one of many by authors, publishers, periodicals and readers on a system which they were nevertheless unable to break down. In the minds of the moral reformers these libraries were considered a potential threat. Hannah More, a noted supporter of various societies for the suppression of vice, so plentiful at the beginning of the nineteenth century, was deeply concerned about the effects of literature on the minds of women and children, and the working classes. She had no such fears for the moral state of the intellectual reader, but was convinced that others would be corrupted by "the hot-bed of the circulating library".[2]

It was against the background of this tradition that the circulating librarian was the guardian of the morals of his readers, that the public library movement gained momentum.

In 1907, the Dewsbury Public Library Committee submitted the following resolution to the Town Council for confirmation:

> "'That the works of Fielding and Smollett be placed in sole and separate charge of the librarian, and that he be instructed to use his discretion as to the issue of the same'. An application was made a short time ago for Fielding's works, which were then in the Reference Library, to be placed in the Circulating Library (i.e. Lending Library), but before the Library Committee determined what to do the members agreed to take a copy of the books in question home. Last week there was quite a scene at the Library Committee meeting, there being amongst other suggestions one that Fielding's works should be burned. The outcome, however, of the meeting was the above named resolution.
>
> Mr. F. Dwyer said the Library Committee had been held up to the derision and contempt of Dewsbury and the West Riding. He was in antagonism to his colleagues on the committee. Mr. Hanson was simply delirious at the meeting, and threw one of Fielding's books down on the table. He (Mr. Dwyer) did not think Mr. Hanson had ever read a work of fiction before unless it had been his 'Parish Magazine', and he (Mr. Hanson) considered that the particular work he had had was disgusting, immoral, indecent, and shameful. The Mayor was simply frozen with horror (laughter), and he (Mr. Dwyer) did not think his Worship had read a work of fiction since he read 'Goody Twoshoes', and he thought probably that that was indecent because she had only got one shoe on (loud laughter).
>
> The Mayor: I shall not allow that. I think it is really too bad. We are discussing business, not frivolity. Mr. Waddington . . . said that notwithstanding the violent fulminations of the self-constituted litterateurs during the past week, the Library Committee was to be congratulated upon its action in proposing to put an embargo upon those works, and the committee were also to be congratulated upon its lack of that fine taste which would enable it to fully appreciate such bawdy and indecent stuff as was contained in Fielding's works. Art derived its dignity from its relations to high thought, but the contents of those works in the lump were base, grovelling, vulgar and indecent. . . . Mr. Gledhill and Mr. Wilby by no means sympathised with any suggestion to destroy the books, because they considered that adults should have the opportunity of seeing them if they desired to do so."[3]

Ann Veronica by H. G. Wells was withdrawn from circulation by the Beverley Public Library Committee in February 1910.

"We are informed that strong indignation was expressed at Beverley that library committees and libraries should find themselves at the mercy of able writers who suddenly put upon the market, as an expression of their deliberate teaching, such philosophy as is contained in *Ann Veronica*. It may be said at once that *Ann Veronica* is by no means food for babes and while one would not go to the length of endorsing either the view of the *Spectator* or the action of the Beverley Committee, it must be admitted that the story of Mr. Wells' emancipated young lady ought not to be handed about indiscriminately. . . . We are informed, too, that as the outcome of the discussion, the Beverley Librarian has advised that in future no work of fiction shall be bought until it has stood the test of twelve months' criticism, and that this view was unanimously adopted. Whatever may be said of *Ann Veronica*, this is certainly a censorship with a vengeance, and we shall be very much surprised if those who are sincerely concerned about books in Beverley, or at any rate concerned with the books issued by the Public Library, do not resent very strongly the action of the Mandarins. How many novels does one care to read twelve months after their publication, and we presume there must be people even in Beverley who are anxious to keep abreast of the literary movements of their times."[4]

Five days later the book was considered by the Hull Public Libraries Committee. The *Yorkshire Post* coyly described it as "a certain new novel by a well-known author".

"The Sub-Committee had decided that five copies of the book which had been purchased should not be put into circulation, but a resolution was moved in opposition to this that the book be issued. In the course of the debate Canon Lambert said he had read the book—it had been his painful duty—and he would just as soon send a daughter of his to a house infected with diptheria or typhoid as put that book into her hands. Alderman Hanger, who moved that the book be issued, argued that it dealt with a problem which would sooner or later engage the attention of the public. . . . Canon Lambert said the Committee were following the example of nearly all the great public libraries in the kingdom. At Birmingham, the book was considered unsuitable for general circulation; Bristol had its withdrawal under consideration; at Cardiff, it was not placed in general circulation; at Leeds, the Librarian refrained from asking the committee to purchase; at Leicester, it was not in the Library; at Liverpool, it was not added; at Manchester, several copies were purchased on the strength of the author's name, but were not to be put into circulation; at Newcastle and Nottingham, the book was read by members of the committee, and not placed in the Library; at Sheffield the book was not purchased, at Bradford it was in the library. Bradford was practically the only one which had put the book in circulation. The question they had to decide was whether they should deliberately circulate a book of this character, instead of allowing those who wanted it to buy it. Up to the present respectable people had had confidence in sending their sons or daughters to the libraries for good books. If that confidence was lost, he was quite sure many people would fight shy of the books in the library altogether. . . . Mr. W. C. Dawson, . . . said . . . 'A novel was read by all sorts of callow youths and girls with unformed characters and undisciplined minds, and it did a terrible amount of harm . . .'.

The resolution was defeated, only three members voting in favour. The sub-committee's minutes were accordingly confirmed, and the book banned."[5]

In 1913, Henry Fielding's *Tom Jones* was banned in Doncaster.

"The Mayor of Doncaster, presiding over a meeting of the Corporation, put forward a motion that a special committee be appointed to inquire into the management of the Doncaster Public Library and the constitution and powers of the Free Library Committee, which has earned notoriety by banning *Tom Jones*. The action of the Committee, said the Mayor, had subjected the Corporation to a great deal of criticism and if they must endure this, then they should have some control over the actions of the Committee.

Alderman J. F. Clarke proceeded to explain the methods adopted by the committee. When this book was referred to, a member objected—it was not he—and extracts were presented, some indecent, impure, and objectionable. The committee decided it was not a suitable book for admission; but whatever might have been the habits 150 years ago, it was not a suitable book for young people—or for old people, either—to have access to in a free library.

The same course has been adopted with regard to other books, and he instanced *The Celibate's Wife*, which was taken out, and by agreement of the committee burned."[6]

In 1926, the *Saturday Review* ran a series of reports which showed that the Press, then as now, could sometimes get its facts wrong. In an article *Prudes in Council*, in the issue of 20th November 1926, it reported:

"The high-minded ladies and gentlemen who prowl our public parks in the hope of detecting indecency have far too long monopolized the world's admiration; and the daily press does no more than bare justice in calling attention to another regiment of moralists who, while we and our companions slept, have been modestly and quietly taking care of our morals. Twelve libraries were visited, says the *Daily News,* and it was found that, at ten out of twelve, 'the librarians exercised private discrimination against many authors. At five, the books had been taken from the public shelves and kept out of sight in locked cupboards or private rooms. At nearly all libraries certain works of Bernard Shaw, Thomas Hardy, and other authors have been excluded'. So much for the general situation, which could hardly be more satisfactory. But there is a greater treat in store for us; for when we come down to particular instances we are afforded a fascinating glimpse of the men who busy themselves, day in day out, in making the suburbs safe for prudery. Unflinchingly, one must suppose, they read these doubtful books; with their long sensitive noses they smell out the offence; and then eyes glistening with joy in a good deed done, they lock it away out of sight and out of reach of those less generously endowed by nature with the power to withstand temptation. What they suffer in this cause, the sacred cause of minding other people's business, only they themselves can know. And they suffer with no thought or hope of reward, unless it is sufficient reward to have protected a few thousands of their countrymen from the wit and sanity of

Bernard Shaw, and from the strength and austere beauty of Hardy's novels; a sanity in which the prurient may cleanse themselves, a strength from which the weak may derive courage.

Let us approach nearer to these admirable librarians and let us in imagination—so far as cold print may assist us—listen to their voices. First of all there is the gentleman who speaks for Croydon: 'We keep a watch on borrowers, and if we find anyone specializing in a certain type of fiction, we put a stop to them having those books'. An enemy might affect to hear in this utterance a note of that insufferable complacency which proceeds inevitably from the union of ignorance and conceit. ... Sure of their mission, undeterred by doubt, unhampered by intelligence, these censors go on quietly and uncomplainingly with their self-appointed task of supervision. In the service of fallen humanity they wear their little brains away; indeed, signs are not wanting that this process is within an ace of completion. *The Prussian Officer* was banned at Bromley, said an official; and he added, by way of explanation: 'An old lady borrower raised an objection to it'. Bromley, perhaps in deference to the wishes of this same old lady, withholds from circulation many novels by Anatole France. But Bromley does not, in its method of procedure, exhibit the admirably unscrupulous cunning employed at Balham, where, we are told, 'there is no open access, but a number index is exhibited by which a borrower is able to tell whether a book is in or out. Many of these numbers are kept permanently turned down to indicate that the books are out'. By means of this masterly mendacity Balham readers are spared the acquaintance of Fielding . . . ."[7]

A week later, W. C. Berwick Sayers, the Chief Librarian of Croydon, replied to the *Saturday Review:*

"Having so delectable a theme to exploit, it was probably too attractive for your brilliant, but uninformed, writer to test the authenticity of the statements in the *Daily News* on which his effort is based. As, however, Croydon is specifically mentioned, and as, among other quite picturesque descriptions of my mental and spiritual qualities, I am honoured as one of 'these illiterate busy-bodies', may I be allowed to say that: (i) the statements attributed to 'a Croydon Librarian' were not made by me or by any responsible member of my staff, and that they are merely perversions of the truth. The statement, for example, that 'we keep a watch on readers of a certain type of book' is fantastic. (ii) I have made a protest to the editor of the *Daily News* and have invited him to publish the actual facts: but, as they are quite undramatic, my request has been ignored.

Your article is in the best traditional *Saturday* style. At the same time, one may ask if truth is not of more consequence than an opportunity to call librarians names, brilliantly and anonymously? Your writer probably knows perfectly well that the whole thing is a trumped-up newspaper stunt, and an old and extremely silly one."[8]

In the same issue Berwick Sayers received unexpected support from a Croydon reader, H. M. Tomlinson:

"If I could add anything to the strength of your protest against the censoring of literature by officials I would do so; but nothing could be added. You are exactly right. . . . But in one particular you are unfair. I know very well you would not be unjust to a man who is, with knowledge and insight, trying to induce in a community a love of things of the mind. I refer only to the Chief of Croydon's Public Library. His work in Croydon is of inestimable value to us here. I should say he is the town's most valuable public servant. He certainly works with enthusiasm and understanding to improve its light. . . . The words, 'we keep a watch on borrowers', are so utterly alien from the spirit of his shelves that until he confesses that they are precisely his own words I shall find it hard to accept them. And so would you, if you knew the library here."[9]

Also in the same issue, the Editor of the *Saturday Review* wrote:

"We need hardly say that we accept without reserve the disclaimer of the Chief Librarian of Croydon and the assurances of those who have written in his support. In fairness to ourselves we must point out that our remarks were entirely based on statements made in an article published on November 15th in the *Daily News* . . . we have since satisfied ourselves that the Chief Librarian of Croydon was never interviewed, and we have his assurance that to the best of his belief no member of his staff was interviewed either. . . . we are assured that at Croydon Public Libraries *all* books are catalogued. . . . Every quotation in our article was taken *verbatim* from the *Daily News* article. Supposing all the facts alleged in that article to have been as stated, our comments on them would have been fully justified."[10]

Further comment on the *Saturday Review's* reports and apologies appeared in *Constable's Monthly List,* January 1927.

"The eternal problem of literary censorship has lifted a new but agreeably characteristic head. In the old days the circulating libraries were the cockshies for all the indignation of the libertarians: their treatment of the 'daring' novel was declared a grave threat to national culture, their standards of criticism were held—alike by Chelsea, Hampstead, and Bloomsbury, (for once unanimous)—to be deplorable. But lately this particular outcry has been stilled. Perhaps the circulating libraries have given less offence. Perhaps (if this is not too much to hope) the undeniable fact has at last been accepted that any man or body of men have a perfect right to offer for sale or paid loan precisely those commodities which they contract to offer and (unless they wish to do so) no others whatsoever.

But into the place of martyr-circulators have today been thrust the public free librarians. Once more the stakes support their burden, once more the flames of bright artistic rage crackle fiercely about the feet of men who dare to assume that every book published is not like every other book, nor can suitably be given into the hands of every man, woman or child. . . . For heaven's sake let us have a little commonsense in this essentially practical matter! A public librarian is perfectly right to exercise his judgment in administering a certain type of book; that is what he is there for. But a publisher has an equal right to publish whatsoever book he cares to sponsor; that is what *he* is there for. A sensible publisher will no more complain of the decision of a sensible librarian than will the librarian attack the publisher for acting as he wishes within his particular province. On the other hand, it does not follow that the librarian and the publisher always exercise their right of judgment wisely; they are liable to err (like anyone else), they have their tastes and prejudices (like anyone else), but at least they put their names to what they do—and that is not quite so universal a habit as it might be. Wherefore let those who have no sin of bad judgment on their conscience throw the first and any subsequent stones at publisher, at author, at librarian. But if they have a speck of dust upon the whiteness of their infallibility, they had better mind their own business; it probably needs minding—and badly."[11]

Stanley Snaith, then Chief Assistant in Islington Public Libraries, contributed to the *Library Assistant,* June 1928. This was an eloquent plea for intellectual freedom in the public library.

". . . I have reached the conclusion that no ultimate good can come of a censorship, or any other agency by which that natural scope is curtailed. I lay this down as a first principle of my argument: the fact that a book repels me is no reason why *you* should be deprived of it; conversely, if *I* want a book I am justified in regarding *your* disapprobation, however reasonable in your own eyes, as irrelevant. The right to force a particular book upon someone else, is a right to which few of us would lay claim. Far less would we be justified in impuning one another's liberty of choice . . . In Comstockery we see the effects of a positive censorship usurping the rights of the statutory censor. . . . An example very near home is that of public libraries. For some obscure reason librarians have taken it upon themselves to decide whether or not a book is fit to read, and whether their borrowers shall be allowed to read it. To keep certain books out of the reach of very young readers is one thing. Gratuitously to coddle the virtue of mature citizens is quite another. To this kind of interference librarians show a growing tendency; and it cannot be too strongly deprecated. No one will deny that a wise discrimination is legitimate; but for heaven's sake let it end there. To become hagridden with the mania for segregating books is to make our profession ridiculous in the eyes of intelligent men and women. Our job is to buy good books. Our job is to avoid bad books. But definitely it is not our job to deny our readers' contact with the facts of life and to help old ladies to preserve their chastity. . . . The dispersion of enlightenment, the promulgation of sane ideals, surely it is to pursue these purposes libraries have come into being? We cannot serve them by officialdom, by suspicion, by obscurantism, by narrowmindedness.

I have heard it objected that to withdraw a book from the open shelves is not necessarily to deny readers access to it. This is surely a quite invalid argument. A large proportion of our readers are at all times shy of coming into contact with authority; and would rather go without a book—particularly an ostracised book—than ask for it. Moreover, it is reasonable to ask at whose instigation a book is removed from access. It appears that in most cases a single dissentient voice is sufficient. Now I suggest in all seriousness that a single complaint, or a dozen complaints, are insufficient evidence of a book's offensiveness. There is one fact of which we must not lose sight; satisfaction is proverbially less loquacious than dissatisfaction. A reader who is disgusted by a book (especially the type of person who is easily disgusted) will say so; whereas the reader who is *not* disgusted will have no reason to make any comment at all. Thus against half a dozen borrowers who complain, there are probably a score who approve. Yet a casual objection appears to be sufficient to cause the Librarian to cast the offender into the limbo of his strongroom. . . . by such a verdict is the common man deprived of the books to which his own purse has contributed. . . . My point is that without mutual tolerance society could not hold together; and such a tolerance is as necessary in judging books as in anything else. To insist upon a book of debatable propriety being allowed to circulate is not at all despotic, for the man who objects to it need not read it (though he probably will). But to threaten free access to a book is despotism most flagrant. Moreover, many librarians, it seems, do not even wait for complaints, but protect themselves in advance by withdrawing anything which they think likely to provoke adverse criticism on the grounds of morality. . . . For tracking out oblique allusions and significant undercurrents, they have an exquisite and phenomenal skill that is worthy of a better use.

Dare we confess that, because we are custodians of books, we regard the morals of the average man and woman as inferior to our own? If so, what condescension, what effrontery; or do we, on the contrary, credit others with the impeccable rectitude which we attribute to ourselves? Whichever attitude we adopt, it is no excuse for setting ourselves up as arbiters of public virtue . . . We are ourselves so godly, or so ungodly, that it never occurs to us to trust him, to leave his personal decency in the best possible hands—his own.

Another point. The Librarian who exercises this function must realize that he is actually helping to make 'dangerous' books more dangerous. It is proverbial that everything subversive thrives upon repression, often attracting, by its very unpopularity, a body of distinguished support. . . . The obvious way to combat an undesirable influence is to leave it alone to perish of its own obscurity and inanition."[12]

In the *East Anglian Daily Times,* December 1934, censorship in libraries was discussed in an editorial.

"The question of a censorship of novels has recently been discussed in various forms. The Westminster Libraries Committee recommend that a British Board of Novel Censors might be set up, something after the manner of the British Board of Film Censors, and most library committees would no doubt support such a proposal if it were practicable. As over 4,000 novels are published every year, it will be seen that there would have to be rather a large staff in the novel censors' department. The question is discussed in the jubilee report of the Aberdeen Public Library Committee, and it is admitted that the need for such a censorship exists. Reference is made in the report to the suggestion of a correspondent in *The Times* that novels might be classed as 'A' novels, for adults only or 'U' novels for Universal reading. This suggestion is regarded as interesting and helpful and it is pointed out with regard to books for general reading that reviews in the Press and even advertised selections of any particular book club are not so helpful as they might be, as reviewers and selectors treat a book from so many different ideals of what constitutes merit. Many libraries have suffered from this sort of thing. Thus, at Ipswich, under the old regime, one of the leading members of the Committee refused to allow the purchase of Ibsen's dramas. Returning to the comments of the Aberdeen report, it is stated that the practice there, as in all public libraries, is to be guided by many factors, the general trend of work and reputation of an author, the topic or main purpose of his story, the standing of the publishers, also, of course, the comments of the reviewers, who can be 'placed' without much difficulty in respect of the periodical in which their work appears. But, best of all, of course, is personal examination of the book, keeping in view always, and without narrowness, that suitability for general public reading is essential." [13]

In fact Aberdeen Public Library's policy on censorship seems to have been a good deal more restrictive than was apparent to the *East Anglian Daily Times.*

"Aberdeen Lovers of the works of Lewis Grassic Gibbon, the famous Scots author who died in February of this year, are angry! *Sunset Song,* the first of Gibbon's Trilogy, *A Scots Quair* an intimate study of the rural and industrial life of North-East of Scotland has been withdrawn as 'unsuitable for general circulation' from the lending departments of the Aberdeen Public Library. The other two units of the trilogy, *Cloud Howe* and *Grey Granite* were never stocked in the Library. This omission to be attributed to the controversy aroused as to the propriety of certain passages of Mitchell's works. The pill has been made all the more bitter to swallow by the fact that Glasgow Public Library possesses nine copies of *Sunset Song* . . . Gibbon has been banned only in his own district. . . .

If exception is to be taken to Gibbon on the score of offensive or excessive realism, it is difficult to see any consistency in the policy of a 'censorship' which admits works so little veneered with false modesty as *Goodbye To All That,* the works of Ethel Mannin, or, to take another Scottish example, Eric Linklater's *Magnus Merriman.* . . . But as an Aberdonian, I do object to the deliberate exclusion of an important contribution to the literature of the North-east of Scotland." [14]

Three books were banned by Bedford Public Library in December 1937. They were Rabelais' *Gargantua and Pantagruel,* Constance May Evans', *The Girl with the X-Ray Eyes,* (a Mills and Boon publication!) and Beverley Nichols' *Crazy Pavements.*

"Mr. J. B. Scrivener, a member of the Library Committee, who made a speech on the subject of censorship at the last meeting of Bedford Town Council, told the *News Chronicle* last night that *Gargantua and Pantagruel* had been removed at his request. 'I object strongly to that book being taken out by boys and girls under 21 . . . since the library was opened in 1924 I have made a point of inspecting other libraries and I have never yet found an unexpurgated edition of Rabelais in the public section . . . Municipal Libraries ought to set some standard of taste . . . I am fond of books. I read a good many and I am no prude.' " [15]

Mr. Scrivener knew nothing about *The Girl with the X-Ray Eyes* or *Crazy Pavements* which had not been removed at his request.

These cases revealed a particular pattern, that of strong control by the library committee, that was to continue until well after the second world war. The librarian might recommend material for addition to the library stock, but the committee made the ultimate selection. This state of affairs was to be expected at the beginning of the century, for the public library movement was still in its initial stages of development—the majority of the nation's public library services were inaugurated between 1890 and 1920. Professional librarians were few in number and opportunities for training were minimal compared with today. So library committees exercised rigorous control over librarian, stock and service, establishing a tradition that would take a long time to break despite the growth of librarianship as a profession.

1. Moore, George. *Literature at Nurse: or Circulating Morals.* London, Vizetelly, 1885
2. More, Hannah. *The works of Hannah More.* London, 1801. Vol. VII, p.205
3. Fielding's works: A Dewsbury Town Council Discussion. *Yorkshire Daily Observer,* 25th October 1907
4. Gossip about books: "Ann Veronica" banned at Beverley: An extraordinary censorship. *Yorkshire Evening Post,* 3rd February 1910
5. Hull Libraries and a debatable book. *Yorkshire Post,* 8th February 1910
6. "Tom Jones" and Morality: passages considered impure and indecent. *The Evening Post,* 6th February 1913
7. Prudes in Council. *Saturday Review,* 20th November 1926. pp.605-6
8. Berwick Sayers, W. C. Prudes in Council. *Saturday Review,* 27th November 1926
9. Tomlinson, H. M. Prudes in Council. *Saturday Review,* 27th November 1926
10. Editorial Apology. *Saturday Review,* 27th November 1926
11. Our Old Friend the Censorship. *Constables Monthly List,* January 1927
12. Snaith, Stanley. Censorship. *Library Assistant,* vol. 21. June 1928. pp.128-142
13. Editorial. *East Anglian Daily Times,* 31st December 1934
14. Banned Books . . .: "Offend public morals". *Sunday Mail,* 9th June 1935
15. Council bans three books. *News Chronicle,* 1st December 1937

CHAPTER 2

The War Years and After
1939–1949

It is hardly surprising that this troubled decade began with reports from a number of libraries of the banning of an edition of Hitler's *Mein Kampf.*

"Eccles Town Council have decided to withdraw *Mein Kampf* . . . apparently· because it does not contain all the 'bits' that appeared in the original German edition, and have been omitted to make it fit for English readers. It is perhaps unfortunate that there is no complete edition in English, but it is at least equally unfortunate that Eccles public are not supposed to be able to read even what there is to be read. To be quite logical the Eccles Council should make another translation and publish a complete edition."[1]

The *Library World* reporting that the edition was:

". . . full of omissions as compared with the original and that the object of the book was to drive British thought towards Fascism."

then continued:

"Would there not have been sufficient books in the library to drive British thought in other directions? In the opinion of the librarian, Mr. Lambert, there are enough and to spare for that purpose."[2]

Comment on this ban came from Frederick Cowles, Borough Librarian of Swinton and Pendlebury, a neighbouring local authority. In his editorial in the *Swinton and Pendlebury Public Libraries Bulletin,* under the heading "The Freedom of Libraries", he wrote:

11

"Naturally the public library is bound to play an important part in the lives of the people of an industrial area. To them it is an inestimable boon, and they make full use of the facilities it offers. But the Library also has a great responsibility to the public. It must place at the disposal of its readers books reflecting all schools of thought in all subjects. It must realize the fundamental truth that a man who knows only one side of an argument knows less than half, and therefore cannot claim to have a considered opinion. When I hear of a library committee banning an important political book because certain members do not agree with the author's point of view, I am tempted to say 'Thank heaven that we, in Swinton and Pendlebury, have a libraries committee with a policy as broad as it is progressive'. It is a short-sighted policy to ban any book, unless it be morally dangerous, and is certain to have unpleasant repercussions in the long-run. Every political book is of value both to the adherents and the opponents of the party it seeks to praise or to attack. Some will be able to accept the views expressed with uncritical minds: others will find it a firm justification for their own attitude of opposition. Stalin will not be overthrown because a libraries committee bans a book on Soviet Russia: nor will the Nazi regime come to an end because of an attempt to prevent a small section of the British public from reading *Mein Kampf.* To ban a book is to give it a wide publicity, and those who attempt to impose such restrictions are defeating their own ends. It is also grossly unfair to deprive ratepayers of the privilege of reading any book that may contribute to their general knowledge of national or international affairs. The ideal public library is one in which the stock is evenly balanced, and does not reflect unduly the political creed of the local authority controlling its activities. The comprehensive freedom of the public library service in this country is its greatest power."[3]

Cowles' comments showed that attitudes among librarians and their committees had changed over the years but it is clear that, even in 1939, complete freedom of expression was not acceptable, for despite his generally liberal attitude, Cowles wrote: "it is a short-sided policy to ban any book, unless it be morally dangerous . . . ." Nevertheless in his March 1939 editorial, he wrote:

"We are living today in a tolerant age, and it is not too much to say that our broad-mindedness is due to the type of books we are able to read. A new literature has come into being—the literature of freedom—and writers are unhampered by any foolish restrictions. Because we are able to get books which explain matters from all angles we learn to appreciate the opinions of those who hold views other than our own."[4]

In March 1939, Hurst and Blackett, publishers of the expurgated edition of *Mein Kampf* which Eccles Council had banned, produced a complete and unexpurgated edition in English, while Reynal and Hitchcock, a firm of New York publishers, produced another complete English version. W. B. Stevenson, Deputy Borough Librarian of Hornsey, London, wrote in "Municipal Library Notes" in the *Library Association Record,* May 1939:

" 'What Lancashire thinks today —'. Eccles Libraries Committee has decided, with great daring, to expose each member to the insidious doctrines of *Mein Kampf* before allowing the public to see the book. It is to be hoped that the book will arrive on the shelves before all its aims are accomplished."[5]

Cowles' feelings about morally dangerous books were shared by Willan G. Bosworth, compiler of "The New Novels of the Month" in the periodical *Librarian and Book World*. For five years from 1938 his column was prefaced by the following statement:

"Purely as an experiment we have commenced a classification of new novels, according to their propriety or impropriety. It would be of interest if readers were good enough to signify their opinion of this classification, or give their version of its groupings if they can form four classes into which novels would more naturally fall according to their authors' treatment. At present the grading is:
(a) Perfectly innocuous from the point of view of decency.
(b) Novels with a sex theme and lacking any objectionable expressions or phrases.
(c) With a sex topic but treated in a serious way.
(d) Novels frankly relying on their sex appeal."[6]

In practice, books reviewed in Bosworth's column were almost invariably classified in category (a) or category (b)!

On the 3rd September, 1939, war was declared against Germany. The war quickly had a profound effect upon people and institutions, including librarians and libraries. Within a short time many chief librarians and experienced members of their staffs, went on active service, as men and later women, were called up. In many instances, their places were taken by unqualified personnel, some very young and inexperienced, who were promoted on a temporary basis for the duration of the war. Total numbers of staff were reduced in many libraries. Those chief librarians who remained in post, and the temporary replacements, found themselves assuming additional responsibilities outside their library work. Some public library buildings were damaged or destroyed in air-raids, or were taken over partly or completely for purposes connected with the war effort. Conditions were extremely difficult and these difficulties were increased by the heavy public demand for books. Probably because of the abnormal conditions, and possibly because the limited resources simply had to be used to the full, there were comparatively few examples of censorship or similar restrictions in the libraries during the war or in the following three or four years. There were some examples, however, particularly those involving the books of P. G. Wodehouse, and also librarians were certainly affected in some degree by censorship brought about by factors outside their control. Instances of this were reported in the professional periodicals throughout the war. The first was noted in the *Library World*, July 1940:

"We came into the news when it was pointed out that recently the use of maps of parts of the British Isles had increased in libraries. We had not noticed this, but the defence authorities have asked that such maps shall be carefully watched and issued only to people whose motives are unquestionable. Some librarians had already taken such steps as it became known that aliens of certain categories—we believe now in all categories—were forbidden to possess these maps. It is indeed a commentary on the type of foe we face. Librarians will always do what their country requests of them."[7]

In October 1940, the editor of the *Library World* wrote:

"Of all the intangible difficulties today none is more awkward than that of the material *in* books and the possibilities of censorship in connection with it. The probability is that the average German is unaware of his poisoned condition or that of the books he is allowed to read; he believes, possibly, that his mind is at liberty. That is the insidious characteristic of all successful mind penetration whatever the end in view may be. There are few outward signs of attempts at censorship in England yet, although we are told by our American friends that it does exist. A few local persons have made objections to certain sorts of books on our shelves—for example, to everything that supports the Nazi thesis whatever it is, and of course there are many books that do that which appeared before last September. There have been a few attempts to stifle public speech and the cruel sentences passed by foolish magistrates for silly expressions tending to 'defeatism' have roused general ire .... We have to win a War, and we shall not do it by sacrificing freedom of thought and expression. This applies with special force to books."[8]

Another problem for the librarian was the censorship of periodicals supplied on subscription from overseas, particularly from the United States. Copies were being received with pages torn out. Herbert Woodbine, Reference Librarian of Birmingham Public Libraries, in his column "Reference Libraries" in the *Library Association Record* asked:

"As we bind all the above periodicals what will happen to our set? Whose work is the deletion, English or American censors, or both? Has anyone asked American librarians to hang on to periodicals they do not bind, and to any duplicates they may have, till after the war, in order that sufficient copies may be available to complete sets? ..."[9]

A. E. Cummins, Acting Librarian of the Chemical Society, answered some of Woodbine's questions three months later in a letter to the *Record:*

"Owing to United States censorship regulations, a number of American scientific and technical journals are arriving with blank pages or with pages torn out. Other journals are held back altogether. It is difficult to see how the multilated journals will be made good after the war, and I have taken up the matter with publishers and with American scientists, who are most concerned about it, and are most anxious to help. The Editor of *Science* has published a vigorous correspondence he has had with the Censorship, and the *Scientific American* aptly points out that if the articles prohibited for export are published at all, enemy agents in the United States have full access to them there. Would it not be possible for British Librarians who suffer from this mutilation of journals to combine to bring to the notice of the appropriate authorities how adversely science and scientific libraries are affected by this policy?"[10]

The *Library Association Record* was able to report in July 1943 that:

". . . the whole subject has been under careful consideration and the Director of Censorship at Washington has now taken a step which will greatly expedite the transit of periodicals from America and should help the war effort by making material available on both sides of the Atlantic. This is, in effect, a ruling that from 1st July all publications available to the general public in the United States may be exported without licence if their contents abide by the voluntary censorship code. We are also very glad to announce that the American Committee on Aid to Libraries in War Areas is making a special effort to obtain copies of those American scientific periodicals which have at any time been mutilated by the Censor, and will keep them until the earliest moment when they can be forwarded to make up the complete files in the subscribing libraries."[11]

Reports of attempted censorship in public libraries, though fewer than hitherto, continued to appear. In January 1940:

"We do not know if the war can be blamed for the extraordinary proposition seriously put forward by the Committee of one Library which shall be nameless in its shame, which we believe is still under consideration, viz., that such periodicals as *The Saturday Review,* the *Spectator,* and others should not be taken at the library because 'No one wanted to read them except professors and would-be professors, and such people could well-afford to pay for them'. This is a 'means test' of library users with a vengeance. We congratulate the librarian on his fight for their retention."[12]

In 1940, Oldham Borough Council approved the Public Libraries Committee's decision to stop taking *Peace News, Action,* the *Daily Worker* and *Tribune* in the Central Library reading room for the duration of the war. On 11th June 1940, a letter had been submitted to the Committee from a wholesale newsagent who supplied papers to the library stating that they had decided not to distribute *Peace News* any longer. The Committee had also been informed that other newspapers were being mutilated and that crude drawings and rude remarks were being written on them by readers, as a result of which the library care-takers had repeatedly to go into the newspaper library and restore order. The Committee had to decide either to close the room or remove the cause of the altercations. After discussion the Committee resolved:

> "That the supply of the four publications now mentioned be discontinued during the war period."[13]

Formal protests were made by the Oldham Communist Party[14] and the Oldham Group of the Peace Pledge Union[15], but the Libraries Committee resolved "that no action be taken on the communication".[16] On 7th August 1940 the Council approved the Libraries Committee's ban by 26 votes to 16, though only after considerable criticism of the move from the Labour and Liberal members.[17] Councillor Kershaw said:

> "That was the first time he had heard of any disturbance taking place. . . . They had no right to ban the papers that had not been banned by the Government."[18]

At the next Council Meeting on 11th September 1940, the Town Clerk wished to submit a letter dated 23rd August from G. R. Strauss, M.P. on behalf of the Board of *Tribune,* but found himself in a difficult position.

> "The Town Clerk . . . said that the subject matter of the letter had been discussed on two occasions during the present municipal year. He therefore could not submit the letter unless the Standing Order bearing on the subject were suspended. . . . The Conservative members voted in a body against the suspension of the Standing Order. . . . The Town Clerk: That ends it. Alderman Whittaker: The freedom of the Press."[19]

The Strauss letter had been forwarded to various members of Oldham Borough Council. It read:

> "Owing to the absence of reports in the London Press I have only just seen the report of the decision taken by your Council to ban the *Tribune,* . . . the decision is an intolerable affront, which carries the most damaging implications."[20]

The Southport Libraries and Art Committee had before it in October 1942, a suggestion that the *Daily Worker* should be taken for display in the Central Library reading room, but after discussion it was decided not to accede to this request. When the decision became known, the Southport Trades Council and Labour Party resolved to ask the Libraries Committee to reconsider its decision.

> "Mr. F. O'Donnell pointed out that the Libraries Committee declined to ban a publication of Benito Mussolini. He saw no reason why the Libraries Committee

should arrogate to themselves the right to prohibit the *Daily Worker*. Councillor A. Hughes, President, who is a member of the Libraries Committee informed the meeting that he was absent from the Committee meeting when the decision was made. He would support the resolution when it reached the Committee."[21]

At its meeting on 16th November 1942, however, the:

"Southport Libraries and Art Committee reaffirmed their decision not to place the *Daily Worker* in the reading room of the Atkinson Free Library, ... The committee, who had previously decided not to entertain new applications for papers and periodicals to be placed in the reading room, declined to make any alteration, as the *Daily Worker* had not been placed in the reading room before."[22]

On 3rd December 1942, the:

"Southport Trades Council and Labour Party . . . decided to send another protest . . . against the Committee's decision not to place the *Daily Worker* in the reading room.
  Allegations were made that the Committee's decision was due to Gestapo methods and political influence. In a democracy, it was urged, minorities had a right to have their publications placed in public libraries.
  'In Mr. Churchill's words, what sort of a people do they think we are?' exclaimed Mr. F. O'Donnell. 'The matter will not rest here. It will be pursued on a question of principle'."[23]

During 1943, the Chief Librarian of Southport received letters complaining that the *Daily Worker* was not available. One correspondent, E. Allen, wrote:

"Being one of Southport's citizens who frequents the Public Library I have often desired to find the *Daily Worker* on the files. The absence of the *Daily Worker* is unjust as well as being detrimental to the war effort, and does not aim at unifying the nation in this critical period when all efforts should be concentrated on the winning of the war. To include the *Daily Worker* in the Public Library would be a stimulant to those of progressive thought and help to achieve victory and a peace that will bring us social security."[24]

Audrey N. Barbasch, in her letter to the *Southport Guardian* of 31 July 1943, pointed out that the *Daily Worker* was available in Buxton, Macclesfield and Blackpool public libraries, and asked why Southport was "so far behind in progressive and democratic principles by banning this vital newspaper".[25]

The minutes of the Libraries and Art Committee meeting of 15th May 1944 read:

"Letters dated the 8th and 12th May, 1944, from the Southport Trades' Council and Labour Party and the Rev. N. C. Oatridge, M.A., Vicar of All Souls' Church respectively, with reference to the *Daily Worker,* were read.

Resolved—That the *Daily Worker* be placed in the Library Reading Room for an experimental period of six months."[26]

The *Southport Visiter* reported the decision:

> "The provision of the *Daily Worker* in the free libraries of Southport has been a matter of keen local controversy for a year or two. There have been frequent debates in the Trades and Labour Council urging representations to be made to the Libraries and Art Committee for its inclusion in the public reading rooms. This demand has also been voiced on numerous occasions at Communist, Labour and Socialist meetings held in Southport and also recently at the meeting of the Southport Jewish Discussion Group.
>
> So yesterday's decision of the Libraries and Art Committee can be regarded as a victory for the supporters of the *Daily Worker.*
>
> Councillor Dr. Betteridge, chairman of the Libraries and Art Committee, told the *Visiter* that yesterday's decision by the Committee was practically unanimous. We have had repeated applications for the *Daily Worker* to be placed in the libraries, . . . but, hitherto, the decision of the Committee has been not to put any extra papers into the libraries at the present time, the shortage of paper and everything else being taken into account. We do not know what demand there is for the *Daily Worker,* but if there is a demand for it the public, of course, have the right to have the paper in the library. The Committee wish to try it and see if there is a legitimate call for it."[27]

Herbert Fielden, who had also written to the Press about P. G. Wodehouse was not entirely satisfied with this decision, as his letter to the *Southport Visiter* of 30th May 1944, showed:

> "This is not satisfactory, unless the paper can be read at the four branch libraries also. Crossens, for example, has a majority industrial population and its ratepayers cannot possibly travel daily to the Central Library. This national newspaper is the only daily that owes its existence to the contributions of the weekly wage-earners! Many people (like the writer) wish to read the opinions of the *D.W.* as well as their own particular paper."[28]

In November 1944, the Southport Libraries Committee resolved that "the *Daily Worker* continue to be placed in the Library Reading Rooms".[29]

In 1943, the Library Association published *The Public Library Service: its post war reorganisation and development,* based on the McColvin report of 1942.[30] In the introduction, the Association affirmed in rather general terms its belief in the library's right to select books freely:

"By the facilities it affords for wide and unfettered reading the public library enables every man not only to enlarge his mind with the refined pleasures of great literature, but in particular (at present a vital need), to secure that understanding of social and economic forces and conditions without which there can be no true realization of the democratic ways of life. Because of its essential freedom, its wide range, its hospitality to all phases of thought and its infinite adaptability the public library can serve each man according to his requirements and safe-guard his development against the dangers of modern standardizing influences."[31]

In addition to its part in the P. G. Wodehouse affair (see Chapter 3) and its ban on the *Daily Worker* in 1942 the Southport Libraries and Art Committee was to be involved in further controversy—over Aldous Huxley's book *The Art of Seeing,* in which Huxley described a method he had used to save his failing eye-sight. The *Southport Guardian* of 28th August 1943 was:

". . . able to reveal that the question of the inclusion of the book in the Atkinson Library was first raised some months ago, when the Committee decided to reject it 'because it might be prejudicial to professional men in the town'. Interviewed at that time, Councillor Paul Carter, Chairman of the Libraries Committee, said: 'We had none of us read the book, but the members seemed to think that it was not advisable to include it in the collection, as it was written by a man with no professional qualifications. We knew it dealt with a cure for failing sight'. Councillor Carter then secured a copy of it and made a detailed reading. Yesterday he told the *Southport Guardian* that his Committee had rejected the book because they believed it would do more harm than good if it were in general circulation from the town's library. "My own opinion is that it is a very sound book, and I see no reason why it should not be available to borrowers'."[32]

The *Southport Guardian* dealt with the ban in its leading article on the same day.

"The banning of books is not one of the proud traditions of old England. Our easy-going and tolerant people do not worry their heads about what others care to read or leave unread. But it is to be hoped that their tolerance has not yet reached the stage where they are prepared to sit back and let the others, in their turn, make arbitrary decisions as to what they themselves are not to read. Library bans on books which ought not to fall into the hands of the young are another matter; nobody disagrees with the refusal of civic authorities to circulate works likely to give offence to the citizens for whom they are trustees. It so happens that Mr. Aldous Huxley has written a number of books which deal in the most outspoken manner with subjects still considered indelicate in a large number of homes. But his new work, ironically enough, does not fall within this category. Instead, it is a straightforward account of how his rapidly failing eyesight was restored by the application of certain methods—partly physical—partly psychological—which have been found widely successful in the United States. He wrote his book in the hope that by bringing these methods to the notice of the British public other sufferers from failing eyesight might perhaps be placed within reach of a cure. It is not necessary to agree with Mr. Huxley's views . . . in order to recognise in him a man of the utmost integrity. If, therefore, he affirms that he has received benefit from certain methods we may know for a certainty that he speaks the truth.

To prevent the circulation of that truth is to risk doing mankind a grave disservice. In any event the only people who can be accounted qualified to make the attempt are the medical profession, and even they have not always shown themselves free from bias in their approach to new and unconventional ideas. . . . But it would seem that certain members of the Libraries Committee have not hesitated to rush in where experts fear to tread—not so much to safe-guard the public against charlatanism, one gathers, as to protect the interest of some professional men in the town. This is a very queer piece of reasoning, and establishes a precedent the consequences of which no man can foresee."[33]

Two months later, on October 12th, the *Southport Visiter* reported that:

"Southport Libraries and Arts Committee yesterday decided to lift their ban on the purchase of Aldous Huxley's book *The Art of Seeing* for issue to library members. Councillor Paul Carter (Chairman of the Committee) told the *Visiter* that by a very large majority the book was added to the Selection Sub-Committee's list approved for purchase, subject, of course, to Town Council confirmation . . . Councillor Carter said in the first instance, some months ago, it was decided to defer the purchase of the book, and in view of this he got a copy and read it. 'It was put on the Selection Sub-Committee's list, but in view of the opinions expressed by a member of the Committee, which carried considerable weight, the Committee turned it down' . . . He added that he was not present at that meeting, being away on holiday. Subsequently most of the members of the Committee took the opportunity of reading the book. . . . 'They knew what they were voting for when the question came up again today, and, after a little discussion, they decided by a very large majority to include it among the books to be purchased."[34]

Alex. J. Philip, editor of the *Librarian and Book World* wrote in his November 1943 editorial:

"There are many signs in different directions of the revival of our old enemy, to censor or to be censored. The matter has become acute at Kidderminster, where the Library Committee refuse to put six books on venereal disease and sex matters on the library shelves. The local Trades Council made strong protest against this decision. Finally, a resolution was passed 'strongly deprecating the action of the Library Committee in banning books on venereal diseases from the Public Library, and urging it to reconsider its decision and acquire books recommended by the Medical Officer of Health'. This is only one case. The war will inevitably enlarge the outlook of everyone. Those who read before the war will want to read with much greater freedom now than they did then: while those who scarcely read, or those who could not be classified as 'readers', will be found to have joined the enormous army of readers of all kinds and classes. Is it the duty of a library committee to see that books on certain subjects are not made available for these readers? It is not exactly a matter of opinion, nor is it a matter of religion, while decency is an entirely elastic term. The laws exist and can be evoked against any offender who departs from what is still a somewhat narrow path. Far be it from us to endeavour to lay down any rules for the guidance of anyone. We can only still adhere to the old, unwritten, but nevertheless very stringent rules:

That a public library recognises no particular sect or religion. That a public library recognises no particular party in politics. And finally, that a public library must, at least, keep pace with changing customs and widening outlooks."[35]

Books by Germans or about Germany in the Cumberland County Library Branch at Keswick caused the Keswick Urban District Council to decide:

"To request the committee which controls the county library scheme in Keswick to consider the temporary removal from the shelves of 'certain books bearing on the German nation'. Mr. Dent said that several rate-payers were concerned at the presence on the shelves of certain of these books. He thought it would be wise for the Library Committee to have them removed for the time being. The Chairman (Mr. Bone) said he personally did not agree with that view, because this country was fighting for freedom of opinion, and if the Library Committee were going to censor the reading of the public it was not in accordance with the principles for which the country was fighting. Mr. C. C. Mayson strongly supported Mr. Dent, and said that, having fought against the Germans in the last War, and having been wounded by them, he was against everything German. . . . When people were losing their sons, brothers and relatives in the war he thought it was a shame that they should have anything in the library concerning Germany. . . . Mr. Hopper said he thought it was a very serious proposition to ask the Library Committee to undertake the censorship of books. There was a censorship in this country of anything that required censoring, and to ask two laymen to go through some books simply because they were written by Germans was asking too much."[36]

However, Dent's motion that the County Library Committee be requested to consider the temporary removal of the books was carried. The *Library Review,* commented on this report:

"Librarians everywhere will agree with Mr. Bone. In war-time the peoples all over the world who are actively engaged in the war have had to sacrifice much of their freedom in the interest of the State. It would be a shocking thing, if in addition to that, we were also to lose our freedom of thought."[37]

Keswick Council's decision did not receive support in the *Cumberland Herald.* 'Silverpen' in his column of 11th November 1944, wrote:

"The Keswick Urban Council looks like stepping in where angels might fear to tread when it starts founding an *index expurgatorius* of German books. . . . I do not know what books these ratepayers object to and it would be a pity if in their somewhat questionable enthusiasm to expel the literary heretics, they should follow the example of Hitler himself, who burned a number of German books because they were non-Aryan in origin, although they might be described as 'bearing on the German Nation'. . . . Has the good taste of Keswick's more sensitive ratepayers been offended by seeing Hitler's *Mein Kampf* staring them in the face every time they approached their literary shrine to borrow a book for the weekend? Personally, I think *Mein Kampf* is very good reading, especially now when Hitler's struggle is not panning out quite as he expected. You can get more laughs to the page out of *Mein Kampf* than out of any book published in Germany for years. . . . I agree with the Council's chairman, who said he disagreed with the proposal, because this country was fighting for freedom of opinion."[38]

In the same issue of the *Cumberland Herald,* Ismay Trimble wrote in a letter to the editor:

"Keswick Urban Council have, I note, decided to adopt a system of 'censoring' the books which will in future be permitted to repose within the sacred (and meagre) precincts of the branch of the County Library in the town, the reason, forsooth, being because certain members of the public frequenting our local Hall of Learning, complain that books are found therein written by Germans. . . . If certain small segments of the public lacking breadth of outlook object to books perpetrated by Huns, why select and read them, and why to goodness try to prevent other people reading them, should such people desire to do so? . . . The whole thing smacks perilously like 'the thin end of the wedge'. Where will it all end? Someone else may object to books about Germany, Japan, etc. Are books by British pro-Germans barred? What of books by red-hot anti-nazi Germans? Are these to be disallowed? Then others may object to certain authors, American, British. Will these books be withdrawn? It opens up a most unpleasant vista! It also savours of Gestapo methods—muzzling, withdrawing, forbidding. If the local authority wished to be consistent in the matter, they should not listen to music by Beethoven, Wagner, Bach. . . . Bouquets are herewith handed to those Councillors who genuinely believe in freedom of choice and action. . . . Surely the whole question of which books are to be 'allowed' in the Keswick Library may safely be entrusted to our most capable and widely read chief librarian in Carlisle. Art, in its many and varied forms, knows no boundaries, countries or frontiers, be it music, literature, art or drama. Hitler and Co. have tried (by burning the books) to trample down certain writings to which they take objection, and authors are in concentration camps. Surely we, who are fighting for freedom, are not taking (certainly a mild one) a leaf from his bloodstained record."[39]

The conclusion of this affair was reported by the *Keswick Reminder,* on December 18th:

"The County Council Library Committee have considered a recommendation of Keswick Council that they should take into consideration the banning of certain German books from the Keswick branch of the County Free Library . . . The Chairman of the County Council, Mr. H. Swinburn, invited to the meeting Councillor G. W. Dent, J.P. who sponsored the resolution at the Council Meeting, the

Chairman of the County Library Committee, Mr. T. Beaton, County Librarian Miss Cook, and local librarian Miss Fulton. . . . The Committee of which other two members are Mr. Mark Hopper, J.P. and Mr. Chas. Bone, decided that it had no authority to censor books issued by the County Library Committee and that it feels strongly that to withdraw books written by German writers would be a denial of the freedom of the reading public, recommended that no further action be taken."[40]

Although the official end of the war in Europe came on 9th May 1945, it was some time before conditions in libraries began to improve significantly. Demobilised librarians began to return to their old jobs or to look for new ones and the situation in book publishing gradually improved.

Originally published in 1944 in the United States, Kathleen Winsor's book *Forever Amber* was published in Britain by MacDonald and Evans in 1945, and was an immediate success. In November 1946, reviewing annual reports in his column "Municipal Library Notes" in the *Library Association Record,* S. H. Horrocks, Borough Librarian of Reading reported that the two most often reserved books were *Forever Amber* and *Jane Eyre*.[41]

The *Library Review* Spring 1947, noted that:

"The Kettering Annual Report has been written up in interesting style . . . Miss Green regretfully observes that *Forever Amber* and the *Green Years* headed the popular novels."[42]

In fact, Kettering had 350 reservations for "that notorious piece of period pornography", *Forever Amber,* within a week of publication.[43] Both Birmingham[44] and Sheffield Public Libraries were reported as having banned it. In Sheffield:

"Book borrowers . . . ask in vain for . . . *Forever Amber*. The book has not been issued for circulation because the Libraries Committee, some of whose members have read it, have classed it as 'unsuitable'. An offer to buy the copies that the libraries hold has been turned down and orders have been given for them to be destroyed."[45]

This announcement was followed by indignant letters to the Press. On 27th December 1946, *The Star* reported the opinions of several correspondents.

"The banning of *Forever Amber* by the Libraries Committee is about the silliest action since the P. G. Wodehouse incident, writes C.B.L. If the Committee feels particularly virtuous will they allow me, I wonder, to go round the library shelves and tell them of the scores of books which, judged by some standards, ought never to have been printed, let alone placed in public libraries?

Also indignant at the local banning of *Amber* is 'Atlantic Charter', who wants to know by what right the Libraries Committee decide what he is to read and what he is not to read. 'These library books' he declares 'are purchased with public money after they have been passed for publication by the proper authority. Had the title been *Forever Red* perhaps there would have been no objection', broods 'Atlantic Charter', adding a footnote that the Committee and not the book should be pulped."[46]

C.D.J. in his letter of 19th December asked:

"Perhaps one of my fellow-readers could tell me the names and ages of the committee who control what books we shall read from the library; and also by whom is this committee elected, if at all. Surely we, as adults and intelligent human beings, are sufficiently responsible to read books by our own selection and not by that of this committee. I see orders have been given for the copies of *Forever Amber* to be destroyed when an opportunity for sale is offered. Is this childish and bigoted action one of the reasons why our Socialist City Council cannot reduce the rates?"[47]

Birmingham and Sheffield Libraries were not alone in banning *Forever Amber* for the book was also banned at Leamington Spa and other libraries. While Leamington Public Library Committee's refusal to purchase the book received little attention in the Press, their discussions over the book *The Rise of Christianity* by Dr. Barnes, Bishop of Birmingham, published in 1947, attracted a good deal. Of the book itself, the Leamington *Morning News* of the 27th October 1947 wrote:

"Independent thinkers, in search of the truth, have throughout the ages met with the enmity of those whom they desired to help. It is an old story, reprinted yet again in the reception of the book *The Rise of Christianity*. . . . Bishop Barnes' book, to say the least, questions the fundamental beliefs of millions of people. His lifelong studies lead him to dismiss the evidence of Christ's physical reappearance after the Crucifixion and discount the Miracles and the Virgin Birth. His conclusions, squarely opposed to orthodox religious thinking, have brought public denunciations from the Archbishops of Canterbury and York. Who is right and who is wrong? Read the book and decide for yourself. That is your privilege. To many it may also appear as a duty. It is, therefore, alarming to read in the local press that the Library Committee seems more than dubious about adding the book to its shelves. . . . The Committee was recently in the news for banning *Forever Amber*—a book read by millions and serialized in the newspapers. The absence of the actual book is not a serious loss, but it is an indication that library users cannot choose for themselves. The banning of *The Rise of Christianity* would be outright censorship of a nature which obviously could not be allowed."[48]

At the Library Committee meeting on the 17th October:

"The Committee Chairman, Alderman C. Davies, had said his view was that, having been repudiated by two Archbishops, he did not quite see how they could give the book their support. Councillor Stubbs: 'It would create great controversy. . . . An important view is that the book is decidedly harmful'. To safeguard the position the Chairman, who had opened the discussion, closed it peremptorily by adding: 'this is a public meeting and, as we should like to think the matter over carefully before making comment, it would be better to leave the matter until we have seen the book'."[49]

The matter then rested until the November meeting of the Library Committee.

"Opposing opinions about the controversial book *The Rise of Christianity* . . . were expressed at a meeting of the Leamington Library Committee, when talk of 'keeping it under the counter' and 'service to truth' clashed with a suggestion that the book was in the same class as the much-discussed *Forever Amber* recently banned from the library's shelves. One of the most forceful arguments for obtaining the book for the library was put forward by the Mayor (Councillor G. Purcell), and after a prolonged discussion his proposal for its purchase—without the customary practice of first obtaining a copy on approval—was carried by a majority of three votes. . . . Councillor L. G. Clayton: Without being disrespectful to the Bishop, I think we should put it in the same class as *Forever Amber*. You remember we said then if anyone wants to read it let them buy it. The Mayor . . . replied that surely it could not be said that it was in the same class as *Forever Amber*. The best service to truth was to admit opposition and point of view. Therefore he moved that the book be received into the library. . . . Councillor W. T. Duckworth said he could not agree. If the book was circulated it would give grave offence to a large section of the public. He thought it was extremely undesirable that they should have a book which offended not only the Catholics, but those of the Church of England and Non-Conformists. It was so controversial he thought it would tend to arouse deep passion and he thought the library was far better without it. They could get far better books which would have a better effect on the minds of the people. If people wanted to read it, they should buy it and not read it with the blessing of this Corporation. The Chairman: We do not actually bless the books. There is no need for people to have the book because it is in the library. But it is our duty to supply all sorts of books. . . . The Mayor's proposal was carried by seven votes to four."[50]

The *Morning News* of 24th November approved of this decision.

"Those who argued against the purchase of the book had, let us admit, some very good reasons, but overriding all was the fact that, unless objection could be taken on grounds of immorality, there was no valid reason why *The Rise of Christianity* or any other volume should not be made available."[51]

Letters to the Press supported the Library Committee's decision. Gilbert Dalton wrote to the Leamington *Courier* on 12th December:

"Congratulations on your decided expression of opinion in favour of adding Bishop Barnes' book to the Library. It is, indeed, surprising that any member of the committee should have opposed the purchase—an attitude which made one murmur "Is this Leamington Spa or Dayton, Tennessee?' The burning of books they did not like by the Nazis is an unpleasantly close parallel. I do not wish to read the book myself, but I would most certainly vote against any Councillor who sought to prevent anyone else from reading it."[52]

At its March 1947, meeting, the Caithness County Library Committee refused to agree to the purchase of C. S. Forester's novel *The Ship*.

"A book by Mr. E. M. Forrester has come under the ban of Caithness Library Committee whose members scrutinise every list of books destined for Wick and Thurso Libraries. At the monthly meeting the Rev. B. Mackay, Free Church of Scotland, . . . said he considered Mr. E. M. Forrester's book entitled *The Ship* was unsuitable for the Library. Accordingly the book was struck off the list of purchases. Humorous aspect is other copies of *The Ship* have been in Wick and Thurso libraries for a considerable time. The banned volume was merely a replacement copy."[53]

However at its next meeting on 4th April 1947, the committee:

". . . rescinded its decision last month to ban a replacement copy of C. S. Forester's novel, *The Ship,* from the County Library. Brigadier G. D. K. Murray, Convener for Caithness, who raised the matter, said that the book was written as a tribute to the cruiser H.M.S. Penelope for its part in a convoy action. It was an excellent piece of naval history, and while there might be one or two passengers which were a little rough, Brigadier Murray thought that it would be a great mistake on the Committee's part to ban the book. Provost W. M. Brims seconded the motion.
    Rev. D. Mackay . . . on whose suggestion the replacement copy was originally banned, said he did not intend to assert that the book was worse than other books in the library. The question was whether they should make some protest against such matters. If it was a question of clean milk for schools they would be deeply concerned about the matter. He thought they should have the same concern about good reading."[54]

Jean Paul Sartre's *The Age of Reason* was the subject of discussions by the Stockton Town Council and its Library Committee at the end of 1947.

"Whether the Public Library Committee should ban a book described by a member as 'filthy, obscene and indecent' was debated at Stockton Town Council last night (2nd December 1947). Under discussion was the translation from the French of Jean Sartre's *The Age of Reason* which Councillor P. Horner moved should be added to a list of new volumes to be purchased. Only one member of the committee, he said, had read the book, and on his recommendation it had been decided not to put it into circulation. Councillor Horner said he had since read the book very carefully and as a novel found it rather dull. Quoting a book by

Rabelais as 'one of the muckiest books that has ever been put into a library'. Councillor Horner added: 'What may be censored in one age seems to become the normal accepted thing in another'. . . . He did not think the Library Committee of any corporation was competent to take upon itself the role of censor. He hoped the Council would ask the Library Committee to formulate some policy whereby they could get a better judgment on books than that of any particular individual. Alderman T. A. Westwater said he had been engaged in reading the book since the controversy arose, and he would say it justified all the adjectives applied to it in committee, but it was not the only book of the kind in circulation at the moment. . . . If, however, they were going to set themselves up as censors, they were going to have a big job. He thought the matter should go back to the committee to be discussed in more detail. Councillor C. R. Booth, Chairman of the Public Libraries Committee, pointed out that it was difficult for the Committee to read all the books that were published. They could only be guided by people who had read a certain number of those books. He was willing, however, to accept a reference back for further discussion by the Committee. This was agreed to."[55]

At the Public Library Committee's meeting of 15th December 1947, however, it was resolved:

"That the previous decision be reaffirmed and that the other book now named (unknown) be also withdrawn."[56]

This reaffirmation came before the Town Council on 6th January 1948.

"Councillor Smith moved and Alderman W. Brown seconded that . . . the words 'that the previous decision be reaffirmed' be deleted, and the following inserted: 'that the book *The Age of Reason* be placed on the shelf'."[57]

Nineteen members voted for this change, and 17 against, and *The Age of Reason* was therefore approved for circulation. The *Evening Gazette*, in its column "Northern Notes" on 8th January 1948, commented:

"To what extent a library committee should exercise a right of censorship over the books it makes available to the public is a nice point and one which for two successive meetings has been hotly debated in Stockton Town Council. . . . Apparently taking the view that to allow the Committee to ban a book would create a dangerous precedent, the Council decided . . . that *The Age of Reason* should be placed in the Library. They allowed to go unchallenged, however, a Committee resolution that a second unnamed book should be withdrawn. It would seem, therefore, that the debate was largely abortive; but no principle has been established; and that the net result is likely to be a rush to read *The Age of Reason* for no better motive than unhealthy curiosity."[58]

S. H. Horrocks, Borough Librarian of Reading, in his column "Municipal Library Notes" in the *Library Association Record,* June 1948, wrote:

"The problem of book censorship is a perennial one. The chaotic state of the international scene and the ranging on opposing sides of the economies of the world have brought up the question of censorship to an unusual degree this Spring. One or two areas are banning communist material, others are banning fascist, while most, it is pleasing to record, are banning neither. At STEPNEY, a deputation from the National Union of Tailors and Garment Workers have waited on the Borough Council to protest against the inclusion of fascist books in the local libraries. The MALVERN Committee are reconsidering the provision of *Union* in the reading room. READING will not add *An Alternative* and *Union*. RICHMOND has refused to display the *Daily Worker*. There are, of course, many reasons why certain newspapers and magazines cannot be added to a public library, but it is reasonable to assume that political affairs govern the decisions in these cases. It has long been the practice for librarians who normally choose books for their own libraries specially to put before the Committee any book or paper of a highly controversial character. This is for self protection, and no-one in the long run can blame the librarian for taking the middle and calmer channel. But because he takes the middle channel he is running in deeper water, and it might be argued that he is evading his responsibilities."[59]

S. H. Horrocks, also wrote an article "Ban the Poison Shelf" for the *Municipal Journal,* January 1949, based on many of the reports he had received and used in his column "Municipal Library Notes" in the *Library Association Record.*

"It is an axiom that the public library stock should be fully representative of current and past literature, should hold books dealing with most subjects and should specialize in the literature of its own area and industries. The primary function is educational, and a nice balance has therefore to be maintained in providing those books which students need, those books the largest numbers need, and those new books about which the biggest clamour is made. The temptation to judge books from the stand point of moral tone and no other quality is a human one, and is resisted less by some than others. But such a principle applied to the choosing of books for the public library serves merely to beg the question as to what is moral tone.

Practice differs from area to area, but in most libraries there will be found, in the librarian's office or some such sheltered haven, a 'poison shelf', on which are placed those books about which some complaint has been made. It might be that the books have been placed there by the librarian, who has been temporarily convinced that they are not worthy of further circulation. The committee might have considered the books—*and* read them—and decided that they shall be withdrawn from further circulation. The books to be found on the 'poison shelf' vary from area to area, but not the pattern. There is always, for instance, a sturdy nucleus of 'modern' novels—those books of not too high a literary standard, written by an author with his or her fingers on the pulse of the majority taste. This nucleus is backed up by some famous classics—I have seen *Candide* there, *The Decameron,* Rabelais, D. H. Lawrence, yes, even Chaucer. Support to these classics is given by Ernest Hemingway, Somerset Maugham, James Hanley ... and others of a similar standing. The remaining works are oddments of novels, some containing bad language, others dealing with a subject which is anathema to some local sect or body, or containing remarks which some person has found objectionable or alarming.

The non-fiction section of the 'poison shelf' consists often of books on sex (the diagrammatic ones are usually treated first), on medical subjects, (such as forensic medicine where the illustrations are rather more than gruesome to the layman), and well illustrated anotomical books designed for the artist or the medical student. Such is the pattern. Now the sex books and medical books are kept there generally because they will be physically damaged if they get into the hands of readers for whom they are not intended. Circulation of these works is not seriously restricted, as each book is often represented on the open shelves by a dummy block and by an entry in the catalogue. The remaining books are segregated because some person or body has protested to the librarian, or the library committee, about the nature of the work in question, usually on the score of its damaging moral qualities. This pressure is to be expected, but it only becomes important when its efforts are successful.

Instances of the local suppression of books are many, and although some receive wide Press publicity, it is rarely that the cold light of history indicates such treatment to have been either intelligent or wise.

It is pleasant to record that these decisions raised a veritable hornets nest, both at home and abroad, and it is likely that the noise thus created had a beneficial effect on the decisions of the many other places which considered a resolution to ban.

The above examples are . . . diverse enough to reveal the nature of the problem and detailed enough to show the working of local censorship. The 'smutty', 'risqué', 'outspoken' book is the real problem, and the solution, it would seem to me, lies in proper book selection, not in the formation of a 'poison shelf'. If a book is purchased because its literary value is sufficiently high to be worth adding to the library, surely its subject matter and its readers can be left to take care of themselves. If the book is frankly pornographic, or appeals only to the lower emotions, it is unlikely to be of a high literary standard, and its claim for a place on the shelves is small. If a book has been chosen for purchase and put into free circulation, and the librarian is satisfied as to its standard, then local authorities should remain firm, and keep it in circulation until it is banned by the State. No amount of pressure from any local worthy should deter them or cause them to change their attitude.

The problem of the book thus resolves itself. The problem remaining is the soothing of the irate councillor or alderman whose taste may well range from Trollope to Galsworthy, but who finds a robustious and picaresque novel like *Tom Jones* of too early a vintage, and Aldous Huxley, Henry Miller and Edmund Wilson too late for his easy digestion."[60]

The *Daily Mirror,* 7th January 1949, drew attention to events in Worthing:

"Grey-haired Librarian Miss Ethel Gerard, 64, doesn't like sexy novels on the shelves of Worthing, Sussex, public libraries. So she chooses fiction with great care. But Councillor A. H. Gorman was incensed when he came across a book in which he read this sentence: 'Suddenly he was beside her. Flinging back the bedclothes he flung himself upon her . . .'.

And last night he told the Council meeting: 'I am no prude. I have seen the seamy side of life. But this book depraves sex. Surely we can take steps to protect our young people from reading such books?'

Miss Gerard, who selects 5,000 books a year, told the *Daily Mirror:* 'Its all a lot of hooey. If the Council is going to throw out every book that has a sex element, we are going to have very few left. Most novels contain some sexy sentences, but they cannot be described as immoral unless the whole chapter is read. I always make sure that we have no 'smutty' books. I personally select every book on the shelves and I do not know of one that is in bad taste'.

Councillor Gorman told his colleagues that twenty-seven people had borrowed the 'sexy' book during the last eleven months. . . . Alderman E. R. Willoughby said last night: 'the book will be removed from the library. We are not telling anybody its title as we have no desire to publicise this sort of thing'."[61]

Alderman Willoughby's hopes were dashed, for the *Evening Standard* of the same day announced:

"The book that shocked Worthing's Councillors is *The Captain's House,* by May Edginton."[62]

Norman Mailer's *The Naked and the Dead* was published in 1949, and in July, in his "Municipal Library Notes" column, S. H. Horrocks wrote:

"The eye of the citizen anxious about the state of public morals has glittered lately at the sight of the pages of a certain American novel. According to newspaper cuttings many public libraries have banned it. BOSTON is busy considering the matter, while TOTTENHAM has purchased a copy, 'but it will not be for general circulation'. LEEDS, on the other hand, has given the book an excellent half page criticism on the first page of their current *Book Guide,* but I have not seen it mentioned in any other book list. NESTON Library has rejected *I chose Freedom* but neither the Chairman nor a member of the committee, when challenged in Council, could recall any specific reason for doing so."[63]

J. F. W. Bryon, Senior Assistant at Beckenham Public Library, wrote in his column, "Off the Record" in the *Librarian and Book World:*

"What have you done with *The Naked and the Dead* in your library? One hears of strange behind-the-scenes scurryings, of Chief Librarians calling on Chairmen of Councils for a private ruling, of special sub-committees, of purchase and subsequent withdrawal, of banning, or ordering second-hand, of ordering one copy for a system with many branches, of copies classified with American literature, of others placed in the Reference Department only. Particularly one would like to know exactly what happened at a provincial library where it is understood, 'restricted' books are graded, and shelved behind locked doors, accessible in turn to

(a) staff only, (b) staff over 21, (c) male staff over 26 and female over 30, and (d) Chief Librarian only. The categories remind one of the rumoured wartime classification of security documents into confidential, highly confidential, secret, most secret, top secret, and Not-to-be-opened-at-all. A colleague envisages an intriguing scene in the library concerned: an assistant is found leaping up the stairs with a glint in his eye. Asked the reason for his haste, he replies: 'It is my 26th birthday today!' The distinction between men and women in category (c) is a quaint survival, and somewhat of an affront, implying presumably that men reach maturity four years before their female colleagues. But perhaps I am misinformed? The colleague who told me of this unusual practice no longer works at the library where it held."[64]

And Horrocks again, in his September 1949 "Municipal Library Notes":

"In August, as I write, the 4th, 5th, 6th and 7th printings of that certain book are promised for the shops shortly . . . The Sunday newspaper which used a portion of its front page on the book has done something. Unfortunately more libraries have banned it: CARSHALTON and LEAMINGTON being two, with BIRMINGHAM's lending libraries sub-committee a close third. Many other libraries have restricted its circulation—LEYTON to the over 21's, and DONCASTER to those who can open a locked glass fronted case. It is evident from the reading of the local press reports that few of those who voted against the book had read it, and certainly the arguments used in favour of non-purchase were specious in the extreme. 'It is not a matter of 'censoring', we are told 'but the *duty* of spending money to the best advantage'. It is certainly a hard thing to resist the temptation to act as a censor, but such a virtue is a *sine qua non* of the holder of a public office. NEWCASTLE-ON-TYNE have decided no longer to display the *Daily Worker* and *Universe*, while LEYTON with a certain practical wisdom, have classified Dali's *Life* with the book not mentioned above as suitable for issue to the over 21's."[65]

In his column for November 1949, Horrocks further reported:

"NEWCASTLE, who banned two newspapers last month, have reinstated them this. WIMBLEDON has refused to buy the new Van der Meersch unread, according to a London newspaper. In this context it might be as well to report that the WESTERN-SUPER-MARE library has decided 'as a matter of policy, that newspapers and periodicals having connections with any religious denomination or organization shall not be obtained or accepted for the Reading Room'. The only comment made about this depressing intelligence by the local newspaper was a caption 'Keeping clear of controversy!'."[66]

1. Dragnet. *Librarian and Book World,* vol. 28. no. 5. January 1939. p.127
2. Hickman, Frank. Topicalities. *Library World,* vol. 41. no. 472. February 1939. p.169

3. Cowles, Frederick (ed.). *Swinton and Pendlebury Public Libraries Bulletin,* vol. 11. no. 11. February 1939. pp.1-2

4. Cowles, Frederick (ed.). *Swinton and Pendlebury Public Libraries Bulletin,* vol. 11. no. 12. March 1939. p.1

5. Stevenson, W. B. Municipal library notes. *Library Association Record,* vol. 41. May 1939. p.232

6. Bosworth, Willan G. The new novels of the month. *Librarian and Book World,* vol. 28. no. 9. May 1939. p.261

7. Editorial. *Library World,* vol. 43. no. 489. July 1940. p.1

8. Editorial. *Library World,* vol. 43. no. 492. October 1940. p.50

9. Woodbine, Herbert. Reference libraries. *Library Association Record,* vol. 44. November 1942. p.171

10. Correspondence. *Library Association Record,* vol. 45. March 1943. p.171

11. Council Notes: American periodicals. *Library Association Record,* vol. 45. July 1943. p.109

12. Philip, Alex. J. War: a serial. *Librarian and Book World,* vol. 29. no. 5. January 1940. pp.101-102

13. Oldham Public Libraries, Art Galleries and Museums Committee. Minutes of meeting, 11th June 1940

14. Banning of the "Daily Worker". *Oldham Chronicle,* 11th July 1940

15. Banned from the Public Library. *Oldham Chronicle,* 23rd July 1940

16. Oldham Public Libraries, Art Galleries and Museums Committee. Minutes of meeting, 9th July 1940

17. Oldham Borough Council. Minutes of meeting, 7th August 1940

18. Action approved after criticism. *Oldham Chronicle,* 8th August 1940

19. No reprieve for banned paper. *Oldham Chronicle,* 12th September 1940

20. Tribune Editor's Letter. *Oldham Chronicle,* 29th August 1940

21. No ban on Mussolini at Library. *Southport Guardian,* 7th November 1942

22. "Daily Worker" ban. *Southport Guardian,* 18th November 1942

23. "Gestapo methods" alleged. *Southport Visiter,* 5th December 1942

24. Allen, E. "Daily Worker" and Library. *Southport Guardian,* 10th July 1943

25. Barbasch, Audrey N. No ban at Buxton. *Southport Guardian,* 31st July 1943

26. Southport Public Libraries and Art Committee. Minutes of meeting, 15th May 1944. no. 1336

27. Libraries Committee and Daily Worker. *Southport Visiter,* 16th May 1944

28. Feilden, Herbert. Libraries' Committee's decision. *Southport Visiter,* 30th May 1944

29. Southport Public Libraries and Art Committee. Minutes of meeting, 20th November 1944. no. 112

30. McColvin, Lionel R. *The public library system of Great Britain.* London, Library Association, 1942

31. Library Association, Council of. *The public library service: its post war reorganization and development.* London, Library Association, 1943

32. Library bans Aldous Huxley's new book. *Southport Guardian,* 28th August 1943

33. That library ban. *Southport Guardian,* 28th August 1943

34. "Art of seeing". *Southport Visiter,* 12th October 1943

35. Philip, Alex. J. Editorial. *Librarian and Book World,* vol. 33. no. 3. November 1943. p.33

36. Keswick wants book censorship. *Cumberland Herald,* 4th November 1944
37. Editorial. *Library Review,* vol. 9. no. 72. Winter 1944. p.241
38. Silverpen. *Cumberland Herald,* 11th November 1944
39. Trimble, Ismay. German books at Keswick. *Cumberland Herald,* 11th November 1944
40. Council Library Committee. *Keswick Reminder,* 18th December 1944
41. Horrocks, S. H. Municipal Library Notes. *Library Association Record,* vol. 48. November 1946. p.283
42. Editorial. *Library Review,* vol. 11. no. 81. Spring 1947. p.250
43. Huntley, Brian. Annual Reports. *Librarian and Book World,* vol. 36. no. 6. June 1947. p.127
44. Craig, Alec. *The Banned Books of England.* London, George Allen and Unwin, 1962. p.112
45. Sheffield ban on "Amber". *Sheffield Telegraph,* 17th December 1946
46. "Silly" ban on "Dull, dreary Amber". *The Star,* 27th December 1946
47. "C.D.J." Letters to the Editor. *Sheffield Telegraph,* 19th December 1946
48. Sitting in judgment. *Leamington Morning News,* 27th October 1947
49. Bishop's Book "decidedly harmful". *Coventry Evening Telegraph,* 18th October 1947
50. Bishop of Birmingham's book for Leamington Public Library. *Leamington Morning News,* 17th November 1947
51. Tolerance prevails. *Leamington Morning News,* 24th November 1947
52. Dalton, Gilbert. The Bishop's book. *Leamington Courier,* 12th December 1947
53. Banned book comedy. *Caithness Courier,* 12th March 1947
54. Banned book will remain in library. *Caithness Courier,* 9th April 1947
55. Should 'bad' book be barred? *Middlesborough Evening Gazette,* 3rd December 1947
56. Stockton Public Library Committee. Minutes of meeting, 15th December 1947
57. Stockton Borough Council. Minutes of meeting, 6th January 1948
58. Northern Notes. *Middlesborough Evening Gazette,* 8th January 1948
59. Horrocks, S. H. Municipal Library Notes. *Library Association Record,* vol. 50. June 1948. p.159
60. Horrocks, S. H. Ban the "poison shelf". *Municipal Journal,* 28th January 1949
61. Hooey, says librarian—but 'shocking' book is banned. *Daily Mirror,* 7th January 1949
62. "It is a highly moral story". *Evening Standard,* 7th January 1949
63. Horrocks, S. H. Municipal Library Notes. *Library Association Record,* vol. 51. July 1949. p.223
64. Bryon, J. F. W. Off the record. *Librarian and Book World,* vol. 38. no. 7. July 1949. p.186
65. Horrocks, S. H. Municipal Library Notes. *Library Association Record,* vol. 51. September 1949. p.283
66. Horrocks, S. H. Municipal Library Notes. *Library Association Record,* vol. 51. November 1949. p.352

CHAPTER 3

The P. G. Wodehouse Affair
1940–1947

The motivation behind the censorship of P. G. Wodehouse's books by a number of public libraries is difficult to appreciate in the less emotive atmosphere of peacetime. It must be borne in mind, however, that this event took place two years after the beginning of the war when the future looked particularly black for Britain; and that it was not easy to ascertain the true facts of the case at the time. In fact it was not until the end of the war that it was established officially that although his broadcasts were inopportune, Wodehouse had not committed a crime; and moreover the facts had been exaggerated and distorted.

It is possible to review the facts of this episode in some detail for it aroused considerable interest nationally. It is of particular interest in that along with a small number of cases involving works by Enid Blyton, W. E. Johns, Frank Richards and others, it constituted a 'miscellaneous' category of censorship falling outside the traditional.

In February 1940, P. G. Wodehouse and his wife went to live in their French home at Le Touquet. In May of that year relatives received letters from him indicating that the situation was becoming awkward; he was now unable to escape from Le Touquet because of the German advance towards the French coast, but he hoped still to be able to get away.[1] His hopes were dashed. He was arrested by the Germans; confined to his home under surveillance and later removed to Germany for internment. During this period he worked on two new books. Towards the end of June 1941 Wodehouse was freed from an internment camp near Breslau and lodged in the Hotel Adlon in Berlin. He was free to come and go as he pleased, provided he did not leave Germany.[2]

On Thursday evening, 26th June 1941, P. G. Wodehouse made the first of a series of five broadcasts over German radio to the United States

34

of America.[3] These broadcasts were entirely non-political in content, and were a humourous account of his adventures in Germany. Coming when they did, the broadcasts caused a great deal of comment and criticism in the Press, and received some attention in the House of Commons.

As the *Bookseller* put it:

> "The acquiescence of Dr. Wodehouse serving the cause of Dr. Goebbels has caused much grief to the countless admirers of his happy genius."[4]

The *Bookseller* went on to quote Ian Hay's letter to *The Daily Telegraph* of 29th June 1941:

> "It was a brilliant idea, and unfortunately my old friend seems to have fallen for it. I have no hesitation in saying that he has not the slightest realisation of what he is doing. He is an easy-going and kindly man, cut off from public opinion here and with no one to advise him, and he probably agreed to broadcast because he saw no harm in the idea and because, after long captivity, he is thus enabled to resume relations with his friends of the English speaking world."[4]

Ian Hay was remarkably near the truth and his kindly letter expressed the view which both the literary and the librarianship press took over the matter. The *Bookseller's* report shows that other writers were not so kind; E. C. Bentley, "unforgiving and malevolent", wanted Oxford University to deprive Wodehouse of his honorary degree of Doctor of Letters which had been conferred in 1939. It appears from Bentley's letter to *The Daily Telegraph* of 30th June 1941 that he had always objected to this award "upon one who has never written a serious line". The *Bookseller* suggested that Bentley had obviously never read P. G. Wodehouse at all, or could not recognise perfect prose and superb humour when he saw it.[4]

The Times Literary Supplement took a similar attitude to that of the *Bookseller,* suggesting that P. G. Wodehouse had been forced into this position by some subtle method of the Gestapo and that there should be a suspension of judgment on Wodehouse until the true facts were known.[5]

On 8th July, questions were asked in the House concerning British subjects broadcasting under enemy auspices. The Secretary of State for the Home Department was asked what arrangements had been made for recording evidence of such broadcasters with a view to their prosecution as soon as they could be brought to justice. The Under Secretary of State for the Home Department confirmed that such broadcasts were recorded and that all practicable steps were being taken for the collection of evidence which might be relevant to prosecutions in the future against any British subject who assisted the enemy. Earl Winterton asked that the Government should make clear by an Order in Council that these people would be liable to prosecution whoever they were "whether famous writers or anybody else". The Under Secretary of State said that he thought the situation was already perfectly clear:

> "Anybody who assists the enemy by broadcasting in their programmes is obviously liable to prosecution if sufficient evidence can be brought after the war, and it is for the purpose of collecting the evidence that we are taking the steps suggested . . . ."[6]

On 9th July 1941 when Mr. Mander asked the Foreign Secretary, Anthony Eden, about the Wodehouse broadcasts in particular, he replied that the Government had seen with regret the report that P. G. Wodehouse had lent his services to the German propaganda machine. However, he would bear in mind Mr. Manders suggestion that he should take such steps as were available to him to bring to the attention of P. G. Wodehouse and others the gravity of their situation by apparently lending their names to the German war effort.[7]

On 17th July 1941, German radio broadcast details of P. G. Wodehouse's position. It was stated that P. G. Wodehouse was now over sixty and no longer eligible for military service and was automatically released from internment according to International Agreement. He was living as a guest of some German friends; his wife, still in France, was expected to join him. The report concluded that P. G. Wodehouse was under no compulsion to make broadcasts over German radio and could stop them if he wished at any time.[8]

The Wodehouse broadcasts came to a rather abrupt end after the fifth. It appears that in a rather roundabout fashion he had received a communication from some of his friends in Britain which told him how damaging to his reputation were his broadcasts from Germany.[9] He was also interviewed in Berlin by a number of American newspaper correspondents—the United States was not at war with Germany at the time—who told him of the damaging effects his broadcasts were having in the United States.[10]

On the 15th July 1941, two days before the German radio announcement on P. G. Wodehouse, William Connor (Cassandra of the *Daily Mirror*), with the full backing of the Minister of Information and much against the wishes of the Governors of the B.B.C., gave a ten-minute talk on P. G. Wodehouse and his broadcasts after the 9 o'clock news. This broadcast brought forth letters of protest to *The Times* and, according to Cassandra, letters of congratulation and agreement to the *Daily Mirror*.[11] Readers' letters to *The Times* attacked the B.B.C. for allowing the broadcast, and also the content of the broadcast. It was described as "ten minutes of irrelevant smearing, pseudo-dramatically delivered".[12] Further letters to *The Times* attacked Cassandra for delivering a "malicious piece of vulgarity" and for condemning P. G. Wodehouse before all the facts and circumstances were known from which a fair judgment could be formed.[13] The Minister of Information, Duff Cooper, took full responsibility for the broadcast, exonerating the B.B.C. While the B.B.C. had felt that "the broadcast was in execrable taste", Duff Cooper felt that "in time of war, plain speaking is more desirable than good taste".[14] Cassandra defended himself in characteristic style and attacked *The Times* for publishing letters critical of his talk.

"Since when has it been bad taste to name and nail a traitor to England? The letters you have published have only served as a sad demonstration that there is still in this country a section of the community eager and willing to defend its own quislings."[11]

Later evidence suggests that Cassandra had not heard the P. G. Wodehouse broadcasts[36] but it was mainly as a result of Cassandra's emotive broadcast and the campaign against P. G. Wodehouse conducted by the *Daily Mirror* that a number of town councils decided to remove the works of P. G. Wodehouse from their public libraries.

Portadown in County Armagh, Northern Ireland, and Sheffield were the first local authorities to take action against P. G. Wodehouse, although in slightly different ways. The *Belfast Telegraph* reported that:

"At their meeting last evening (16th July 1941) the (Portadown) Urban Council unanimously decided to instruct the Library Committee to withdraw from circulation all of P. G. Wodehouse's books. Mr. Edward M'Cann, who raised the matter, said the Library Committee had been talking some time ago about banning books, and he thought they had a good opportunity now. P. G. Wodehouse, the humorist, was now giving propaganda talks from Germany, and he thought that from what they had heard from a BBC talk on Tuesday night that there was no doubt that they should ban Wodehouse's books. 'They are no longer funny', Mr. M'Cann added. Mr. George Johnston agreed, and said Wodehouse was no friend of the state at the present time."[15]

The motion was passed unanimously. In a letter to the *Northern Whig and Belfast Post* two days later, G. R. Lloyd of Belfast said:

"For a long time now a possible Nazi invasion of Britain has been in the news, and we are told that Britain is prepared. What is not generally realized is that there is a more subtle form of invasion which has already taken place. No Nazi paratroops have landed in Britain, yet there are many signs that a spiritual penetration by Nazi ideas and methods is in progress. The fact that it comes gradually and unnoticed makes it all the more menacing. The most recent symptom is the Portadown Urban Council's ban on Wodehouse's books from the Public Library. This may seem a small thing, but it is symptomatic of an attitude of mind which is far more dangerous to our country than a Panzer division. . . . Some of the remarks of the Portadown Councillors are in the very best Goebells tradition. For example Mr. M'Cann, as reported in the press, stated that Wodehouse's books 'are no longer funny'. Just how the humour of books written years ago can be affected by the recent actions of the Author is hard to understand. My remarks are prompted not by any interest in or sympathy with Wodehouse, but by concern at the dangerous results which would follow if the people of our land swallow the nonsense and hysterical stupidity of the Portadown Council. An appeal to people not to buy books written by Wodehouse would perhaps have been reasonable, but the banning of the books from the Library is undemocratic and childish. . . . A spark of humour would have saved Portadown Council from making itself a laughing stock."[16]

A month later the Larne Regional Education Committee resolved to ban all books as published and edited by P. G. Wodehouse from circulation from the schools in the area under the Committee's jurisdiction, and also that the Antrim County Library Committee were to be informed of this action.[17] The banning did not spread any further in Northern Ireland, however, and it is notable that no action was taken against Wodehouse's books in the one large urban library system in the Province, Belfast Public Libraries.[18]

Also on the 16th July 1941 the Libraries, Art Galleries and Museums Committee of the Sheffield City Council unanimously decided that no more books by P. G. Wodehouse would be bought for the City Libraries. Alderman J. Hawnt, Chairman of the Committee stated that the ban would operate until Wodehouse substantiated his claim to be a Britisher. The decision expressed the Committee's determination not even to appear to give support in the remotest degree to a writer whose loyalty to this country was very questionable.

"I cannot find any excuse for a man who would make any plea for, or give any support to, a body of administrators who have debauched the minds of the children and young people of Germany, and deprived them of any guidance or teaching as to their relationship and duty to God."[19]

The Committee did not propose to take any action over the copies of P. G. Wodehouse's books already in Sheffield City Libraries. Alderman Hawnt, in a letter to the Sheffield *Telegraph and Independent* later explained the point of view of the Libraries Committee in deciding to buy no further copies of books by P. G. Wodehouse.

"Library readers can decide for themselves whether or not they read the Wodehouse books already in stock and the Committee express no views on this point. As representatives of the citizens of Sheffield, however, the Committee feel sure that they will be interpreting the feelings of the great majority in deciding not to use public money to subsidise a man who is acting with the enemy, since a proportion of the cost of every new book they buy goes to the author."[20]

There is no doubt that Cassandra's broadcast on Wodehouse created a great deal of hatred and disgust at Wodehouse's action, as it was obviously intended to do. Certainly it created a great deal more ill-feeling than did the Wodehouse broadcasts themselves. A letter to the *Telegraph and Independent* printed the day after the Library Committee's decision reads as follows:

> "As a former admirer of P. G. Wodehouse I am sure I express the loathing and disgust which must be felt by every decent Briton after listening to the broadcast by Cassandra on Tuesday night. Within ten minutes every book in my possession written by the literary quisling was destroyed and placed in the dustbin. Never again will I read a novel by this traitor—a vow which, I am sure, will be made by millions more. Surely it would be a proper gesture if the public libraries withdrew from circulation all books written by this cowardly comfort-loving pro-Nazi."[21]

While the Sheffield Library Committee's decision received little local or national publicity not all those who knew of it were happy about it. W. Glynne Jones, wrote in the *Telegraph and Independent:*

> "When Germans burnt the books of anti-Nazi authors we condemned this violence to liberty. The deplorable case of P. G. Wodehouse has now brought forth in this country a boycott upon his books. I note that the Libraries Committee has decided to buy no more of his works. If this action can take place re non-political and extremely comic literature, to what depth of intolerance will it lead us?"[22]

New books by Wodehouse were not added to the stock of Sheffield City Libraries for another thirteen years, although the subject reappeared in the Minutes of the Libraries Sub-Committee on 8th December 1953:

> "P. G. Wodehouse. Correspondence was submitted from borrowers commenting on the present policy of the Sub-Committee in connection with books by P. G. Wodehouse, and requesting that such policy be re-considered. The Sub-Committee agreed that the matter be deferred for further consideration in three months' time."[23]

The Minutes of 9th March 1954 read:

> "P. G. Wodehouse. Pursuant to their decision of 8th December last, the Sub-Committee reconsidered their policy in connection with books by P. G. Wodehouse, and they decided that such books be now admitted to the City Libraries."[24]

Thus the Sheffield ban on new works by Wodehouse was lifted. There appears to have been no comment in the local press about this decision nor any reaction at the Council Meeting where the Libraries Sub-Committee Minutes received final approval.[25]

The Sheffield and Southport libraries committees were exceptional in that they eventually took formal decisions to rescind the ban on Wodehouse's works, whereas the ban on his works by library committees in other towns appears to have been forgotten in time, his works being reintroduced in these libraries without any formal committee decision.

In Southport, the Book Purchasing Sub-Committee of the Libraries and Art Committee had been asked to approve the purchase of a number of books, one of which was P. G. Wodehouse's latest, *Quick Service*. The Sub-Committee decided not to add this book to the public libraries, and on 21st July 1941 the main Committee resolved that all P. G. Wodehouse's books be withdrawn from circulation until further notice. The Libraries and Art Committee's decision was reported to Council on Tuesday 5th August 1941 when Councillor Mrs. Haigh put forward an amendment to the effect that the works of Wodehouse already acquired should be put back into circulation in the library. Mrs. Haigh agreed with the decision of the Book Purchasing Sub-Committee but said that she thought that the decision of the Libraries and Art Committee to remove all his books:

> ". . . 'was going a bit too far. All the books of Wodehouse that we have here were purchased before he was taken from France into Germany and became 'Nazified'. . . . The books written by him before he was a Nazi, . . . would be all right for 'blackout nights'. . . . I think to move these books would show that stupidness which the Nazis have shown in burning Bolshevic books."[26]

She went on to say that if the Council was going to regard the political bias of all the writers they would have a big task in putting their libraries straight. From the point of view of fair-dealing they should keep the books written before Mr. Wodehouse became a Nazi, and she moved that these be restored to circulation. Alderman Dr. H. Coates said that he had taken part in getting the resolution of the Libraries Committee passed and argued that:

> ". . . the literary merits do not affect the situation at all. There is only one thing, that this man has hired himself to aid and comfort our enemies to the extent he is acting against us in this war for the one and only object of his broadcast was to undermine our resolution to prosecute this war until Hitlerism is destroyed. There is only one way in which we can show our disapproval of his action, that is to decide to have nothing to do with him or any of his works."[26]

Councillor P. Carter said that when the Libraries and Art Committee had decided to remove all Wodehouse's books from the library, the entire Committee with the exception of Councillor Mrs. Haigh voted in favour. Mrs. Haigh's amendment to restore his works was defeated.

Councillor R. A. C. Greaves then put forward an amendment that Wodehouse's works be disposed of as surplus paper for pulping:

> "I am amazed that anyone in this council chamber should get up and support that books by Wodehouse should be left on our shelves in the public libraries. What we want is to get rid of anything connected with those who have acted in such a way in order to get better treatment for themselves. I do not think the public want to read them, and the better thing is to turn them to useful war purpose. His name will stink in the nostrils of any right-minded person."[26]

He suggested that the Libraries Committee had not gone far enough and he concluded with the proposition that "this peculiar type of humour is not what is required by British people."[26]

Councillor Greaves' amendment was accepted by nine votes to four—thirty six members of the Council abstained from voting. Thus ninety books by P. G. Wodehouse in the library were earmarked for pulping. The Town Clerk took Counsel's opinion however and reported to the Libraries Committee in October 1941 that as trustees they had no authority to destroy public property. The Committee therefore decided to adhere to its resolution that the books simply be withdrawn from circulation and it left any further action to the Town Clerk.[27] In the light of the legal opinion, the Libraries Committee directed the Chief Librarian to preserve the books.[28]

Although the decision of Sheffield Public Libraries to discontinue buying new books by Wodehouse appears to have gone almost unnoticed nationally, Southport's decision to destroy its entire stock certainly did not. Letters and articles appeared not only in the Southport newspapers but in a number of national dailies and periodicals although surprisingly little comment appeared in the professional library journals. Much of the correspondence was opposed to Southport's decision and there was very little in favour of it. "The Watcher" of the *Oldham Evening Chronicle* pointed out two days after the Council decision, that there was a time when the Atkinson Free Library (Southport Central Library) was one of the best managed and most progressive in the north-west, but that this decision seemed to be a mistake. After all, how would it harm Wodehouse?

> "Let me state that I hope Wodehouse will be suitably dealt with after the war, and that the Government will look upon him as one of that vile race of Quislings so appropriately denounced by Mr. Churchill, who promised that they would be proceeded against. Thus I would never again support the expenditure of public money on any more Wodehouse publications, but the books at present in the library I should leave. After all, the public will decide, and probably most of them will be left on the shelves."[29]

Many Southport residents called the Council decision "childish" and "unnecessary"[30] and many people suggested that Wodehouse's books should not be pulped but should be presented to hospitals or other institutions or indeed be passed on to the troops who "in the coming winter will urgently need light-reading matter."[30]

On the other hand, some residents were in favour of the ban and one, Herbert Fielden, wrote to the *Southport Visiter:*

> "The decision of the Town Council might be carried further, and the books of P. G. Wodehouse be banned indefinitely from Southport's public libraries. . . . Nine to four against with thirty-six abstentionists, in such an important issue is a very grave reflection on the courage of members of the Council. If they are not at total war—then I suggest that they have no right whatsoever to sit upon such a public body in wartime. No incident and no propaganda against our cause is too small not to affect our men's lives one way or the other. Let us be thankful that the thirty-six abstentionists and the four who voted for Wodehouse are not essential for the success of our war effort."[31]

Arthur Thompson of Teignmouth, a journalist and long-standing friend of Wodehouse and the author of a number of letters in the press at this time was not in favour of the ban.

> "All fair-minded men will deplore the action of the Southport Town Council in withdrawing the novels of P. G. Wodehouse from their Library on account of his broadcasts from Germany, where he is a prisoner. It has always been a characteristic of the British race to give fair play to both sides; it has also been an old axiom of English justice to say 'Every man is innocent until proved guilty'. Another attribute of our race was not to condemn a man who cannot answer back. . . . Faced with the harassing difficulties of the position he was placed in, as a prisoner in enemy hands, far from his home and his friends, I venture to say that there is not one of his detractors who would have done any other than he has done, in the matter of non-political broadcasting in exchange for a measure of liberty. 'Plum' Wodehouse was never a politician, neither was he a soldier. . . . He, as an author, only asked to be left alone. He is a delightful fellow, quite apart from his books; and everybody knows that in his literary gifts, as a humorist, he stands far above all others. He is the most popular funny writer in the English language, and he will continue to be so in spite of the attacks of a small minority. To prove this, one has only to count up—on the fingers of one hand—the small number of towns that have banned his works. They amount to three. A little place in Northern Ireland that nobody ever heard of; and in England, Sheffield and Southport. Like banning any kind of book, the public will want it all the more. His circulation will go up by leaps and bounds. Already in the West of England there is a bigger demand for his works than ever. 'Twas ever thus. And I do hope his opponents will be perfectly satisfied."[32]

'Pall Mall' in *The Daily Mail* (Hull) agreed with Arthur Thompson when he wrote:

"But will the Southport decision be all that is intended? To sweep the books from the library and to say: 'no more Wodehouse', is surely to stimulate a sharpened appetite for his works. Ban any mortal thing and you create an increased desire for it. The unobtainable is always preferable to the things that can be had at will. As for the novelist himself, he is not likely to be unduly perturbed, even though every library in Britain follows Southport's example. He will reason that his position as a writer is assured and that all will be forgiven after the war."[33]

"Rate Payer" writing to the *Southport Guardian* on the 16th August may well have provided the necessary stimulant to the Town Clerk to take Counsel's opinion concerning the legality of the decision to destroy Wodehouse's books.

"It would be interesting to know whether, legally, the votes of nine members of the Town Council, four opposing, and the others looking uninterestedly on, are sufficient to have public property destroyed. Since the Wodehouse books are public property, and do not belong either to nine or the whole sixty members of the Council, the question as to whether the legal right to have this property destroyed vests in the Council is of considerable interest."[34]

Mrs. A. Wright in a letter to the *Southport Visiter* considered that the Committee had gone:

". . . outside their province. Their duty is to see that the library has a supply of books which the public needs, either for instruction or recreation. Mr. Wodehouse's books are good, clean, rather sarcastic humour, a real recreation, and are quite a valuable tonic to tired minds. The Committee have nothing to do with what occurs outside the library, and their ill-considered action unfortunately has the effect of making Southport insular and somewhat ridiculous."[35]

On 23rd August Arthur Thompson returned to the defence of Wodehouse.

"Now that the broadcasts from Germany have been done all over again at a popular time . . . on the German wave-length in order to let British listeners hear what it is all about, I feel sure that some of the mighty heroes, who have been swash-buckling and sabre rattling, must be sorry they spoke. Surely there was not one single word in the humourous talks on his prison experiences that could either aid the enemy or undermine our own war efforts? Little details about prison smells, catching trains with ten hours to spare, sleeping on straw, eating poor meals of variegated soups, etc., and travelling in horse trucks, could hardly effect the war in any way whatever. . . . I am afraid, your Town Council rushed into this matter like a bull at a gate, before they knew the real facts. The fact remains . . . that not only has £20 to £30 of rate-payers money been thrown away, but also a very dangerous precedent has been introduced into local government. If a small number of our elected representatives can decide what we are going to be allowed to read, where does our English freedom come in? This smacks of Nazi-ism and Hitler tyranny, if ever anything did. And yet, this is supposed to be the thing we are fighting. We in the West are very sorry indeed for the poor ratepayers of Southport. Their Library Committee, backed by their Town Council, and tacitly supported by a large band of indifferent Councillors who were too frightened to vote, have taken it into their inexperienced hands to dictate, forsooth, as to what the folks who pay the piper should, or should not, read. Was there ever such a silly exhibition of bigoted prejudice? When this war is over, someone is going to be sorry."[36]

Readers letters continued to suggest that P. G. Wodehouse's books still possessed great entertainment value for hospital patients, members of the forces, etc. Despite these letters, the Southport Council was not prepared to change its decision until the Town Clerk persuaded it to do so on legal grounds.

After the controversy over the Southport decision had died down the matter rested until the January, 1947 meeting of the Libraries Committee, which recommended that the books be put back into circulation. The Council met on Wednesday 5th February 1947 and carried an amendment to defer consideration of the Libraries Committee recommendation until a special committee had reported on the reasons why the original decision to destroy the books had not been implemented. Notwithstanding the setting up of a special committee however, the Council also decided that the books should be returned to the shelves and they were in fact freely available to the public on the day after the Council meeting. The Special Committee met briefly a few days later when the facts, including Counsel's opinion, were outlined and it was accepted that no blame attached to the librarian or the Committee for not carrying out the terms of the original minute of 1941.[28]

The banning of Wodehouse's books was confined almost entirely to libraries of the north of England. On the 22nd July 1941, the Blackpool Public Libraries Committee resolved: "That the Public Librarian be instructed to withdraw from circulation in the libraries under the control of this Committee, the works of P. G. Wodehouse".[37] This resolution was later confirmed by the Council. There is no surviving record to show that the books were destroyed and in the opinion of P. Dunderdale, Chief Librarian of Blackpool, they were not. The ban on Wodehouse presumably was ignored shortly after the war when a new Chief Librarian was appointed. There appears to have been no public or Council reaction to the re-introduction of Wodehouse's books to Blackpool Public Libraries.

Following in the wake of Southport and Blackpool, the Public Library and Baths Committee at Colne, Lancashire resolved on 7th August 1941:

"That all the works of P. G. Wodehouse now in the library be withdrawn from circulation and disposed of as waste-paper."[36]

In Council on the 3rd September 1941, Councillor Duckworth referred to the Minute and asked the Chairman of the Library Committee the reason for the withdrawal of the works, the number of volumes and the approximate cost.

"Were the Committee going through all the volumes in the library? He wondered if it was in connection with the salvage drive. The Chairman of the Libraries Committee, Councillor J. Y. Ball, said he was sorry if Councillor Duckworth was not conversant with the writings of so notorious a character as Mr. Wodehouse. He did not wish to discuss anything in regard to any matter he may have written in the past, but it was what he was writing and doing at the present time. As to these 28 volumes it was not a point of theirs (the Committee) to try and make any money in connection with anything he might have written. 'If it would help in the cremation of Wodehouse . . . I would be quite prepared to get a match for that purpose'. Councillor Phillips asked: 'Is it true that he is a pro-German?' Councillor Ball replied: 'I could not say. I have not had the opportunity of meeting him, but would be prepared to do so if he could make an appointment'."[39]

The Council confirmed the Committee decision.[40]

The *Colne Times* commenting on the decision was not sure whether the Colne Library Committee was acting on the suggestion of some organisation to which it was affiliated or, whether the Southport example was considered a good one to follow. Wodehouse had certainly "blotted his copy book" but it was questionable whether that called for the kind of action taken by the Libraries Committee. There might have been some who thought that there were already a lot of books on the shelves of the library which should not have been there—books which boosted the Nazi regime and its leading figures, others which glorified fascism and Mussolini, all written by Englishmen.

"In this changing world the time may come when there will be a demand once again for the works of Wodehouse, in which case the ratepayers will have to find the money for a new set."[41]

The Colne decision like that at Southport generated a good deal of correspondence for and against the ban. "Endurum Perpetua" in a letter to the *Colne Times* pointed out that only three years previously people were "expressing amusement at similar puerile antics indulged in by the Nazis"[42] and that now they had the pleasure of witnessing the same antics on their own doorstep. The letter continues:

"Whatever may be Wodehouse's ignominious crimes—and I think most people who heard or read the broadcasts will agree on their rather inculpable nature—the action of the Committee seems to be a case of cutting off the nose to spite the face, and the operation will hardly add to its intellectual pulchritude. One would be safe in saying that the Wodehouse books are amongst the most popular in the library. . . . If the Committee can find in these books any subversive qualities, they might as well complete their self-appointed 'purge' and burn nine-tenths of the remaining stock. We can then queue up for the pleasure of choosing such obscure titles as 'The True Meaning of Democracy' and 'The Rights of the Common Citizen'. The Committee might take a further step, which would leave even the Southport Authorities a little breathless, by railing off some of the surplus ground outside the library and starting a small concentration camp for obstinate readers. This would be fine propaganda and would greatly clarify our war aims."

The Editor of the *Burnley Express* commented:

"Believing that members of Burnley Town Council possess average intelligence, if not the super-intelligence which some electors demand of them, we do not expect them to repeat the grave error of Colne Town Council. . . . Because he (Wodehouse) loses his self-respect in Berlin in time of war, the citizens of Colne are to lose the cheerful companionship of Bertie Wooster, Psmith, Lord Blandings and all the other comic characters created by P.G. in days of peace. The humble rate payer, who pays for the books in the public library, who reads them, but who does not choose them, he, of course will instantly perceive that the only person to suffer by this display of municipal wrath is himself. . . . All that remains for the Colne Library Committee to do is to rid the shelves of the works of all other authors who have been suspected of moral turpitude—and then close the library doors."[43]

On the 17th October the *Colne Times* reported Counsel's opinion given to the Town Clerk of Southport that the Committee had no authority to destroy public property. This decision was no doubt noted by the Colne Library Committee for there is no record of the Colne books having been destroyed either.[44]

The Committee of the Colne Literary and Scientific Society having written to the Town Clerk of Colne, asked the *Colne Times* to print the text of the letter:

"Having considered the decision of the Public Library and Baths Committee . . . to be entirely indefensible the Society registers an emphatic protest against it, regarding it as harmful to the community . . . to destroy exactly that factor for which this war is being fought: the freedom of each individual to think for himself; to read what he will and to hold whatever opinions conscience and knowledge dictate."[45]

This was to lead to yet another battle in Council. Councillor Doyle asked what action had been taken. Had the books been destroyed or put into cold storage? Councillor Duckworth demanded to know whether the Committee had the power to destroy the books. The Mayor finally admitted that the books had not been destroyed.[46]

The ban on P. G. Wodehouse no longer exists in Colne, as at Blackpool it probably fell into abeyance soon after the war. Peter Wightman acquired a full set of Wodehouse's books on his appointment as Librarian at Colne in 1959 and there was no public or council reaction to the readdition of Wodehouse's books.

On 16th August 1941 the *Oldham Standard* stated:

> "The philosophic calm of the Oldham Libraries Committee Meetings proved quite equal this week to the attempt to foist a controversy upon the members. They were asked at the last Council Meeting if they would consider the advisability of burning the books of a certain British author who is now broadcasting from Berlin. The works of the author, which are of a light, humorous nature far moved from any ideologies, have been popular, and the Libraries Committee in their service to the reading public of Oldham have placed these books on their shelves and there, they decided this week, the books will remain for any reader to borrow. It is a minor decision which interprets democracy's principle of the freedom of thought. The Committee have preserved a sense of proportion. Southport have burnt this author's books, a foolish, almost a pagan, gesture which does the author no harm and the reading public no good. If you object to your baker's religion you do not burn his bread. You can always change your baker."[47]

The matter had been first raised at the Oldham Town Council Meeting of 6th August 1941, by Councillor Arnold Tweedale who asked:

> "Whether the Libraries Committee would consider handing over Mr. Wodehouse's books to the Carrying and Cleansing Committee to help the national effort."[48]

Alderman Bainbridge, Chairman of the Libraries Committee, promised that he would report on the matter at the next meeting of the Committee. Six days later on 12th August the Libraries Committee considered Councillor Tweedale's suggestion. The Chairman reported that he had been asked at the Council Meeting whether the Committee would consider following Southport's decision. A ban on Wodehouse's works would have affected over one hundred volumes in the Central Library alone. Councillor Graham said that he had listened to two of Wodehouse's broadcasts and he considered that he had not said anything wrong against this country. He suggested that "they should postpone the matter for a month and try to obtain reports of his broadcasts". The Director of Oldham Libraries, Mr. S. Deem, said:

> "The books were amongst the most popular they had in the library, were in a humorous vein, and there was not the slightest sign of politics in any of them. Councillor H. Buckley considered it would be cutting off their noses to spite their faces to destroy one hundred books. Mr. Wodehouse might be broadcasting with a pistol at his back. He moved that they should carry on as at present with the books

but do not purchase any more. They should hear both sides of the case before judging the man. Councillor Bradbury did not see any reason why they want to ban the books until they got further information."[49]

Councillor Buckley, seconded by Councillor Graham, put forward a motion that no further copies of Wodehouse's books be obtained and this was carried unanimously. The existing stock was to remain on the shelves of the library. Oldham's decision was thus similar to that taken by Sheffield.

After the first wave of decisions totally to ban Wodehouse's books or at least to buy no more, Wodehouse's name was to appear on the agenda of Library Committee and Council meetings in various parts of the country, but, in nearly every case, he emerged unscathed.

Blackburn was quite definite in its view regarding the withdrawal of the books by P. G. Wodehouse. Alderman F. J. Greeves, J.P., Chairman of the Library Committee, told the *Blackburn Times* on the 7th August 1941 that he did not see any reason for such a policy and that he did not think that his Committee would withdraw any books because of a disagreement with an author's views. There was still a moderately large circle of interested readers but he felt that the books were no longer the great draw of former years. Throughout its history the Blackburn Public Library had not found it necessary to ban any book of merit because of an author's personal beliefs.[50] Three weeks later 'Rambling Robin', in his *Blackburn Times* column, 'Around the Town' agreed with the Library Committee views, asking:

> "What good would it do to send Wodehouse to a literary Coventry? . . . Surely there are many volumes one thousand times more fitting for the waste-paper basket—that prize package of lousy literature "Mein Kampf"?"[51]

At the end of the month, a representative of the *Bolton Journal and Guardian* interviewed the Chief Librarian of Bolton, H. Hamer, who told him that action against P. G. Wodehouse had been taken by the reading public themselves and that no official action was being taken. The interviewer agreed with the wisdom of this decision. Hamer told him that he had never seen so many copies of Wodehouse's books on the shelves and it was obvious to him that readers were boycotting this once popular author and experience had shown him that once an author lost the goodwill and interest of his public he rarely came back.[52]

The *Library World* for August 1941 made two references to the Wodehouse affair. The first, in the Editorial, stated:

> "Even if our correspondent, Eratosthenes, who has vivid memories of the attempt at suppression during the Great War, writes somewhat heatedly about what may seem to be the not very important recent criticisms of the humorist Wodehouse, hi

general contention is one of supreme importance to librarians. Hardly a day passes in which the librarian is not advised, even ordered, to remove some author's works because of their want of quality, their political or religious views, their sex or other morality or want of it; and so on. Yet the whole purpose of the war is to preserve men's right to free minds and the free expression of them. Not a week passes when the librarian himself is not displeased by something in some book or other. But the prevention and not the promotion of undue censorship is the very essence of his work. A 'censoring mind' is a closed mind and a librarian with such a mind has got into the wrong profession." [53]

In the same issue Eratosthenes, a pseudonymous regular contributor, devoted a whole page to his anger at the censoring of Wodehouse's works.

"One despairs at times, as this sort of thing seems to prove that our life-work as librarians is a vain thing. These reflections are forced upon men when I contemplate the pother over the iniquities of P. G. Wodehouse, and the literally childishly-vulgar public expressions by Press and wireless upon this writer." [54]

Not that he approved of Wodehouse's broadcasts; what worried him was the lack of faith shown in the cause of librarianship by those who imagined they could sustain it by banishing his books from their libraries. He attacked Southport Town Council and asked what its action would achieve, and in defending Wodehouse, wrote:

"He is a writer who never dabbles in any form of politics, who never pretended to draw characters which are serious portraits of men and women. He is the creator of one of the legendary figures of literature—Jeeves. Do our important seaside gentlemen think they annihilate Jeeves by pulping the physical paper on which his record is given? Wodehouse is one of the most perfect writers of English alive . . . I hear, even in my own library, that certain old women of both sexes, mercifully very few in number, have a sense of nausea when they see Wodehouse, whom of course they have not read, on my shelves. They are of the same breed that burned *Tom Jones* and even *Jane Eyre* . . . they have existed in all ages and will exist until commonsense becomes an attribute of the human race. . . . Meanwhile, they have deprived hundreds of readers of innocent mirth in choice English, which has no relation whatever to the war, except that it cheers some intervals in our endurance of it. A *most* patriotic achievement! This attempt to suppress men through books must be resisted by all means we have. Otherwise we lose all for which we fight. We cannot expect the muddleheaded to understand this, but freedom in this, as in other things, is vital to us."

At the end of August a motion that the works of P. G. Wodehouse should be withdrawn from Thurrock, Essex, Public Libraries was defeated. Councillor J. H. Freeman, the mover, said that the man was the worst kind of traitor. Councillor W. H. Edwards, Assistant Head of a public school, and a teacher of literature said that Wodehouse's works had no permanent value.[55] Mr. E. Hanford said:

> "He did not know whether Mr. Freeman realised that he was proposing that the Council should destroy £40 worth of books. ... The proposal represented a hysterical view, the sort of view they got from a mob. These books were written long before the war, and there was nothing objectionable in the contents."[56]

Similar discussions took place in committee at Crompton (Lancashire); Leicester[57] and Llandudno[58,59] with no further action being taken.

At the Chertsey Urban District Council meeting in September 1941 Mr. W. J. King moved the following motion:

> "That the Librarian of the Chertsey Public Library be instructed to remove all writings of P. G. Wodehouse, and after having severed the leaves from their binding, to hand them over to the Salvage Department for disposal, and all other owners of such literature be offered the same facilities for disposal upon delivery of such books to the library."[60]

Mr. King justified this motion by asking his fellow Council members to judge Wodehouse not by his writings but by his actions. He was not worthy to have his writings on the bookshelves of the Chertsey Library with those of such patriots as Shakespeare, Scott and Dickens. The Country was at war, and in Mr. King's opinion Chertsey should take a firm line. Opposing, Mr. Jenkins professed himself greatly surprised at the attitude taken by Mr. King; and considered he had lost a due sense of proportion.

> "There were a great many other books in the library, the writers of which had offended against laws of decency of this country. If they were going to take away poor old Wodehouse from their library, they should do the same to the others.
>
> Mr. Payne looked upon books as works of art, which gave them benefit and pleasure. He quite agreed with a great deal that Mr. Jenkins had said . . . but the old man had no doubt chosen the easiest way out. They might have done the same if they had been in his position. They would do a very silly thing if they denied themselves of his books.
>
> Mr. Seccombe said that Wodehouse was a leg-puller: his whole attitude was part of his stock in trade and the whole thing was an elaborate leg-pull. They might take a different view of the case later on."

Mr. King's motion was finally defeated by eight votes to three. Wodehouse remained on the shelves of Chertsey Library.[60]

"Hydra" writing to his friend "Glauco" in his regular column in the *Library World,* October 1941 asked:

"Has your Committee talked about Mr. Wodehouse yet? I see that many prominent towns have distinguished themselves further by ordering a blitz against his books. Somehow I cannot bring myself to think with equanimity of *The Indiscretions of Archie* blazing on a bonfire. I used to think we left that kind of work to the gallant Marshal Goering and his henchman Goebbels. Who knows, we may even yet be flinging out Wagner and dictionaries of German/English. It is not the place in these fair pages to speculate upon the action of Mr. Wodehouse in his broadcasting, but even when they have been pitched out many people will give a wry recollection to his many volumes of profound nonsense, and think of Wooster, Mulliner, and the Empress of Blandings. My own Committee has so far kept silent upon the subject, and I have from time to time wondered what I would tell them if they mooted a banishing from our own shelves."[61]

It would not be correct to leave the Wodehouse affair at this point, although with the exception of a few post-war incidents and Sheffield's long continued ban the public library side of the matter was more or less complete. News on P. G. Wodehouse continued to filter through spasmodically, and in December 1943 the BBC placed a ban on the revival of certain musical comedies because Wodehouse had written the lyrics.[62] On the 20th November 1944 P. G. Wodehouse and his wife were arrested by the French Police in Paris, where he had finally been sent by the Germans to live under Gestapo surveillance. The police charged him with "undertaking propaganda in favour of the German Reich and German Policy on the radio."[63] Questioned by the police about his broadcasts, Wodehouse said that they were a voluntary effort to let his friends know his circumstances. They were made at his own request, were not intended as propaganda but as humorous descriptions of the experiences he underwent in the five German prison camps through which he had passed in one year after his arrest at Le Touquet.[64]

In the House of Commons, 6th December 1944, the Foreign Secretary Anthony Eden stated that the P. G. Wodehouse case was being closely watched by the Ambassador in Paris. Wodehouse had been arrested on 20th November on the grounds that he had broadcast from Berlin and had been released on 24th November on condition that he resided in a hospital under surveillance. He had been visited by the Embassy staff and relatives who reported that his health was good and that Wodehouse had not expressed a wish to return to Great Britain. The Foreign Secretary was also asking the French Government to state the legal grounds for this residence under surveillance. There was no question of a trial or of a charge now by the French police. The Foreign Secretary was asked whether P. G. Wodehouse should be brought to Great Britain for full investigation and trial. He replied that the Home Office had gone into the whole affair and had advised that there were no grounds upon which legal proceedings could be taken against Wodehouse. This being the case there was no question of asking the

French Government to hand him over for trial. Mr. G. Nicholson, M.P., suggested it would be better if Wodehouse were relegated to obscurity.[65] There were those in the House however, who were not prepared to relegate Wodehouse thus. On 15th December Mr. Quentin Hogg again raised the question of Wodehouse's broadcasts, stating that he thought the Government's legal advisers had a wholly mistaken view of the law. Sir Donald Somervell, the Attorney General, contended that the vital part of the offence of treason was the intent to assist the enemy. P. G. Wodehouse's case had been considered carefully on the evidence available and it had been decided that his conduct did not constitute an offence. If further evidence showed that Wodehouse had committed treason, he would not hesitate to prosecute.

Wodehouse remained under surveillance in Paris until 6th March 1945 when the Paris police released him, having decided that there was no basis for further action in his case.[66]

At the end of April 1947 P. G. Wodehouse left France for New York with his wife. On his arrival he stated that he intended to stay in the United States for a long time writing plays and books.[67]

The Wodehouse affair was almost complete. The re-instatement of his books in various libraries which had banned them has already been discussed. The Bolton Chief Librarian's comment on his loss of popularity was proved invalid in the long term for there is little doubt that P. G. Wodehouse's writings are as popular today as they were before the 1939-1945 war.

P. G. Wodehouse celebrated his ninetieth birthday on Friday, 15th October 1971. Michael Davie of *The Observer* interviewed him a few days before this event and some of Davie's comments make a penultimate postscript to this chapter.

"(Mrs. Wodehouse) raised the subject I hadn't had the heart to mention to Wodehouse: the Berlin broadcasts. She was evidently aware that some people in Britain, even today, have the impression that Wodehouse behaved discreditably during the war, without being able to remember quite why.

These strange events point to the central Wodehouse puzzle, . . . How has he managed to remain so well insulated from the world both in his books and in his life. However innocent the motives, the Berlin broadcasts were still an act of incredible obtuseness. The clue may be that the Wodehouse temperament is of a peculiar kind—a peculiarly *English* kind, one might say. He combines innocence, which is partly a lack of self-awareness, with a talent for dodging unpleasantness: a combination to be found also in bishops, school-masters, and occasionally in aristocrats—people who feel enclosed in a safe institutional framework. . . . The weakness of Wodehouse's policy of universal good will was exposed by what he has called his 'German troubles', when his instinct for minimising unpleasantness went altogether too far, though in a way that damaged no-one except himself. But on the whole it has served him well. Like one of his own characters to whom nothing seriously unpleasant ever happens, he gives the impression of having escaped life unscathed. While society disintegrates around him, he has evidently found a formula for living that allows him to carry on undisturbed. His novels, to him, are what the pig was to Lord Emsworth."[68]

At the time Michael Davie penned those comments, no one could foresee the final reinstatement of Wodehouse into "respectable" society. For in the New Years Honours List, 1975, P. G. Wodehouse received a Knighthood, at the age of 93. The *Daily Mirror,* perhaps rightly choosing to forget its efforts to brand Wodehouse as a traitor in 1941, and which contributed to the unusual sequence of events that make up this chapter, devoted its front page of the issue of 2nd January to the news that both P. G. Wodehouse and Charlie Chaplin, both men with controversial lives and both exiles from this country for many years, were to receive their ultimate accolades.[69] The *Mirror*[70] gave a brief history of Wodehouse's background, without reference to its own involvement, and felt that Britain had not acted overhastily in reaching this decision. Both *The Times* and *The Guardian* of the same day positively welcomed the news, seeing the Knighthood as an act of official foregiveness "done with good grace before the solitary surviving English literary comic genius . . . is beyond the reach of other men's opinions".[71] And that, *The Guardian* felt, was a "cause for rejoicing among all generous men". *The Guardian* was able to remember the attacks of Cassandra of the *Daily Mirror* clearly, however.

The Times considered Chaplin and Wodehouse to have fair claims to being considered "the funniest men in the world",[72] and agreed that the Knighthoods were richly deserved. *The Times* reported Wodehouse's own comments about the broadcasts in 1941: "Of course I ought to have had the sense to see that it was a loony thing to do to use the German radio for even the most harmless stuff, but I didn't. I suppose prison life saps the intellect."[72]

There were many "loony" things done during the 1939-1945 war, not least the war itself. In retrospect, Wodehouse's "crime" must have been amongst the most insignificant and harmless of the "loony" acts committed at that time.

Alas, official forgiveness came only just in time, for Sir Pelham Grenville Wodehouse died on 15th February 1975, only six weeks after the Knighthood was announced. He was engaged on his ninety-fourth novel at the time of his death. He, however, must have been content, for in a filmed BBC interview after the knighthood was announced, said that he believed that an author became "recognised" when he had a Knighthood and a place in Madame Tussaud's—and he now had both!

1. P. G. Wodehouse at Le Touquet. *The Times*, 27th May 1940
2. Mr. Wodehouse freed from internment. *The Times*, 27th June 1941
3. Broadcast from Berlin by Mr. Wodehouse. *The Times*, 28th June 1941
4. Notes and News: Wodehouse. *Bookseller*, 3rd July 1941. p.5
5. Notes and News. *The Times Literary Supplement*, 5th July 1941. p.1
6. Parliamentary Debates, Commons. 5th Series, Vol. 373. 8th July 1941. Col. 32
7. Parliamentary Debates, Commons. 5th Series, Vol. 373. 9th July 1941. Cols. 145-146
8. Mr. P. G. Wodehouse. *The Times*, 18th July 1941
9. Wodehouse Broadcasts end. *Colne Times*, 10th October 1941
10. Parliamentary Debates, Commons. 5th Series, Vol. 406. 15th December 1944. Cols. 1578-1588
11. Cassandra's postscript. *The Times*, 23rd July 1941
12. Barraud, Ronald F. Taste on the air. *The Times*, 18th July 1941
13. Taste on the air. *The Times*, 19th July 1941
14. Minister and B.B.C. *The Times*, 22nd July, 1941
15. Portadown bans Psmith. *Belfast Telegraph*, 17th July 1941
16. Lloyd, G. R. Wodehouse banning. *The Northern Whig and Belfast Post*, 19th July 1941
17. Wodehouse banned in Larne Schools. *Belfast Telegraph*, 1st September 1941
18. Letter from D. Wort, Deputy City Librarian of Belfast, to the author, 27th August 1971. (Unpublished)
19. No more of his books. *Sheffield Telegraph and Independent*, 17th July 1941
20. Hawnt, J. Libraries committee and Wodehouse. *Sheffield Telegraph and Independent*, 28th July 1941
21. W.A.B. P. G. Wodehouse. *Sheffield Telegraph and Independent*, 17th July 1941
22. Jones, W. Glynne. Wodehouse books. *Sheffield Telegraph and Independent*, 24th July 1941
23 Sheffield Libraries, Art Galleries and Museums Committee. Minutes of the Libraries Sub-Committee of 8th December 1953
24. Sheffield Libraries, Art Galleries and Museums Committee. Minutes of the Libraries Sub-Committee of 9th March 1954
25. Letter from J. Bebbington, City Librarian of Sheffield, to the author, 15th January 1971. (Unpublished)
26. Wodehouse books to be pulped. *Southport Guardian*, 6th August 1941
27. Southport and Wodehouse's Books. *Colne Times*, 17th October 1941
28. Letter from E. G. Twigg, Chief Librarian of Southport, to the author, 18th January 1971. (Unpublished)
29. 'The Watcher'. Jeeves off the shelf. *Oldham Evening Chronicle*, 7th August 1941
30. They want reprieve for Jeeves. *Southport Guardian*, 9th August 1941
31. Feilden, Herbert. Wodehouse books for pulp. *Southport Visiter*, 9th August 1941
32. Thompson, Arthur. A personal note. *Southport Visiter*, 9th August 1941
33. 'Pall Mall'. Off the shelves. *The Daily Mail* (Hull), 11th August 1941
34. 'Ratepayer'. Destruction of public books. *Southport Guardian*, 16th August 1941
35. Wright, Mrs. A. Wodehouse books for pulp. *Southport Visiter*, 16th August 1941
36. Thompson, Arthur. That Wodehouse controversy. *Southport Guardian*, 23rd August 1941

37. Letter from P. Dunderdale, Chief Librarian of Blackpool, to the author, 14th January 1971. (Unpublished)
38. Colne Public Library and Baths Committee. Minutes of the meeting of 7th August 1941
39. Colne Town Council: disposal of author's works. *Colne Times,* 5th September 1941
40. Colne Municipal Borough, Minutes of the meeting of 3rd September 1941
41. Works of P. G. Wodehouse. *Colne Times,* 5th September 1941
42. 'Endurum Perpetua'. Books of P. G. Wodehouse. *Colne Times,* 12th September 1941
43. Cutting off the nose. *Colne Times,* 19th September 1941
44. Letter from P. Wightman, Borough Librarian of Colne, to the author, 15th January 1971. (Unpublished)
45. Halliwell, S. K. Books of Wodehouse. *Colne Times,* 17th October 1941
46. Colne Council 'Breeze'. *Colne Times,* 31st October 1941
47. Philosophic calm. *Oldham Standard,* 16th August 1941
48. Wodehouse's books in library. *Oldham Chronicle,* 9th August 1941
49. Jeeves reprieved. *Oldham Evening Chronicle and Standard,* 14th August 1941
50. Not banned. *Blackburn Times,* 7th August 1941
51. 'Rambling Robin'. Around the town. *Blackburn Times,* 22nd August 1941
52. A snub for P.G. *Bolton Journal and Guardian,* 29th August 1941
53. Editorial. *Library World,* vol. 44, no. 501. August 1941. p.18
54. Letters on our affairs. *Library World,* vol. 44, no. 501. August 1941. p.32
55. Wodehouse not 'waste paper'. *The Star,* 3rd September 1941
56. No censorship at Grays Library. *Essex Weekly News,* 5th September 1941
57. No Wodehouse ban. *Leicester Evening Mail,* 3rd September 1941
58. Burning question for the Urban Council. *Llandudno Advertiser,* 19th July 1941
59. Those Wodehouse books. *Llandudno Advertiser,* 20th September 1941
60. Should Wodehouse books be removed? *Surrey Herald,* 26th September 1941
61. 'Hydra'. Letters on our affairs. *Library World,* vol. 44, no. 502. October 1941. p.51
62. News in brief. *The Times,* 23rd December 1943
63. Mr. P. G. Wodehouse—arrest and release in Paris. *The Times,* 23rd November 1944
64. Mr. P. G. Wodehouse on his broadcasts. *The Times,* 24th November 1944
65. Parliamentary Debates, Commons. 5th Series, vol. 406. 6th December 1944. Cols. 499-502
66. Mr. P. G. Wodehouse released from provisional confinement. *The Times,* 7th March 1945
67. Telegrams in brief. *The Times,* 28th April 1947
68. Davie, Michael. Wodehouse at ninety. *The Observer,* 10th October 1971
69. Knighthoods for the two clown princes of laughter. *Daily Mirror,* 2nd January 1975
70. Hagerty, Bill. Cheerio, Charlie . . . Pip-pip, PG. *Daily Mirror,* 2nd January 1975
71. Barker, Dennis. A funny thing happened on the way . . . *The Guardian,* 2nd January 1975
72. A very happy new year double. *The Times,* 2nd January 1975

CHAPTER 4

1950–1954

In the late 1940's and early fifties, the 'cold war' situation gave rise to concern in the West regarding the growth and influence of communism in Europe and there was a tendency in some quarters to view with disquiet the possibility of its gaining a foothold in Britain. This probably explains the very large number of reports in the early fifties, of attempts to censor newspapers in public libraries on political grounds.

In Greenock, members of the Library Committee strongly refuted any suggestion that preference was being given to Labour papers and periodicals in the public library newsrooms, after a protest had been made against the withdrawal of certain newspapers.

> "Mrs. Robinson . . . gave a list of the publications mentioned, which were mostly Scottish District papers or Irish papers, and said that it had been suggested at the ward meeting that the number of Labour papers purchased should be cut down and some of these papers restored. Provost Robert Boyd said that there was obviously misunderstanding of the position. 'There appears to be the idea . . . that we in the Labour Party are eliminating the opposition in the fashion of the Kremlin. We are doing nothing of the sort. Some time ago we found that a certain number of papers were not being used at all. They had been kept on for a long time and although they may have been read in the past the new generation is not interested in them and they are therefore superfluous'. Bailie John Reed added that the Library Committee had had a report from the Librarian before cancelling these newspapers. They only reduced those that were not being read to any great extent."[1]

In Llandudno, *Soviet News,* which had been available in the public library for nine years was withdrawn.

> "The Council decided this at their monthly meeting after a question by Councillor C. B. Arnold, who asked: 'In the Public Library the other day I saw a copy of *Soviet*

News. Is it our wish that it should continue to be displayed in our Library? The Library Committee chairman, Councillor H. S. Edwards: 'I am astounded to learn that there is such a paper in the Library, especially as every application for papers comes before the committee. With your permission I will suggest its withdrawal at our next meeting'. The Council however, decided on swifter action and, on the proposition of Councillor G. Curtis, seconded by Alderman Arthur Hewitt, resolved that it should be withdrawn immediately. The Librarian, Miss K. M. Cooks, said that the journal had been taken for 9 years since the time when Russia was an ally."[2]

Strong opposition was recorded in Millom, Cumberland, when the Millom Rural District Council by a majority vote decided to recommend to the County Library Committee that communist literature should be removed from Millom Public Library. At a meeting of the Millom Trades Council on 2nd March 1951:

"It was generally agreed that a dangerous precedent was being established when a county local authority banned any particular national newspaper from a public reading room, especially when the Government of the Country had not issued a directive against the publication. It was also stated that the action of the Rural District Council was a reflection on the intelligence of the people and their lack of ability to discriminate between the political propaganda either of the Right or of the Left present in practically every daily newspaper with a national circulation."[3]

These were but a few of the many reports of such cases during the first 18 months of the decade. They were sufficiently worrying to give rise to a question in Parliament on 8th May 1951, when Mr. David Llewellyn, Conservative M.P. for Cardiff North, asked the Minister of Education:

"Whether he will introduce legislation making it illegal on the part of local authorities to ban any political newspapers and periodicals from libraries under their control.
In a written answer, *Mr. George Tomlinson, Minister of Education* replied: No. It is for local authorities to decide what newspapers and periodicals shall or shall not be made available in those public libraries which they administer."[4]

The increased incidence of reports concerning the banning of newspapers was to continue until 1954 after which they decreased, partly as a result of the lessening fears of communism and partly because many libraries were closing their newsrooms and dispersing their newspaper collections. In November 1951, the Bromley Library Committee turned down an offer of the Soviet magazine *News*.

"Explaining why the offer was rejected, Councillor L. C. Winterton, Chairman of the Public Library Committee, said it was felt *News* would not be a valuable addition to the library. He quoted from an article 'My English Visit' in one issue that stated that Liverpool had 'not suffered damage from bombing' during the War. Councillor Clayton moved the reference back of the minute containing the committee's decision. 'It implies that they have set themselves up as censors . . . It seems to me this is going to create a very dangerous precedent for the future'. It was no part of the Government's policy to legislate against ideas, however unpopular they might be, and it was no part of a Library Committee's duty to say what should be on their shelves, so long as two basic tests were covered: that there should be no offence to public morals, and that anything displayed should be of likely interest to readers. . . . Councillor R. S. Shillingford said it was obvious that the publication was sent over from Moscow for one purpose only—biased propaganda. Replying to the debate, Councillor Winterton said Councillor Clayton had made a point about promoting friendship between the two countries. The Library Committee, who had considered the matter very carefully on two occasions, felt that acceptance of this periodical would have exactly the opposite effect."[5]

Only two councillors voted in favour of referring the Committee's decision back and *News* was thus decisively rejected.

"Peace News banned in Library", reported the *Southport Guardian* in December 1952 when the Southport Borough Council decided that this pacifist weekly should not be displayed in the Central Library:

"Councillor Arnold Townend maintained that the paper merely expressed the views of the Quakers whose movement is above reproach, but Alderman Sir Herbert Barber objected that many of its articles were communist inspired. Opposing a Committee decision banning the paper from the public libraries, Councillor Dr. Sidney J. Hepworth said it was not part of the Library Committee's duties to select reading material for the public. Library Committee leaders emphasised that the ban was imposed only after a month's adjournment to allow members to read the paper. They found nothing in it not already covered by other publications in the libraries and there had been only one request for it. The Town Council approved the ban."[6]

Criticism of a different kind caused the Caithness County Library Sub-Committee to remove the *Daily Worker* from the Wick and Thurso library reading rooms, where it had been among the papers available since shortly after the war.

"Moving that it be banned, Mr. J. Abrach Mackay, Castletown, said that on Tuesday that he was approached by two ratepayers, who drew his attention to the fact that the *Daily Worker* was in the library. 'They charged me with being one of a company assisting in the dissemination of poisonous ideologies in the libraries of Wick and Thurso and said that on going into the Library the first paper that one saw was that Communist Paper the *Daily Worker*. . . . We are a Protestant County, and believe in the British way of living and dying. Why should the rate payers of Caithness be asked to pay for this rag? It is seething with atheism and Communism and all ideologies that follow in their miserable train'."[7]

The Chairman said that the Thurso Librarian had told him that the *Daily Worker* was never used. As the paper was not being read he felt another paper should be bought in its place. The Dean of Guild, George Sinclair, proposed that the paper remain in the library but this was defeated, a large majority of the Committee voting for its removal from the reading room.[8]

During the following few months, press reports of further banning or restricting of newspapers, were to be over-shadowed by two major topics related to censorship. The first was the activities of Senator Joseph McCarthy's special investigators in Europe, Messrs Cohn and Schine and their attempts to dispose of all Communist material in American Libraries throughout the world. The second, the publication of the Kinsey report on the sexual behaviour of the human female.

Apart from the bannings of newspapers, there were examples of library censorship in respect of other materials. Dr. F. W. Robertson, County Librarian of Caithness, denied that a book was "sneaked into" Wick Library without the knowledge of the Library Committee.

> "The charge was made at a meeting of Caithness Library Sub-Committee by Councillor Alexander Miller, of Wick. He said he had been told that a book about Father Theobald Matthew 'issued by the Catholic Truth Society' had recently been added to the Library. Dr. Robertson, who is a Catholic, replied 'Father Matthew was founder of the teetotal movement'.
>
> Councillor Miller: 'I object to the Catholic Truth Society pitching these books into the Library'. Dr. Robertson said the book went through the annual report a year ago, and when Councillor Miller said it was not mentioned by name Dr. Robertson replied that it was impossible to mention all books individually. Retorted Councillor Miller: 'We should not allow these Jesuitical things to be sneaked into the Library'.
>
> Dr. Robertson: 'I do not worry very much about Mr. Miller's language. The book is not published by the Catholic Truth Society. It is an ordinary publication'. Said ex-Bailey James Mulraine, Wick: 'This discussion is ridiculous'. And there the matter was left."[9]

The book critic of the *West London Observer,* on the 21st March 1952, demanded that censorship by librarians should stop.

> "I drew attention in this column, not so long ago, to the banning of Edmund Wilson's *Memoirs of Hecate County* by a certain public library. I was not aware, at the time, of the extensive censorship operated by the librarians at the instigation of local councillors. And when I remarked that many of the (morally dubious) classics of literature were, perhaps, only preserved for us through the illiteracy of officialdom I did not realize then how frighteningly near the truth my remarks had come. I now find that this was no isolated case of excessive puritanism; other public libraries also banned the *Memoirs*.
>
> At another West London Library two recent American novels *From here to*

Eternity by James Jones and *Barbary Shore* by Norman Mailer, were banned, presumably because they deal with sexual relationships in an uninhibited way. These are examples that have come to my attention, but I am sure there must be many other books which public libraries, fearing to embarrass the local vicar, tactfully omit to buy. Such a state of affairs seems to me quite intolerable. We used to say proudly when complaining of film and theatrical censorship that at least literature was free from the restrictions of officialdom. This seems to be no longer true. With so many people having to depend entirely upon public libraries for their reading, insidious forms of censorship of the kind I have mentioned can effectively ban books as far as certain sections of the public are concerned. It seems to me that it is the duty of a public library to buy all outstanding books and leave it to the reader to judge whether crudities of expression and unusual outspokeness are, in their context, justifiable or not." [10]

Following protests by Paignton Ratepayers Association Devon County Libraries withdrew from circulation all copies of Robert Merle's book *Weekend at Zuydcoote*. The ratepayers association wrote to the County Council complaining that the book was "profane, blasphemous and unfit for a public library". Robert F. Ashby, then Borough Librarian at Kettering, commented in the *News Chronicle:*

"What sort of behaviour is this, when a County Council bans a book on the say-so of a ratepayers association? Anyone who has read *Weekend at Zuydcoote* knows that it is an honestly written accurate account of soldiers at war. What will the Paignton Ratepayers Association be encouraged to tackle next—works on politics which do not accord with their views? There is nothing in the Public Libraries Acts which permits a library authority to exercise censorship." [11]

"Bookmark" writing to the *Trade Circular* in January 1953, suggested that it might be worth while for publishers to investigate the system of buying books for public libraries, for it appeared to him that the books purchased were not necessarily those which the public wanted to read.

"I recently asked at my local Library for a copy of *Picaroon,* by Ernest Dudley. I was informed that it is unsuitable for library circulation, so I purchased a copy of the book, found it comparatively innocuous, and offered it free to the library, in case any other ratepayer might wish to read it. The offer was refused.

The Public Libraries state that they cannot buy every book asked for by the ratepayers, yet they purchase hundreds chosen by librarians and by their own special county selection committee. This seems to offer loop-holes for all sorts of abuses, both moral and commercial. It amounts, in fact, to a virtual dictatorship on what the public shall read.

As a ratepayer I am compelled to subscribe some £2 a year towards the public library, which in return renders me a service far inferior to that offered by a local chain library for 12s. 6d. One cannot help but suspect immediately that large sums are being absorbed in paying salaries to officials who exercise this most unreasonable censorship over our reading."[12]

A common pattern of events can be discerned in many of the cases involving public libraries and the acquisition of controversial books. The Press gives sensational publicity to a book on or appertaining to sex and having given its views on the book itself, then turns its attention to what public librarians are doing about the provision of the book concerned. The first notable instance of this during the period 1950 to 1954 occurred following publication of Dr. Alfred Kinsey's report on *Sexual Behaviour in the Human Female* in October 1953.

> "The Kinsey Report on sex behaviour in the human female, publication of extracts from which in the Sunday Press has been criticised by church authorities, social workers and some influential newspapers, is not likely to be dealt with any differently from other books by the Libraries Committees serving Birkenhead, Bebington, Neston, Hoylake and the Wirral Urban District. A previous work by Dr. Kinsey on sex behaviour in the human male, published four years ago, is included in the Reference Department of Birkenhead Central Library and in the reference library at Chester.
>
> It has been there since its publication and the librarians have not noted any exceptional demand for it. Practice in Birkenhead and the Chester County area is for the chief librarian to submit to his committee books which are recommended for purchase for the libraries. The committee do not make any exhaustive analysis of the long list of books which must necessarily be submitted in areas which have such extensive library facilities.
>
> They accept the judgment of their chief officers and in any event the committees do not claim nor desire the functions of censors. So far as they are concerned, the first Kinsey report and other similar specialized works are available for those who may require them for serious study and they are not put into general circulation.
>
> No decision has yet been taken in Birkenhead or Cheshire on whether the new Kinsey report will be purchased, but it is not expected that the notoriety given to it by some of the Sunday papers will cause the Libraries' Committees to depart from their policy of supplying their reference departments with books which are reputably published."[13]

The policies of the library committees of authorities in Cheshire, referred to in this statement in the *Birkenhead News,* were not typical of the country as a whole. In Colchester, 'a woman ratepayer' reserved a copy of the work in the library and as a result the Borough Council set up a special sub-committee.

> "The sub-committee's job is to decide whether Kinsey shall be placed on the shelves. Its all male members are a Baptist Minister, a Canon of the Church of England, a school groundsman, a railway clerk and a retired engine driver.
> Chairman of the Libraries Committee is Alderman C. Jolly, a 72-year-old retired

engine driver, who has been a church warden for 17 years. He said yesterday: 'We shall hold a round-table conference to consider the request to read the book. We are all married men with families. My opinion is that it is our duty to satisfy the reading requirements of the public, and if there is a demand for this report we ought to meet it. I am sure that having it in the Library will not affect the morals of our town'."[14]

The *Daily Mail* reported that public libraries were in a quandary—"their biggest yet". The paper reported that: "they have been inundated with inquiries for the Kinsey report. And they just don't know what to do".[15] The *Daily Sketch* of 11th September 1953, carried the following report.

"Unmarried people are to be barred from borrowing Dr. Kinsey's book on sex from Luton public library. When a copy reaches the library, it will not go on the shelves but it will be locked in a cupboard. The ban on the book *Sexual behaviour in the Human Female,* was decided by the town's chief librarian, Mr. F. M. Gardner. He said last night, 'I don't think it's suitable for children, adolescents or unmarried people. The book will be issued only on application. I shall decide if the person is suitable to read it. I think the only people who should read it are young married couples, doctors, marriage guidance councils or people with a scientific interest in it."[16]

The *Daily Mirror,* commented on the *Daily Sketch's* report:

"Pity the poor Librarian! He will run into heavy weather applying this typically British ruling. Either library books are available to the public or they are not. Certainly there may be a case for labelling some books 'for adults only'. But there is no case for discriminating between one library member and another. Censorship is a perilous game. Luton library chiefs should grow up and think again."[17]

The *Daily Mail's* statement that public libraries had been inundated with enquiries for the Kinsey report did not appear to be true of all parts of the country. Librarians in Camberwell, Lambeth and Southwark reported that no requests for the report had been made.[18] The Librarian of Wimbledon, Miss Helen Bishop, said:

"I have not had any written applications for it. In a book like this I should bring any request for it before the Committee. I don't like anything on the shelves which might be harmful to young people."[19]

In Banbury, Alderman T. Haskins, Chairman of the Borough Library Committee said that they would certainly not object to the report being stocked by the Borough Library, providing the public showed that they wanted to read it.

"Who are we to censor what the people in Banbury and district want to read anyway? If they want Dr. Kinsey's Report we shall only be too willing to provide it for them."[20]

On the 23rd March 1954 *The Times* reported that the Chelsea Public Library had been involved in a dispute about the admission to its shelves of the Kinsey report.

"The dispute will reach its last stage tomorrow, when the Borough Council will consider a member's motion that 'no book of a lawful character, for which there is a reasonable demand, shall be denied a place in the circulating library on the grounds that its religious, social, scientific, philosophical or factual content are disliked, disputed, or opposed by certain sections of the reading public'. The public library committee of the Council are agreeable to the motion being accepted, provided that the word 'circulating' is omitted in order to make clear that the right to decide into which section of the library any book shall be placed remains with the committee."[21]

Replying to the motion the Libraries Committee stated:

" 'Whilst we endeavour to meet the reasonable needs of all sections of the community in the childrens, lending and reference libraries and whilst evidence of a reasonable demand for any particular book is considered, we would not refuse to purchase a book solely on the grounds that its contents were disliked, disputed, or opposed by a section or sections of the reading public'. Councillor Dixon told the Council that he appreciated the decision of the Committee. He said: 'While not completely logical, the action taken does make this valuable but controversial book available to those who wish to read it, while doing something to allay the misgivings of those who do not wish to read it'. . . . The Committee recently decided to supply the Report in their Reference Library only, after virtually banning it for three months."[22]

The *Birkenhead Advertiser,* 17th October 1953, reported an attempt to ban from Birkenhead public libraries books which did not reach 'a proper standard of decency', by Councillor Austin Power.

"Reference to the move was made by Councillor Power at Tuesday night's meeting of the Prenton Literary and Debating Society. Mr. Power had previously raised the matter of the ban on library books at a meeting of the Libraries Committee under 'any other business' the same evening. This followed similar comment to the Committee a month previously when he had asked members to express their opinion on one particular book. Mr. Power told the Prenton Society that he had objected to books which presented a perverted way of life as a normality. This book was written in a good literary style and was therefore, more dangerous than a trashy type of literature. Some members of the Libraries Committee, who had read the book, had said they were not prepared to support him in his case for its withdrawal from the library . . . Committee members had expressed themselves unfavourably disposed to any form of censorship, but Mr. Power suggested there was no reason why they should not withdraw the book from circulation and refrain from buying such literature.

Mentioning that this was only one of a number of books he could name, Mr. Power said: 'My object is to get them removed from the shelves of the Library on the grounds that they are dirty books'."[23]

Similarly, Councillor H. Roote, Chairman of Ilford Libraries Committee was quoted as saying:

"If there are any books of an obscene character in the libraries, then for heaven's sake let me know. I shall put my foot down."[24]

Raymond Parkin, editor-in-chief of the *Northamptonshire Evening Telegraph* gave an address on "Censorship and Citizenship" to members of the North Midland Branch of the Library Association at Kettering on 22nd October 1953.

"Freedom of the Press has never included, and ought never to include the right to encourage crime, or to so offend public taste that a breach of the peace is caused. That is the test: whether a writer is exercising his freedom in a manner which harms other people. The law says that any policeman can lay a complaint against anyone—including a librarian—whom he believes to be offering reading matter which has a tendency to deprave or corrupt those whose minds are open to such depraving or corrupting influences and into whose hands such reading matter may fall.

Have you had a look through some of the modern novels on your shelves lately? Are you quite happy that they are all completely free from 'anything which has a tendency to deprave or corrupt'."[25]

Parkin's editorial on the following day was on the same subject.

"Books that have been 'banned' are subjects that can be discussed at length from a variety of viewpoints, and no final conclusion can be reached because times change, and we with them. Censorship must be closely affected by contemporary taste.

Librarians are naturally inclined to blame on some sections of the Press the fuss and bother arising around some books. But a free Press has the right and the duty to discuss all matters of public interest—which must include books of every type, including those that are 'banned' in some areas as a result of local prosecutions.

One Librarian's way of discouraging people from applying for books that have been 'banned' is worth quoting. In a loud voice he says, 'Let's see, Mr. So and So, isn't this the book that the Magistrates described as filthy? I'll see if we can get it for you—if you really want it. But, of course, not many people locally would want to read that kind of stuff'. The applicant, we can well believe, slinks away to hide his blushes—and seeks other means of satisfying his prurient curiosity about books that have been 'banned'."[26]

A 79-year-old retired clerk, Mr. A. E. Shaw, started a local campaign against obscene literature in a letter to the *Blackburn Times* on 30th October 1953:

"For at least 65 years I have been a reader of books and I cannot help comparing the sentimental novels by Silas Hocking and those of a more robust type by such as Rider Haggard and Jules Verne etc. with the novels of today whose authors frequently chose 'sex' for their theme. Many times I have wondered how far the latter will be allowed to venture before the authorities cry a halt.

Quite recently I obtained a book from my customary source—the Blackburn Public Lending Library, and after reading the first four pages I just stopped and—gasped! As I read on, I learnt that those four pages formed the foundation of the whole structure of the book. Believe me it was one of the most debasing and vulgar books I have ever read.

After some consideration I sought an interview with our Librarian—Mr. J. W. Thomas, I showed him the book, indicating the portion which I wished him to read, and asked if he would give his opinion upon it. He did by using precisely the same word as used by the others—FILTH. And, without prompting he said that the book would be instantly withdrawn from circulation. It is with his approval that I use his name in this letter, and he desires it to be widely known, that if any of his borrowers come across an obscene book, he would be very grateful to be notified, so as to assist in his efforts to keep the public library clean. Why not get at the roots of this pornography by killing it at it's source? The horrible book to which I have referred has the publisher's name upon it, so what more is needed?"[27]

The campaign gained support:

"Twenty-four women's organizations in Blackburn are to discuss the growing threat to family life presented by the infiltration into lending libraries and bookshops of obscene novels. The type of book with which they will be specially concerned is that which, says Mrs. J. Stirrup of the Women's Conservative Association, 'masquerades under the plain cover of an ordinary novel'. Reactions by the various units of the Women's Organization Council to a suggestion by Mrs. Stirrup that an approach be made through Blackburn's M.P.s to the Home Secretary urging that publishers be prosecuted for the publishing of objectionable books, may be heard at the December meeting. The action followed the banning at a Blackburn bookshop-lending library of a new novel by an internationally-known authoress. Mrs. Stirrup, who produced the book at the last meeting of the Council, described it as being unfit for anyone to read. 'We feel that a book-seller selling or a Librarian lending such books is blameless in the matter. He cannot, after all, be expected to read every new volume that becomes part of his stock. Objectionable literature should be killed on the spot by the publisher's readers, and legislation to that effect should be introduced'.

The Borough Librarian, Mr. J. W. Thomas, told the *Blackburn Times* 'Every possible precaution is taken to keep the public libraries "clean", but as the majority of people will agree, that is a formidable task. Out of an annual fiction intake of 5,000 books one could say that only about 5 were withdrawn as objectionable after complaints from borrowers'. They were at liberty at any time to bring before him any book they considered to be offensive. Similarly, he received complaints from intellectuals who resented the fact that books they considered invaluable to their studies, but which some other borrowers regarded as obscene, were not available at the public library. Books that were blatantly obscene by any yardstick, if found in the Library, were immediately withdrawn from circulation, and any serious complaint was always brought to the notice of the Libraries Committee."[28]

More reports concerning newspapers and periodicals in public libraries appeared at the end of 1953 and early in 1954. A move to reinstate the *Daily Worker* in Richmond public libraries, where it had been discontinued six years earlier, was turned down.[29] The Keighley Libraries Committee decided to recommend the withdrawal of political periodicals from the library reading room, though this ruling did not apply to daily newspapers which were already displayed there.[30] In Watford however, it was resolved that one publication from each of four recognized political parties be displayed and the earlier Library Committee policy of excluding political publications was to that extent modified.[31] The Bromley Public Libraries Committee was criticized at a Council Meeting for having reduced the number of donated periodicals in the reading room. One of the periodicals which the Committee proposed to reject was *Peace News*. During the argument Alderman Gibbs interjected: "I oppose anything in the way of pacifism or communism in the Library. Let us keep our heads." The Library Committee report was adopted by the Council.[32]

In January, 1954, Richmond public libraries featured again when the Library Sub-Committee recommendation that D. W. Cory's book *The Homosexual Outlook* should be bought, was rejected by the full committee:

"Councillor H. J. Stickland said they should not concern themselves with what the reader was likely to get out of the book. The subject was very much before the public now and if people wished to understand the underlying factors of such an abnormality it was up to the committee to cater for such demand and buy the book. . . . Alderman Herman Courlander asked if it was their duty to open people's eyes to the subject. It was a most dangerous book and there would be a demand for it.

Mr. Turner (the Borough Librarian) told the Committee that the doctor who suggested the book was a regular attender at the library and on previous occasions when he had suggested a book, his choice had always been of a careful and serious nature. Alderman Wilton said that the book might do harm to many people if they read it. He also did not like the title. It did not seem to him to be a title which a valuable book would have. He disagreed entirely with the view that they had to get whatever the public might happen to want. They had always taken the line as a committee that their aim was to set up a certain standard. The case for the book was not sufficiently strong to justify departing from their usual practice of having a very high standard of books in the library.

Councillor Morell said that shelves of the Library were open to any 16-year-olds and it could do a lot of harm if they picked the book up, even in innocence. Councillor Stickland suggested that they should adjourn the matter for a month so that they might study more reviews on the book and give the Librarian time to read the book so that he could give his impressions on the book. Alderman Wilton said he did not think the responsibility should rest with the Librarian. Even if the committee rejected the book there was nothing to stop them bringing up the matter at a later date.

The Committee were asked to vote and they rejected the book by 7 votes to 5."[33]

In his Presidential Address to the North-west branch of the Library Association at Chester on 3rd March 1954, Mr. E. H. Mason, County Librarian of Cheshire, discussed the wave of book suppression by pressure groups, which was affecting Librarians in the United States, and continued:

"Let us constantly be on our guard against any effort to introduce such a sorry state of affairs to Britain and let us hope that the Library Association will lift its voice in vigorous protest even as the American Library Association has done against those who would ban and burn."[34]

He further commented on the increase in the sexual content of novels, even those by well-known best-selling authors and from reputable publishing houses.

"This was a serious problem . . . and although Librarians were not custodians of morals they had an obligation to their employers and readers to provide books which reach a minimum standard. 'The volume of publishing in this country at the present time is so great that it is quite impossible in the average Library for all books which are added to stock to be read . . . It will be interesting to see how far publishers can go before public opinion, already beginning to make itself heard in odd corners, forces them on to a higher plane'. It was essential to buy only the best, . . . and he suggested that a weekly evaluative list of the best fiction might be provided by co-operation."[35]

The *Worthing Gazette* of 31st March 1954, reported:

"Mr. L. M. Bickerton, Worthing Borough Librarian, is leading a move to prevent pornographic literature from getting into public libraries. He would like to see an independent book reviewing panel set up. At a recent meeting of the London and Home Counties Branch of the Library Association Mr. Bickerton tabled a motion regarding the panel. Mr. Bickerton's action has been approved by the Worthing Town Council Library and Museum Committee. Mr. Bickerton said this week: 'An increasing number of these books are appearing today. It is impossible to read every book we get and occasionally we get complaints from borrowers. Sometimes there is nothing objectionable in the book, others we throw away. This question arises in other libraries as well and I feel it should be dealt with on a national scale. It may be done in conjunction with the British National Bibliography which issues a weekly list of details of books."[36]

In March 1954, a series of letters from readers protesting against censorship in public libraries appeared in *New Statesman and Nation*. With the running title "Hidden Censorship" the series was started by Mary Wedd who wrote:

> "It may be of interest to your readers to know that at my local public library I was told that I could not have a copy of Alfred Haye's novel *In Love* because a member of the Library Committee had objected to its inclusion in its fiction list. This book had an exceptionally enthusiastic review by Mr. McLaren Ross in the *Sunday Times* . . . on the face of it, it seems absurd that a book which did not shock the *Sunday Times, The Observer* or the BBC and which was requested, I believe, by some dozen library members, should be denied to them as unfit to read by some unknown and perhaps quite unliterary councillor. It would interest me to know how he obtained his copy."[37]

The following week, *New Statesman* printed a reply from Geoffrey Finsberg, Chairman of the Public Libraries Committee of the Hampstead Borough Council.

> "Mary Wedd alleges she has been unable to obtain a copy of *In Love* from the Hampstead Public Libraries. First, I must point out that there are three copies of this book in circulation and, secondly, that there has never been any question of censorship. The purchase of books is made, not by a committee as such, but by the Chief Librarian. No member of our staff with any knowledge of the system could have made such a statement, and I venture to suggest that your correspondent might have verified the facts of the case before rushing into print and casting a most unwarranted slur upon the service which is provided."[38]

Mary Wedd replied:

> "I should be very sorry to cast any unwarranted slur on the public library service, for which in general I have the greatest respect. I was under the impression that, in inquiring from the staff of my library, I was attempting to verify the facts of the case. I saw the librarian concerned consult a notice pinned up over the desk and find the name of this book, together with one other title on it, both of which I understood were not to be available. In reply to my query, I heard the explanation I have given. However, if the Chairman of the Libraries Committee tells me that I must disbelieve the evidence of my own senses, I have no means of proving him wrong. As far as I am aware, no-one has suggested that the purchase of books is made by the committee 'as such'.
>
> I am interested to learn that there are now three copies in circulation, particularly as I have before me the post-card which was sent to me after I had put in a card for this book and which first caused me to make the above enquiry. The post-card is headed with the name of the Borough and Branch and then reads

Author: HAYES
Title: *IN LOVE*
I write to inform you that the above book which you reserved is not represented in
our fiction stock, and I am therefore unable to supply a copy. Borough Librarian."[39]

The correspondence ended with a letter from N. R. Tillett of Norwich:

"As an elected member of the Libraries Committee of this City, I have followed this
correspondence with great interest and entirely agree with your critics that there
can be no justification whatever for operating an unofficial censorship of books
within the City Hall. In my view, no committee member has any right to attempt to
substitute his own standard of taste for that of the reading public, deplorable
though he may sometimes privately think that standard may be. He is, however,
faced with another difficulty, the nature of which, I feel, is not fully appreciated by
your correspondents. Every public library has its cupboardful of books placed
officially on 'restricted issue'—which means they can only be borrowed on personal
application to the librarian. In our own public library, the 'blue chamber'—as it is
charmingly referred to by the staff—contains works by Kinsey, Stopes and others of
a familiar character which can be obtained by any responsible adult student if the
Librarian is satisfied that he, or she, may safely be trusted with them. This is not in
any sense a censorship of morals: it is simply to ensure that the book is reasonably
likely to come back in safe, undamaged or undefaced condition.

Some years ago, I remember the experiment of placing a popular book on sex
education on the open shelves was made. But after three successive copies of the
book had been borrowed and returned with the chapters on birth control torn out,
the committee reluctantly decided the only thing to be done was to place it under
lock and key. It is extremely difficult to know what to do about ratepayers who insist
on working off their inhibitions in their library books. Popular sexy novels will, as
often as not, be returned with their juicier passages heavily underscored in indelible
pencil. If the offender can be discovered, he can, of course, be prosecuted under the
bye-laws: but it is not always easy to find him.

Complaints from ratepayers, usually the same ones, about certain works of
popular fiction are not infrequent, and to avoid repetition the temptation to take
the easy road and simply hide the book away is very great. Committees, too, have
their shockable members who are only too glad to seize any opportunity to impose
their private opinion, in the name of 'decency', on the general body of citizens. I
have no sympathy with them at all; at the same time the dilemma must be
recognized. How are we to protect what is, after all, the property of the citizens
against theft, or mutilation by a few irresponsible ratepayers?"[40]

At the Scottish Library Association annual conference on the 1st
June 1954, Dr. W. R. Aitken stated:

"One cannot help noticing that in the prosecutions that have been reported
recently a frequent plea of the defence is that 'copies of the books in question are, in
fact, on the shelves of the public library'. Some of the prosecutions, of course, may
have been misdirected and the books may not be out of place on the library's

shelves. Even more ill-advised, it seems to me, are the attacks on certain books launched by newspapers whose own reputations are not always above reproach. These attacks frequently not only give undue prominence to books that, without such publicity, would be read by few people and attract little attention. No man cries stinking fish. Another favourite pastime of the Press is to attack what it describes as 'censorship in public libraries'. Let us be quite clear on this matter: no librarian, no Library Committee can ban a book. They cannot stop its publication or distribution nor can they prevent its being read. The librarian and his committee say that, in their opinion, this book or that, is not suitable for circulation from the open shelves of a lending library. They may place the book for a variety of reasons, and not only, and indeed, not even frequently, for the one reason usually in mind when the censorship of books is under discussion, under controlled circulation in the lending department, or under an even stricter control in the reference department. They may decide that the public money they are entrusted with is better spent on buying another book altogether, and although the wisdom of their judgment in a particular case may be questioned, we cannot deny their right and their responsibility to judge."[41]

The most important of the prosecutions referred to was the case of Regina v. Secker & Warburg and Others at the Old Bailey before Mr. Justice Stable on the 2nd July 1954. Three defendants, Secker & Warburg, Limited, Frederick John Warburg and the Camelot Press Ltd., were charged with publishing an obscene libel in the novel *The Philanderer* by Stanley Kauffman. The jury returned a verdict of "Not Guilty". The *Bookseller*, commented:

"This verdict, which has given great satisfaction to thoughtful opinion, followed a wise and far-sighted presentation of the issues involved by Mr. Justice Stable, whose summing-up must be regarded by all who are concerned with books as the most significant judicial utterance on the subject, since Lord Chief Justice Cockburn's definition of the test of obscenity in 1868."[42]

Less than a month after the verdict on *The Philanderer,* Swindon Magistrates ordered a two volume edition of *The Decameron,* seized from a local bookshop, to be destroyed as obscene. It was pointed out by the defence that the same edition was in the Swindon reference library.[43] The *Bookseller* commented:

"The decision has provoked wide-spread comment in the press, the general tenor of which has been strong criticism of the law as it now stands which could make such a decision possible. The defending solicitor in the Swindon case submitted that the police would be held up to the ridicule of the whole country if *The Decameron* were judged obscene. The newspapers in ther turn have pointed out that the Swindon Magistrates have . . . 'demonstrated why our rules on this subject make England the laughing stock of civilised nations'.
    The Navarre Society edition of *The Decameron* is available to the public in the

Swindon Public Library. Mr. Harold Jolliffe, the Borough Librarian, stated that it would not be withdrawn."[44]

J. E. V. Birch, the Borough Librarian of Taunton wrote to the *New Statesman and Nation,* which published his letter under the heading "The Librarian's Daughter", on 14th August 1954.

"From time to time we read in the national press a brief report that a public library committee somewhere in the country has withdrawn a book from circulation. The book is invariably one which deals frankly with sex, and the report usually suggests by its tone and headlines that readers will no doubt be amused at yet another example of provincial narrow-mindedness. They are, of course, and note the book in their library lists. Yet, though to sophisticated metropolitan readers such acts of censorship would seem silly and maiden-auntish, there would generally be found to lie behind them a sincere and entirely laudable concern for the moral wellbeing of the community, and more especially of the younger members of it. . . . But the problem, towards a solution of which these sporadic acts of censorship are, as it were, vague and inadequate gestures, is an important one and merits serious consideration.

Like most other Librarians, I get occasional complaints about books in my library. These complaints have recently become rather more numerous. At the moment of writing I have on my desk four books which have been referred to me as 'unfit for circulation' or as 'not suitable for a public library' or even (in the case of a book enthusiastically reviewed on the radio) as 'too disgusting to read'. Now these complaints always involve a concern for the possible harmful effects upon the third parties. I cannot recall a single case in which the complainant has confessed that the reading of the book in question, or of similar books, has done him, or her, irreparable moral harm. As a result no one can ever produce any sound evidence that books have a harmful effect. I usually point out that it is one of the librarian's duties to read carefully any book which is a subject of complaint, and that so far as I am aware librarians are not especially distinguished for their vicious and depraved conduct. And yet they do not claim to any godlike incorruptibility or moral supremacy over the common run of mankind. At this stage of the discussion—I always invite complaints to have a friendly chat—the librarian's daughter is invariably introduced. 'Would you be happy' I am asked, 'if you knew your daughter was reading stuff like this?' The question is a fair one and one day it will be an extremely pertinent one—at the moment my daughter is not yet five. So I do my best to project myself into the future. . . . Now, is 'stuff like this' going to help her, or not? A good friend of mine, who has a vast experience of young people, says decidedly: 'No'. He objects very strongly to young people reading, not books which represent (as they surely must), that making love is a pleasant, desirable and healthy activity but those books which might instruct them in amatory techniques.

He would keep out of their hands any such books until they were at least 16 or 17 years of age. . . . If my friend is right, obviously I should do something to protect these young people from premature enlightenment. At present I allow them unrestricted access to the shelves of the adult lending library after they reach the age of 14! But is he right? One tries desperately to recall one's own adolescence.

But, of course, we were all models of purity and innocence, otherwise we would have not have grown into such decent people. One vaguely remembers some third party boastings which, if true, would have indicated that some of one's coevals were exceptionally precocious. But well-bred children of our day made their amorous discoveries gradually and naturally.

What is the truth of the matter? I dare say no permanent psychological damage will be done to my young readers if they have to wait another two or three years before they are allowed the books which their parents find so entertaining and profitable. But I have a horror of being fatuous, even in the cause of virtue. I shudder to think of the headlines. Will some kind reader advise me?"[45]

Two readers responded to Birch's plea. The first, Robert Wood of Littlehampton, wrote:

"No doubt most of your readers will sympathize with Mr. Birch's difficulties in connection with his work as a librarian. It should, however, be pointed out that this matter is much deeper and more important than the ridicule of the well-meaning but ingenuous on the part of the more sophisticated. It is not necessary to question the good faith of those who object to the public circulation of novels dealing with sexual themes, but neither is it necessary to accept their standards, still less to permit them to impose these standards on the community. After all, total abstainers, vegetarians, opponents of dancing and the theatre, are all, no doubt, equally sincere, but society is surely wise in according a permissiveness wider than these creeds. The plea of protecting young people sometimes seems to be in the nature of a rationalisation, for if this were the real purpose the simple expedient of issuing certain books to adults only would solve the problem. What is really at stake is freedom of expression, and the right of adult men and women to choose what books they wish to read. This is surely the policy that Mr. Birch should support."[46]

The following week 'Sixth Former' also replied to Mr. Birch.

"I have often wondered if those who advocate the banning of books for the purpose of protecting the morals of the young ever consult the people for whom their concern is felt. I am convinced that no intelligent boy or girl of 15 or 16, brought up in a happy and cultivated family environment, would take harm from reading any book on the shelves of the normal public library. It is, surely, upon those less happily situated, or less intelligent, that books of the type to which Mr. Birch refers might have an ill-effect; upon such people as are less likely to make regular use of library facilities than their more fortunate fellows, and I would deny emphatically that the answer to their problem lies in closing the adult section of the Public Library to all those under 17.

As an example of what is, in my opinion, the right method, obtaining what, I hope, are fairly satisfactory results, I would cite the Library of my own Grammar School which is open without reservation to boys of 11 and upwards and to girls of 14 and upwards from the neighbouring High School. Among other 'dubious' works available, *The Canterbury Tales* (in translation) and *The Decameron* have recently been added to stock. It is true that the demand for them has been high, nor would I attempt to deny that, in the majority of cases, the motivating force behind the request has been not a love of classical literature, but, in the words of one reader, a desire 'to see what all the fuss is about'. It is amazing how frequently, however, *The Decameron* is returned with a laconic 'read half a dozen and you've read the lot', an attitude which, if a trifle unfair to Boccacio, is scarcely that of the determined seeker of sex instruction. There can, I feel, be no doubt that if Mr. Birch's daughter turns out according to his forecast, his wisest plan will be to allow her to read what she likes, and to discuss or criticise her choice only upon her invitation."[47]

The Caithness County Library Sub-Committee decided at their meeting of the 3rd September 1954 to withdraw Bruce Marshall's novel *The Fair Bride* from the County library service, although 200 readers had already borrowed it.

"Two months ago Councillor Owen R. Owen, drew attention to the book and described it as 'the most revolting book I have ever read'. Since then, the book was circulated among the members of the Library Committee and at last Friday's meeting they were invited by the chairman, the Rev. R. R. Sinclair, to give their opinion.

Following a motion that the book be banned, the Rev. Douglas Briggs, said that he had read the book. He added: 'One of the objections stated at a previous meeting was that it contained Roman Catholic propaganda. I do not think that it contains this propaganda at all. I don't see how anyone could write about the Spanish Civil war without writing about the Roman Catholic Church. The Book is disgustingly sexy, but it is no worse than a lot of other books going into the library. The literature of the present day is turning more and more to that kind of thing because it seems to be what sells. If you are to ban this book on those grounds then you will have to go over a lot of books. To set up a censorship committee would be to create a precedent which would ultimately not be for the good of the people.' 'If the book was obscene', said Mr. Briggs, 'the attention of the police ought to be drawn to it. I would willingly see the last of this book, but I don't think that this Committee should ban one particular book unless we are prepared to ban all which touch on the disgusting'. Bailie D. B. Millar said that there were much worse books to be picked up at public book stalls.

The chairman, Rev. R. R. Sinclair, said that he had read parts of the book as a duty. 'I found it to be permeated with moral filth . . . it seems to me that the author and publishers have catered for a section of the public who will read anything however gross. I recoil from the very thought of this book being read around the Christian fireside and I cannot conceive a minister of the Gospel having any word to say by way of conserving this book for the Library. You talk about keeping it from the young. I would keep it from the over-70's. Everyone has morals and the old are just as much in need of moral protection'.

Asked by Mr. Alexander Miller, Wick, to express his opinion, the County Librarian Dr. F. W. Robertson, reminded the members that the choice of books was the responsibility of the Book Selection Committee. Continuing, Dr. Robertson said, 'If I thought a book was immoral I would draw the Committee's attention to it. Bruce Marshall's book was passed by the Committee. It was reviewed in practically every newspaper in Great Britain. It became the "Book of the Month" and was favourably reviewed in *The Times Literary Supplement* which is the soberest paper in Britain. Technically, *A Fair Bride* is not an obscene book. The book has been read by over 200 readers during the past year and a half and I have not received a single objection to it.'

Mr. Miller asked Dr. Robertson: 'Would you let your family read it?' Dr. Robertson: 'If either of my children were old enough I would give it to them to read, because it would show them the type of world they are going into. The children of the coming generation should be prepared.' Rev. Mr. Sinclair: 'There is no reason why they cannot write about civil war without permeating the story with filth.' Dr. Robertson: 'I don't see how they can deal with war without referring to these matters. Are you going to suppress it and tell your children that such things do not happen?'

Mr. Alexander Miller then seconded the motion that the book be removed from the library. Rev. Mr. Briggs moving a direct amendment, said that he was not standing as an upholder of this book. 'It is typical of a certain class of book which passes as literature to-day. As a member of the reading public . . .'. Rev. Mr. Sinclair: 'I would remind you that you are here as a member of the Book Committee.' Mr. Briggs: 'You have also reminded me, that I am a minister of the Gospel. What I have to say is this: If it was the mind of the Committee that all books of that kind should be banned, I would support it to the hilt. But I object to this book being taken out and others equally harmful being left.' There was no seconder to Mr. Briggs' amendment and the motion was declared carried.

The Rev. Mr. Sinclair said that the committee by their majority decision had given public manifestation of the fact that they disapproved of such books. Mr. Briggs remarked: 'Your words are rather giving the impression that I would approve of this book being circulated. The fact that I have not a seconder does not worry me in the slightest. I have made my own position clear, and I now make it clearer by moving that it be remitted to the Book Committee to take into consideration the question of whether there are any other library books in the same class which will have to be banned.' Mr. John S. Banks, John O'Groats seconded, and the motion was unanimously approved."[48]

The Sub-Committee's decision to withdraw the book was confirmed by the County Education Committee on the 8th September 1954.[49] However, the matter was discussed further at the Library Sub-Committee's meeting on 8th October 1954.

"The suggestion that books unworthy of being taken into the family circle should be reported to the Director of Education with a view to their being withdrawn from the County Library, was made at last Friday's meeting of the Education Library Sub-Committee at Wick. The sub-committee, however, decided to make no change in the present system of book selection whereby the County Librarian Dr. F. W. Robertson submitted lists of new books to the Book Selection Committee. When a member suggested that Dr. Robertson should draw the committee's attention to any book containing 'Romanist propaganda', . . . Miss Louise M. Kennedy, Thurso, said: 'You are forgetting that there are Roman Catholic ratepayers in Caithness and that their tastes must be catered for'.

The Chairman, Rev. R. R. Sinclair, said that the censoring of books was a very difficult task and added: 'It has been my custom to go along to Dr. Robertson and ask his opinion'. Dr. Robertson said: 'Public Libraries do not stock books of an obscene nature. Because they value the goodwill of the libraries, the booksellers advise us privately of any doubtful books'. After further discussion, the committee agreed to a suggestion put forward by Mr. Hugh R. Stewart, Director of Education, who said that the booksellers could be asked to take special care in recommending books for Caithness Library.

The three copies of Bruce Marshall's *The Fair Bride*—banned by the Committee last month—are to be produced at the committee's next meeting and arrangements for their disposal. When this was decided, Mrs. E. Mackay, Thurso reminded the committee that it had been agreed that *The Fair Bride* should be read by each member before any decision was taken. I was not given the opportunity of reading the book, . . . and I would like to read it now. The chairman replied: 'Legally it is banned'."[50]

But at the Caithness Education Committee meeting on 10th November 1954 it was found that:

"Caithness County Library's three copies of Bruce Marshall's *A Fair Bride* are still circulating among members of the Education Committee, who recently banned the novel as being 'disgusting' and 'not fit to be taken into the family circle'. At last Wednesday's meeting of Caithness Education Committee, Councillor J. A. Mackay, . . . asked why the banned books had not been produced and dealt with, as requested by him, at a previous meeting. He added: 'I am led to believe that the books are still in circulation. I am determined that these volumes be withdrawn from circulation forthwith and placed on the table'. When the chairman, Councillor Walter Sinclair, asked Councillor Mackay what he proposed to do with the banned books, Mr. Mackay answered: 'They should be publically burned in the Town Square'. Councillor Sinclair replied: 'I would never agree to the books being destroyed'. There was no further discussion on the matter.

Interviewed after the meeting, the County Librarian, Dr. F. W. Robertson, said: 'The three library copies of *A Fair Bride* are still circulating among members of the Education Committee, who will no doubt decide what is to be done with them'."[51]

On 17th September 1954, at the Central Criminal Court, fines totalling £1500 were imposed on Hutchinson & Co., publishers; Taylor, Garnett, Evans and Co. Ltd., printers; and Mrs. K. H. Webb, director of the companies for publishing an obscene libel in the book *September in Quinze* by Vivian Connell. The case was heard by the Recorder of London, Sir Gerald Dodson. In his summing up, the Recorder pointed out that the test of obscenity was whether the tendency of the matter charged was to deprave and corrupt those whose minds were open to such immoral influences and into whose hands the publication of that sort might fall.

"In other words . . . the definition is designed to protect the weak rather than the strong. A book which might not affect the mind of an Archbishop might well affect the mind of a callow youth, or girl just budding into womanhood."[52]

The book had been published in 1952 and Thomas E. Spurgeon, a Director of Hutchinsons "agreed that the book had been circulated by well-known libraries and that no complaint had ever been made that it was obscene". The implication of this case for the librarian was that all copies of the book had to be removed from circulation, otherwise he would also have been guilty of publishing an obscene libel.

> "A spokesman at the Library Association, London, said that no general ruling would be given as to whether libraries should withdraw the book. 'But surely, . . . it would be wisest to withhold the book from libraries, at least temporarily'."[53]

Also in September 1954, the Wiltshire Quarter Sessions Appeals Committee at Trowbridge, allowed the appeal against the Swindon Magistrate's decision that *The Decameron* should be destroyed as obscene. The *Bookseller* commented: "That decision will for a long time remain, literally the 'classic' example of book banning". The Chairman of the Appeals Committee, A. W. Northey asked Counsel for the Director of Public Prosecutions, Mr. J. T. Moloney, whether he considered it would be perfectly proper for the copy of *The Decameron* to be in the Swindon public library. Moloney replied:

> "I say it would be, because, although I have failed to discover it, I gather the literary merits of this book are considerable, and it is perfectly right, I concede at once, that students of Italian Social History should have access to it."[54]

In a talk to the Swindon Round Table, Harold Jolliffe, Chief Librarian of Swindon, declared: "If you start banning you will go on banning until the whole community rises up and says 'this has gone too far'." He thought the law dealing with obscenity was rather stupid.

> "We are not necessarily writing and publishing books for a girl of 14. We produce books for an adult world. I personally feel all this business has got out of hand. The librarian's job in public libraries was to stand apart from politics and pressure groups of any kind and present the books available for all to read. The librarian had no axe at all to grind."[55]

Jolliffe's article, "The Dangers of Book Censorship" appeared in the *Municipal Journal* of 22nd October 1954:

> "Today we are living in one of those periods—and they come round quite regularly—when books are subject to attack on the grounds of morality. Whenever this sort of thing occurs the would-be censors always have good reasons to offer. . . .

Mr. Justice Stable's summing up in the recent *Philanderer* case came as a clean wind, driving away many of the unhealthy fogs which beset the subject of censorship. Furthermore, he defined the function of the novel very completely indeed, and described the public for whom the novelist caters, namely, an adult one. This needed to be done and the only unfortunate aspect of the matter is that it was not done by one of the organisations of the book world. It is strange, to say the least, that at the recent Library Association Conference censorship was referred to only in passing. The greatest danger in any form of censorship is that once it has started it is difficult to stop.

Almost as great a danger, too, is the effect of censorship on the book world, and all connected with it, be they writers, publishers, printers, book-sellers or librarians. Banning of matter considered possibly offensive can ordinarily only succeed in sending it 'underground'; but no writer of imaginative literature, for instance, can work satisfactorily with the constant threat of prosecution by his side. It is rarely possible to write what may prove to be a major work and at the same time conform to a strict formula that has been evolved, perhaps arbitrarily by an outside body."[56]

The Programme Committee of the North-west Branch of the Library Association had given E. T. Bryant, Borough Librarian of Widnes, the "difficult and delicate" task of preparing a report on book selection and censorship in public libraries and this report was delivered at a Branch meeting in Bury on 28th October 1954. His paper was divided into two sections. The first consisted of general comments upon the related problems of book selection and censorship and the second comprised the results of a survey by questionnaire circulated to all libraries in the North Western Branch area—the questionnaire contained a list of twelve book titles and asked for information on their availability in the libraries.

"Generally speaking, censorship covers three types of reading matter—political, religious and moral. I think it is true to say that political censorship is, at present, the least of our worries. No librarian in this country, so far as I know, has had to defend himself for retaining on his shelves books issued by the Left Book Club, or perhaps the Right Book Club depending upon the political complexion of the Council.

Religious censorship strikes much nearer home and is a problem that faces many of us today. Yet the right to criticise religion is surely as important as the right to criticise political or social beliefs and any group that attempts to suppress criticism in this field must be regarded with suspicion. We can ignore the scurrilous, but a serious criticism of the beliefs of any particular church is surely deserving of a place upon our shelves.

It is, though, in the moral field that we enter the most difficult territory. The increased number of police prosecutions during the last few months has drawn public attention to this problem, and there is little that I can usefully add to the large amount of newsprint devoted to the subject. The great difficulty of course, is that any decision upon the alleged obscenity or pornography of a book is reached mainly as a matter of taste and belief.

Public opinion is always fluctuating, as we well know, and many people feel that Cockburn's definition of 1868 is too sweeping. Many of us would be much more sympathetic to the remark of Justice Qua of Massachusetts, who said: 'A book placed in general circulation is not to be condemned merely because it might have an unfortunate effect upon some members of the community who might be peculiarly susceptible'. It would appear that Mr. Justice Stable took a similar view earlier this year, when summing up in the case containing the *Philanderer* for he said: 'Are we to take our literary standards as being the level of something that is suitable for the decently brought up young female aged 14? Or do we go even further back than that and are we to be reduced to the sort of books that one reads as a child in the nursery? A mass of literature, great literature from many angles, is wholly unsuitable for reading by the adolescent, but that does not mean that a publisher is guilty of a criminal offence for making these works available to the general public'. The line between honest and sincere writing and obscenity is not easy to draw.

It has always been my experience that complaints are always about the potential harm to *other* people, generally referred to as 'girls of 16' or 'somebody else's daughter' etc. I will admit that this kind of thoughtfulness for other people's susceptibilities always finds me dubious. If the complaint refers to page 2, the reader has always found the moral strength to finish the book. A quotation from Carnovsky is relevant here: 'If the book is simply offensive, the remedy is simple—we can close the book. Happily the freedom to read includes the freedom to desist from reading. But many of us will not desist, and that is what the censor truly fears: not that we will be offended but that we will be pleased'. It is a threadbare cliché to say that 'to the pure all things are pure' but I am sure that many of the passages about which complaint is lodged would not be understood by the innocent mind. If a teenager does understand the full import of a page, chapter or book of this nature, then I feel that our book stock cannot harm him or her; the damage, if such it can be called, has already been done. It seems to me that young people can learn much more of the baser side of sex from court cases reported in certain Sunday newspapers than from a whole library of books. When a complaint *is* made, verbally or, as some librarians insist, in writing, we have several courses of action open. We can read the book, or the part of it that has caused complaint and if we decide that the criticism is unjustified, return the book to the shelves. This may require courage, but if we believe our judgment, is the proper answer to the complaint. Some librarians I know, allocate such a book to another branch of the system, where it may well get worn out by a succession of readers without a second complaint ever being raised. If, however, we feel that the complaint has some justification, there is no alternative; the book must be taken off the open shelves. If it is well-written and apparently sincere, we are justified in retaining it in reserve stock, though issues from here will probably be fairly infrequent. On the other hand, if the book has no particular literary merit, then it is best withdrawn and forgotten. This may seem a contradiction of my earlier defence against censorship, but I think I am consistent. The book with serious intent, well-written, should be retained. The novels mentioned in the questionnaire have all received objection in some quarters, yet I feel that all deserve representation in our book stocks, because their virtues outweigh their possible vices. This plea for courage, though primarily addressed to librarians affects committee representatives and councillors also. We all feel so vulnerable, since any attack, however unjustified, may lead to unpleasantness of one sort or another."

In the second section Bryant discussed the answers to his questionnaire:

"My conclusions from the survey must be limited and obvious. Generally speaking whether there is a book selection sub-committee or not, book selection is primarily the responsibility of the librarian. The Librarian who is go-ahead in professional matters appears to be equally go-ahead in book selection. If my figures are correct, it is the medium-sized libraries that have the most liberal attitude to the problems outlined this afternoon.

You will have noticed the large proportion of books that are shown as being available upon application, and which are not displayed upon the open shelves. I do feel that it shows an attempt by librarians to include books in their stocks that might be open to some criticism by certain people. It is, in fact, a compromise, to keep certain books out of the hands of adolescents. How far that is a desirable object you must decide for yourselves.

Let me wind up by repeating that the public libraries in a true democracy must be prepared to include works by 'no' men as well as 'yes' men, to represent as far as possible all shades of religious and political thought and to include a wide selection of literature of all ages and types.

We live in an age of pressure-groups and both councillors and librarians need resolution to withstand such groups when any question of censorship arises. The temptation to forestall such criticism by not purchasing a book is very attractive at times, but every time we submit to this, the less worthy we become of our position. It means that readers who may be interested are to suffer for those who may object. Both are imponderables, but surely we should take the positive course of providing the book and deal with any protest as it arises, rather than cross our bridges long before we reach them. The lack of provision of books that intelligent readers have a right to expect in our libraries is public relations at its worst, and should worry us far more than the possible protest of a single person or group of persons. The latter will create bad public relations also, but if we are convinced of the book's value, then we should retain it in stock, even if we agree under protest to take it off the open shelves. We must be prepared to be co-operative, but may providence protect us from becoming abject appeasers to each and every reader who makes a protest."[57]

1. No Kremlin discrimination in newspapers. *Greenock Telegraph,* 22nd April 1950
2. After nine years. *Llandudno Advertiser,* 23rd September 1950
3. "Red" literature ban is criticised. *North Western Evening Mail,* 2nd March 1951
4. Parliamentary Debates, Commons. 5th Series, vol. 487. 8th May 1951. Col. 207 (Written Answers)
5. "Censorship" accusation against library committee. *Bromley and West Kent Mercury,* 30th November 1951
6. Peace News banned in library. *Southport Guardian,* 3rd December 1952
7. Banned by Caithness. *The Scotsman,* 7th March 1953

8. "Daily Worker" ban. *Glasgow Herald*, 12th March 1953
9. Row over "teetotal" founder's book. *Scottish Daily Express*, 6th October 1951
10. Censorship by librarians must stop. *West London Observer*, 21st March 1952
11. What sort of behaviour is this? *Trade Circular*, 3rd May 1952
12. "Bookmark". Unreasonable censorship by public libraries. *Trade Circular*, 10th January 1953
13. Dr. Kinsey causes them no headaches. *Birkenhead News*, 12th September 1953
14. X asks library for the Kinsey Report. *Daily Sketch*, 7th September 1953
15. Tanfield's Diary. *The Daily Mail*, 10th September 1953
16. Library bar Kinsey to unmarrieds: *Daily Sketch*, 11th September 1953
17. Grow up! *Daily Mirror*, 21st September 1953
18. Kinsey Report—no one wants it, they say. *South London Observer*, 1st October 1953
19. Kinsey Report "too dear" for library. *Wimbledon Borough News*, 2nd October 1953
20. "Kinsey Report" for Banbury if demand is big enough. *Banbury Guardian*, 8th October 1953
21. Admission of books to Chelsea library. *The Times*, 23rd March 1954
22. Lawful books not to be denied. *Publishers' Circular*, 3rd April 1954
23. Councillor seeks ban on obscene library books. *Birkenhead Advertiser*, 17th October 1953
24. Any obscene books? *Ilford Recorder*, 22nd October 1953
25. Libraries face 'daring book' problems. *Northamptonshire Evening Telegraph*, 23rd October 1953
26. When books are banned. *Northamptonshire Evening Telegraph*, 23rd October 1953
27. Shaw, A. E. Filth in books. *Blackburn Times*, 30th October 1953
28. Obscene books: Stop them at the source. *Blackburn Times*, 13th November 1953
29. Ban stays on paper. *Richmond Herald*, 12th December 1953
30. Political journals may be banned at library. *Yorkshire Post*, 2nd January 1954
31. Watford libraries to get political periodicals. *West Herts and Watford Observer*, 8th January 1954
32. Library committee under fire. *Bromley and Kentish Times*, 5th February 1954
33. Reader's suggestion puts library committee in a quandary. *Richmond Herald*, 16th January 1954
34. Cheshire Librarian hits at "hysteria" of book-burning. *Liverpool Daily Post*, 4th March 1954
35. Modern novels. *Manchester Guardian*, 4th March 1954
36. "Blue" books—he wants them checked. *Worthing Gazette*, 31st March 1954
37. Wedd, Mary. Hidden censorship. *New Statesman and Nation*, 27th March 1954
38. Finsberg, Geoffrey. Hidden censorship. *New Statesman and Nation*, 3rd April 1954
39. Wedd, Mary. Hidden censorship. *New Statesman and Nation*, 10th April 1954
40. Tillett, N. R. Hidden censorship. *New Statesman and Nation*, 24th April 1954
41. Librarians' problem of 'doubtful' books. *Glasgow Herald*, 2nd June 1954
42. The modern test for obscenity. *Bookseller*, 17th July 1954. pp.512-516
43. Order to destroy The Decameron. *The Times*, 29th July 1954
44. Swindon magistrates order The Decameron to be destroyed. *Bookseller*, 7th August 1954. pp.664-666

45. Birch, J. E. V. The Librarian's daughter. *New Statesman and Nation,* 14th August 1954

46. Wood, Report. Obscene books. *New Statesman and Nation,* 21st August 1954

47. Sixth-Former. Obscene books. *New Statesman and Nation,* 21st August 1954

48. "A Fair Bride" is banned from Caithness Library. *Caithness Courier,* 8th September 1954

49. Ban on Fair Bride. (Aberdeen) *Evening Express,* 8th September 1954

50. Book choice system to remain as before. *Caithness Courier,* 13th October 1954

51. Banned books. *Caithness Courier,* 17th November 1954

52. Old Bailey jury find "September in Quinze" obscene: £1,500 fines. *Bookseller,* 25th September 1954. pp.1040-1042

53. "Obscene" book—£1,500 fines. *National Newsagent,* 25th September 1954

54. A book can be obscene in one place and not in another. *Bookseller,* 25th September 1954. p.1047

55. Banning of books may get out of hand . . . *Swindon Evening Advertiser,* 24th September 1954

56. Jolliffe, Harold. The dangers of book censorship. *Municipal Journal,* 22nd October 1954

57. Bryant, E. T. Book selection and censorship. *Librarian and Book World,* vol. 44, no. 4. April 1955. pp.65-76

CHAPTER 5

Blacking Out

The obliteration of racing news from newspapers in public library reading rooms, or "blacking out" as it was commonly known, was a practice adopted by many public libraries over a considerable period from the late nineteenth century. Its purpose was that of discouraging "betting men" from frequenting the newsrooms of public libraries where they tended to monopolize certain newspapers. This "undesirable element" did create problems in a newspaper library and its activities were often contrary to the bye-laws of the library. However, by 1939 the practice was in decline; and although it continued after the second world war, the number of cases steadily decreased until 1968 when no records of this practice could be traced.

A paper on "blacking out" read to the Library Association at the end of the nineteenth century, but not published, shows that the practice was in existence before the turn of the century.[1]

In August 1915 the *Library Association Record* reported that the members of the Greenock Public Library Committee had recently discussed the advisability of obliterating all betting news in newspapers in their reading room.

"A report on the subject was submitted by the Librarian, who said that he had been in communication with a number of library authorities in Scotland and England who carried out such a policy. The 'blacking out' was seldom regarded as a hardship by readers, and appeared to have been the means of discouraging betting men from frequenting the newsrooms of these libraries. In Greenock the Public Library newsroom was regularly resorted to by several men for the purposes of getting betting information, and often they became a nuisance to other readers by monopolising the newspapers. The Librarian recommended that the Committee should experiment for a time by obliterating betting news from all papers. He suggested that the method adopted might be the pasting of gummed strips on which advertisements from local tradesmen might appear, and a small revenue be thus

82

obtained. It was unanimously agreed to adopt the Librarian's suggestion for an experimental period of six months."[2]

In 1932 Horace Goulden, Librarian and Curator of Huddersfield Public Library and Art Gallery, produced a report on the obliteration of racing news, built up from a series of questionnaires he had circulated amongst librarians.[3] This showed that a number of authorities were blacking out in the days when Greenock was considering it, although some of them discontinued the practice during the first world war.

In May 1932 the Exeter Public Library Committee agreed to continue the practice recently adopted, of obliterating all betting news on the grounds that it had resulted in a less congested reading room.[4] In Galashiels, less than a year later the Library Committee turned down a recommendation by its Book Committee that all betting news should be blacked out in the newspapers displayed in the reading room.[5]

Obviously the Huddersfield questionnaire on blacking out was published at an opportune time for in "Municipal Library Notes" in the *Library Association Record,* January 1933 the following comment appeared:

"A very old and hardy perennial has recently again burst into bloom. I refer to the controversy whether the betting news in the daily papers should be 'blacked out'. I have before me a thick wad of press cuttings in which most of the pros and cons are thoroughly propounded. Undoubtedly, many libraries find that the presence of the betting fraternity is a grave nuisance and interference with the normal public, and several have, quite recently, decided to black out. One Borough Council has even gone further and, resolved to be thoroughly democratic and logical, has ordered that Stock Exchange information should also be hidden from view.

Let us be logical too. Would we tear out the pages of a book if they offended or if they attracted undesirable readers? No. We should either take steps to keep the book away from the undesirable readers (or vice-versa), or we should not have the book at all. Since it is obviously difficult to keep any type of reader away from our newsrooms, if we can't do so let us stop taking the attracting papers. At once three objections, at least, will be raised: (a) that those who want the papers, even racing papers, help to pay the library rates, and are entitled to have what they want; (b) that there are many who can't afford to buy a daily paper for themselves; and (c) that to stop taking these papers will be a hardship to the unemployed who consult the 'Situations Vacant' advertisements.

(a) Involves the principle that none of us has ever recognised—though we might pretend that we do. Do we give all sections of the public the *books* they want? Of course we don't. Why should we apply a different principle where newspapers are concerned.

(b) Is equally illogical. Is it the function of a library committee or of any other local or national body to give people the things they can't afford just because they can't afford them?

(c) It is time that we realized that whatever functions we have to perform, one of them is not that of being an Employment Bureau. There were no Employment Bureaux when most of our newsrooms were established, and no doubt in those days they rendered a valuable service. Nowadays we would be helping such people best by diverting them from the newspapers—which, moreover, are by no means free from bogus and misleading advertisements—to those agencies, public and private, better able to assist them.

My newspaper cuttings are full of discussions on the ethics of betting. To my mind that has got nothing to do with the case. We are concerned with maintaining order in our rooms and in spending our money to the best advantage. To 'black out' may serve the first purpose, but it leaves the library authority open to criticism for partisanship. To discontinue taking and displaying the papers in question is to draw attention to the fact that we have little enough to spend on more legitimate requirements."[6]

The conclusions reached by the Peterborough Public Library Committee in attempting to find an alternative to blacking out, a practice of which the Committee did not approve, were summed up and criticised in a cartoon[7] published by the *Northern Dispatch* in October 1933 (see p. 85). Only a week later the following letter appeared in the *Yarmouth Mercury*.

"It would be interesting to know if the Library Committee are considering the idea already adopted in other towns, of detaching the racing news pages from the papers in the reading room and filing them all together for the use of the racing fraternity who frequent the room solely for the purposes of 'looking for winners' (or losers), thereby preventing genuine readers from making use of the papers. The above method seems a likely solution to a rather vexatious problem."[8]

As a result of the *Betting and Lotteries Act* of 1934, British newspapers no longer published details of the Irish Sweepstakes. However, such details continued to appear in the Irish editions of Irish newspapers (although editions of Irish papers for sale in Great Britain did not contain this information), and in certain newspapers published on the continent. As a precaution against prosecution under this Act for displaying such information, a British librarian who took any newspaper which contained details of the Irish Sweepstake should have protected himself by obliterating or removing them before the newspaper was displayed in the library.

G. M. Fraser, Chief Librarian of Aberdeen Public Libraries replied to a number of letters in the *Evening Express* concerning the monopolising of certain newspapers in the reading room by people wanting betting news:

"There is no doubt that in Aberdeen, as in all other towns, advantage has been taken of the facilities of certain newspapers . . . in the reading rooms for betting purposes, but to a less extent in Aberdeen than in many other towns for the reason

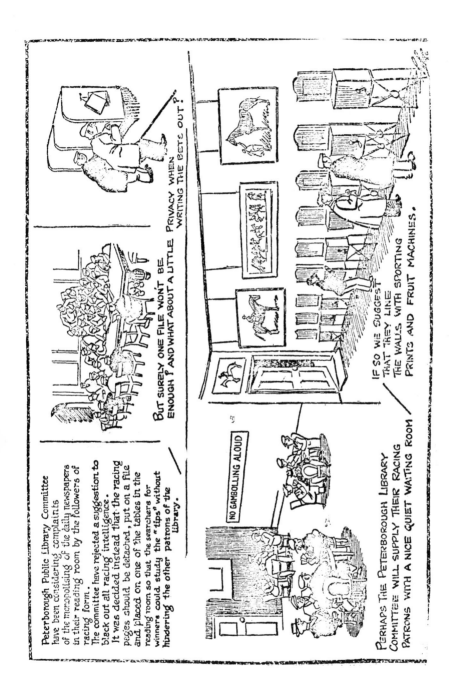

A Tip for Librarians. Cartoon from the Northern Dispatch, *Darlington, October 1933*

that personal control is kept on persons so acting by the reading room attendants. The practice of making use of the reading room for such a purpose is against the library by-laws, and this is well-known to the persons who indulge in it and they keep their eyes on the attendants accordingly. The 'blacking out' of betting news is a gross and unsatisfactory expedient, and, although followed in certain towns, is not as efficient as personal oversight properly gone about.

With a view to putting a complete stop to this objectionable practice in the reading rooms in Aberdeen more stringent instructions were issued recently to attendants in the reading rooms. Consultation has also taken place with the police authorities, who know exactly how to act whenever an actual case happens in any of the reading rooms, but since the issue of the recent instructions no such case has occurred. The result, so far, has been a marked diminution in the practice . . . and it is not anticipated that prosecutions to any number will be necessary."[9]

In April 1937 at the Newcastle-under-Lyme Council meeting, criticism was made of the following recommendation of the Free Library Management Committee:

"That the Librarian be instructed to obliterate or remove from all daily papers exhibited in the Library, the racing news, betting news and Stock Exchange information. Mr. A. H. Furnival moved the reference back of this, describing it as an attempt at 'grandmotherly legislation' and questioned its practicability. He held no brief for betting, but he thought people ought to be able to read news of the Stock Exchange, which was part and parcel of the commercial life of the country. Mrs. F. R. Deakin said she did not think Stock Exchange news should be approved and racing news condemned. Gambling was gambling wherever it took place.

Mr. W. Parton (Chairman of the Committee) said the proposal to obliterate gambling news was his own and was the result of complaints that newspapers in the Library were being monopolized by people who used them to study racing. The inclusion of Stock Exchange news in the recommendation was the decision of the Committee and was, he suggested, put forward 'out of spite'. He was quite willing to take the recommendation back. The reference back was carried."[10]

In the following year, 1938, the Library Association produced a list of public libraries which obliterated betting news in newspapers, showing that the number of libraries "blacking out" was considerably less than that given in the Huddersfield survey of 1932.[11]

The L.A. list showed that only partial obliteration took place in the Dudley newspaper room. This practice was to change in 1939.

"A severe blow has been struck against the convenience of certain regular frequenters of the newsroom at Dudley Public Library, by the decision of the authorities to delete betting news from copies of the daily Press in the room. For some weeks a group of men met daily in the newsroom to read and discuss 'dead certs'. Ignoring requests to observe silence in the room; entirely indifferent to the comfort of other users of the public reading facilities, they talked and argued and even defaced newspapers by writing. By far the most deplorable feature of this abuse of privilege, they chalked the names of their chosen 'winners' on the walls of the entrance hall and newsroom.

This was really too bad, and the Librarian (Miss M. Southall), reported the matter to the Public Libraries Committee of the Town Council. Now—well, no betting news, no more disturbances; peace and silence have been re-established in the news room. Alderman J. L. Hillman, chairman of the Libraries Committee, told our reporter: 'Betting news was blotted out of the papers as an experiment, but now it has had the desired effect, it will be blotted out in the future from now on'. Approval to the measure has been given by the Town Council." [12]

The (Ipswich) *Evening Star* of 27th June 1939, discussed betting activity in public libraries.

"There is a place for everything, but if there is one spot where discussion on the merits and chances of contending racehorses seems out of place, that place is surely the reading room of a public library. Not only for the general benefit is silence enjoined in such institutions, but where, as is not infrequent, these discussions are waged, no doubt for ready reference, before an opened paper, perusal of the periodical by people who desire to use it for its proper purpose is prevented. Nobody wishes to deny the unemployed man an interest in the 'sport of kings' but whether a person on the dole is justified in backing his fancy at the expense of the nation and his family is a very different matter. Certainly he ought not to be allowed to obstruct the individual who frequents the public library in the hope of finding employment. Some correspondents would like to see operated at Ipswich the system in vogue in the public reading rooms of many other towns, where in order to remove the attraction the racing news has for a certain type of person it is purposely made illegible. While this action may prove effective in its aim, it certainly has its objections, one of which is that sporting news ought to be available to those interested equally with other forms of information." [13]

The actual process of blacking out was undertaken by library staff in a number of ways. The pasting of strips carrying advertisements from local tradesmen over the offending material and the use of brown gummed paper were two methods, and the *Library World,* June 1944, mentioned two others in common use.

"Some libraries pasted strips of white paper over the betting news, others blacked them out with rubber rollers and printing ink." [14]

The termination of the second World War brought to an end the practice of blacking out in many of those libraries listed in the Library Association's 1938 list, though the practice continued in a few places for a number of years. The *Librarian and Book World* for May 1948 reported:

"Dundee Public Libraries committee have decided to lift the ban on racing news in their seven reading rooms for a trial period of three months. For the past twenty years it has been blacked out."[15]

Two years later however:

"People at Leyton and Leytonstone can no longer read the racing columns of newspapers in the borough libraries. Leyton Council have decided to re-introduce the practice of blotting out all references to betting."[16]

At the Leyton Council Meeting on Thursday, 6th April 1950:

"It was decided to re-introduce a 1909 resolution authorizing obliteration of betting news in newspapers in local public libraries. Councillor Brockbank said that the Library Committee had been informed that the libraries were being used by people wanting betting news. The 1909 rule of obliterating such news had not been enforced since 1938—when many race meetings were discontinued—but it was now thought desirable, for the convenience of other people who used the libraries, that the regulation should again be enforced."[17]

On Wednesday, 14th June 1950, the St. Helens Libraries Committee decided that the blacking out of betting news in the newspaper libraries was to be discontinued for a six month trial period.

"At the previous monthly meeting of the committee, a complaint had been made that the blacking out of betting news interfered with the reading of the Parliamentary Report in *The Times*. The committee then decided to experiment with gummed paper strips over the betting news, so that the reading matter on the reverse side of the page would not be interfered with. On Wednesday Alderman J. E. Hughes moved that they no longer blacked out or obliterated the betting news. He thought it had been shocking and disgusting in the past. They would have to leave it to the good sense of our people not to mutilate the papers. Not only did they black out one page, but two or three pages. The blacking out, with all due respect, was clumsily done, Alderman Hughes said. They had blacked out as many as two or three pages and spilled over into the adjoining columns. He said the original reason for blacking out was because the racing columns had been cut out or torn out. Mrs. R. Houghton, a co-opted member said that was not the original reason for blacking out. Crowds had collected round particular papers creating a hubbub and a din.

Supporting Alderman Hughes, Councillor J. Hand said it was distressing to see all this business. He thought they ought to give it a trial because in some of the outside libraries it was felt there was no bother with the racing news. He thought the Central Library was a different proposition, but it ought to be given a trial. It was eventually decided to give the non-blacking-out idea a six month trial."[18]

H. C. Caister, Chief Librarian of St. Helens, informed me in his letter of 3rd July 1972 that the practice was not re-introduced.[19]

Although many librarians did not consider blacking out to be the answer to their problem in the 1950s, the newspaper library continued to be a source of trouble.

"The Chief Librarian at Cradley Heath, Mr. J. Wilson Jones, has appealed to the public to help in stamping out the nuisance caused by a group of men who use the library's reading room to place bets on horse races. A library official told the *County Advertiser* that the library staff had had their suspicions for some time that certain 'undesirables' were using the room for something more than merely reading newspapers. Their suspicions were borne out by complaints passed on to them from the Town Clerk's department. A Council spokesman commented: 'It is very difficult to catch these people red-handed, for as soon as anyone who even looks as if they have authority puts in an appearance all suspicious activity ceases. . . . I think practically every library in the country has this trouble some time or another, but usually it can be stamped out with little difficulty, particularly if there is the full co-operation of the law-abiding public. The notice that Mr. Jones has put up at the entrance of the library headquarters of the Rowley Regis library service, is as follows: 'Any use of this room for the purpose of studying horse-racing or the placing of bets is an offence under the bye-laws and police regulations. Members of the public are requested to give information about any persons using the room for selection of form, placing of bets, paying out cash or audibly conversing on horse-racing. Kindly give information at the lending counter for action to be taken'."[20]

The last traceable reports on "blacking out" refer to the situation in Kirkcaldy, where in 1962 the Public Library Committee approved the Librarian's recommendation that newspapers displayed in the library reading room should have the racing news blacked out since the Librarian felt that some patrons "were using the newspapers for following racing and not just news".[21] The newspapers were four months late in reporting the lifting of this ban in 1968—the decision was taken by the Library Committee in March but was not reported in the Press until 9th July 1968.

"Kirkcaldy Librarian, Mr. Ronald McLaren, has lifted the ban on racing tips in newspapers provided at the Central Library. But he is confident that the absence of black ink obscuring the betting hints will not turn the reading room into a 'home from home' for punters. He said today: 'The Library Committee agreed to remove the ban on racing tips which was imposed by my predecessor some years ago, and after two months trial, I am convinced that racing fans are not monopolising the papers to the detriment of news readers. I have instructed the library assistant in that part of the building to advise me if there is any difficulty but there has been no trouble so far. I am quite sure that the lady who held this post previously had good grounds for censoring the tips when she did. But the tipsters' articles were left uncovered and anyone who read these could gather all the information they needed, even if no starting prices were shown'."[22]

The practice of "blacking out" arose in the first place because of considerable interest in the betting news associated with the mass unemployment of the first half of the century when many of the unemployed had few places to go, apart from the public library reading room. There is also little doubt that the reading room formerly appealed to a very much wider range of readers than is the case today. The necessity for blacking out has now disappeared as many public libraries have closed their newspaper rooms and incorporated the newspapers and periodicals once found in the newsroom in appropriate reference and other departments. In those news rooms which remain, the "betting fraternity" no longer cause the congestion and nuisance that they once did.

"The clever C. E. Montague, 34 years ago, could write thus: 'Pinn spent half the net gains on a Free Library, set in the heart of a working class district, a greater boon than he knew to many, who, but for it, might have walked far, or waited long, to learn the starting prices'. The muddle-thinking of which is obvious, since starting prices are useless if not known well in advance. There was formally a wave of faith in the evil that newspapers in our rooms did to the maligned working class who, as a class, are much less adicted to betting than the classes who are a little-more-than working class."[14]

1. Frank Campbell. Rough subject-analysis of Papers read before the Library Association. *Library Association Record*, vol. 1, part 1. January 1899. pp.14-15
2. Miscellaneous. *Library Association Record*, vol. 17, no. 7. August 1915. pp.376-377
3. Huddersfield Public Libraries and Art Gallery. Report on the obliteration of racing news: Summary of returns. 1932
4. Betting news ban. *Western Morning News and Mercury*, 31st May 1932
5. Betting news in papers. *Edinburgh Evening Dispatch*, 3rd February 1933
6. Municipal Library Notes. *Library Association Record*, vol. 35, no. 1. January 1933. pp.24-25
7. A tip for librarians (cartoon). *Northern Dispatch*, 19th October 1933
8. The Library Reading Room. *Yarmouth Mercury*, 28th October 1933
9. Betting news in reading rooms. (Aberdeen) *Evening Express*, 1st July 1935
10. News in library. (Hanley) *Evening Sentinel*, 8th April 1937
11. The Library Association. Public libraries which obliterate betting news in newspapers. May 1938
12. They have now to buy newspapers. *Dudley Herald*, 6th May 1939
13. "Spotting the Winner". (Ipswich) *Evening Star*, 27th June 1939
14. Editorial. *Library World*, vol. 46, no. 532. June 1944. p.166
15. Here's news . . . *Librarian & Book World*, vol. 37, no. 5. May 1948. p.155
16. All dark horses now. *The Star*, 10th April 1950
17. No 'tips' at libraries. *Leyton Express and Independent*, 7th April 1950
18. No black-out of racing news. *St. Helens Newspaper and Mid-week Reporter*, 16th June 1950

19. Letter from H. C. Caistor, Chief Librarian of St. Helens, to the author, 3rd July 1972. (Unpublished)
20. Librarian determined to stamp out betting nuisance. (Brierley Hill) *County Advertiser and Herald,* 18th August 1956
21. Racing is on again in the library. *Scottish Daily Express,* 9th July 1968
22. They're off! Library lift racing tips 'black-out'. *Edinburgh Evening Express,* 9th July 1968

CHAPTER 6

1955–1959

Following the series of prosecutions in 1954 in which reputable British publishers were charged with publishing "an obscene libel", and in the light of Mr. Justice Stable's summing up in one of these cases, namely that involving Secker and Warburg Ltd., and their publication, *The Philanderer* by Stanley Kauffman, the Society of Authors formed a Committee under the chairmanship of A. P. Herbert, to prepare a draft Bill to amend the law relating to obscenity in literature. The draft Bill was submitted to the Home Secretary at the beginning of 1955 and according to the Bookseller, was "widely welcomed".[1]

The Bill proposed that, in any procedings, the author, publisher and printer should have the right to call expert evidence in defence of the book. Secondly, the words "obscene" and "corrupt" were to include any matter which, whether or not related to any sexual context, unduly exploited horror, cruelty or violence, whether pictorially or otherwise. Thirdly, and this was relevant to the position of the librarian, the character of any person charged and the nature of his business was to be taken into account before he could be convicted of trafficking in obscene printed matter. Fourthly the general character and dominant effect of the published matter was to be considered, not just selected passages. The Bill formed the basis of the *Obscene Publications Act, 1959.*

In December 1955, Alderman Hermon Courlander resigned from the Richmond Libraries Committee in protest against its decision to stock Peter Wildeblood's book, *Against the Law.*

"Copies of it have already been bought by the Twickenham librarian and will soon be included on the book shelves. Yet when a Richmond reader suggested the book be bought by the borough's library, it created a fuss during which Alderman Courlander crumpled his committee papers into a ball, threw them on the floor and

92

stormed out of the committee room shouting: 'I resign. I leave the room. That is what I think about the matter'. He made his decision to resign after Committee chairman Councillor A. D. Maddocks had given his casting vote in favour of buying the book.

Moving that the Committee did not purchase the book, Councillor Mrs. Vera Boursot said that she did not think there was any demand for books of its type. There was a danger also, she added, that it might fall into the hands of adolescents. Councillor A. Allee however, pointed out that it had been reviewed in the national press, during which it had been said that the book could do nothing but good."[2]

" 'Succulent popsies' not for Oxford" ran the heading in *The Guardian* of 17th January 1956

"Unswayed by the presence in the Council Chamber of a double page 'pin-up' in colour of the Swedish film star Anita Ekberg, Oxford City Council yesterday refused by a substantial majority to ask the Library Committee to reconsider its decision not to take *Picture Post* in the reading room of the public library. The photograph, from a recent copy of the magazine, had been pinned up before the debate by Alderman Mrs. Kathleen Lower, the Mayoress, together with other pictures on the crime wave, the cost of living, and commercial television. Moving the reference back of the Committee's report, she said: 'I picked up those copies in my doctor's waiting room. If a doctor can have them, then they are perfectly suitable for the public libraries'. She thought this was a magazine for the general reader and that the real reason for the Committee's decision was that someone had suggested that the magazine was 'not in quite right taste'. Councillor Lionel Harrison, who seconded the motion, said he would be 'failing in my duty to those who elected me if I deprived them of the opportunity of seeing that photograph of Diana Dors'. Councillor Michael MacLagan; 'On a point of information, Sir, I believe it is a Miss Ekberg'.

Councillor Michael Foote criticized the magazine for what he called 'its rapid alternation between succulent popsies on one page and oleographs of saints on the next', and Councillor Mrs. Caroline Goulton-Constable thought *Picture Post* had been 'quite a reasonable paper' when it was first brought out but now it was 'just rubbish'. To this Councillor Ronald Owen replied: 'Now we see what we are really up against. The Library Committee are exercising censorship over the type of periodical it brings into the library. People's opinions of rubbish differ. How dare anyone call that lady's photograph 'rubbish'! I believe she is called 'the Swedish Iceberg'. Everybody knows that two-thirds of an iceberg is hidden from view'. Councillor MacLagan: 'On a point of information, Sir, I believe the correct figure is seven-eighths' . . . Councillor MacLagan said that the main reason for the Committee's decision had been the discovery that few people ever looked at *Picture Post* in the reading room and secondly that the magazine had fallen off. 'It now indulges in a great deal of what I believe is referred to in the vernacular of the newspaper world as 'cheesecake'. This is the depiction of attractive ladies in positions which could possibly be described as provocative and very rarely fully clothed'."[3]

In May 1956, Marie Mares of Canterbury, wrote to *Books and Bookmen:*

> "In theory we have no book censorship, but in practice can we be sure that the functions of censorship are not invested in public librarians? It is their task to decide, in sub-committee, which titles requested by borrowers shall in effect be 'banned'. It seems to me there are only two valid reasons for refusal to buy requested books; their non-availability and the library's inability to pay for them. Once librarians leave these two grounds they are placed in the sorry position of becoming involved in the question of what constitutes unsuitability. Let nobody suppose fiction is the only victim, non-fiction has its casualties too. The individual book does not matter; the specific subject does not matter; the principle of freedom to read what one pleases emphatically does.
>
> No, we can all sink into the quicksands of shifting opinions and tastes when we try to decide what others shall not read. Let our librarians add their own choices to borrowers requests, but such requests should be met without question so long as the books are in print and within the means of the purchasing authority . . .".[4]

Murray Shoolbraid replied to this letter in July:

> "The provision of all books on demand brings up the whole question of the purpose of the public library: should obvious trash be provided and public money spent on the worthless? This is a result evidently desired by Marie Mares; but I hope this is not what she meant. There must of necessity be some discrimination. The library that bought every item requested would probably sooner or later find itself in possession of an unrivalled collection of cheap ephemera. It is not the public library's business to provide the novelettes and even more ambitious books which are the province of the newsagent and the subscription library. As for books which are 'experimental' and/or specialist, the librarian will have to decide whether or no it is good policy to obtain them when they may be limited in their appeal. Personally I believe that all controversial books should be acquisitioned, since from the merely historical viewpoint some will wish to know what the fuss was all about. If need be, they might be kept in a separate sequence, away from impressionable youth—I admit this separation seems another form of censorship, but it is the best the librarian can do, and he, poor fellow, notwithstanding periodical appearances to the contrary, means well."[5]

L. C. Guy, Assistant Librarian, in charge of the Central Lending Library at St. Marylebone Library, replied to both:

> "I am a librarian spending some hours every day attending to reader's requests and supervising a large and busy lending department. The only 'censors' are the other readers, not the librarians. The latter are on the whole willing and indeed eager to purchase any and every book, except pornography, but no library in this country receives anything like enough money to allow such a happy ideal. Look what happens when we put a 'controversial' book on our shelves—by the time the library committee meets next month, the librarian, the chairman, the Town Clerk will all

have received letters demanding the withdrawal of this 'disgusting', or 'ridiculous', or 'unintelligible', or 'dreadful', or 'unseemly' book. Not one little comment by the professedly more advanced on how nice it is to see such a wide representation in the stock; not one letter in the local press defending the right of a minority to its choice. What other course then have the elected representatives of the ratepayers than to withdraw or restrict the issue of the book and to discourage such an event in future?

However, if an authority will not purchase a particular book, and they are quite entitled to refuse whatever they wish, then the reader is not prevented from obtaining that book through the public library. Librarians have been enlightened enough to produce the most extensive scheme of co-operation existing in all public service so that not all libraries have to purchase all books. The ability to provide a book does not cease at one's local centre."[6]

In 1956, political newspapers were still a source of controversy particularly in the last few months of the year, following the Soviet invasion of Hungary. At the monthly meeting of the Fleetwood Town Council on 7th November 1956, an attempt to defeat the Library Committee's decision to allow *Soviet Weekly* to be displayed in the public library failed by 13 votes to 7.

"Councillor T. Smith, opposing the resolution, said he refused to have his mind poisoned by Russian propaganda. 'I refuse to accept this paper as a contribution to peace, for, on the contrary, it is a most flagrant contradiction of the Commandment forbidding us to bear false witness against our neighbour'. The Council had a duty to the public to reject any publication if they had serious doubts about its contents. Alderman J. I. Kennedy said: 'The council would be aiding and abetting the cancerous growth of Russian doctrine if they did not ban the paper'. Take no chances with our Christian and democratic heritage, he urged. Other members said the reading public should be free to make their choice and argued that to ban a publication would only create curiosity and a determination among a section of the people to see it.

Councillor W. Wright, Chairman of the Library Committee, said he had read the publication and had not found anything contrary to Christian teaching. If there was anything of that kind he would be the first to suggest that they withdraw it from the library."[7]

Councillor J. Howel Williams, a member of the Caernarvon Town Council, admitted at a meeting of the Council on Tuesday 4th December:

"That he deliberately destroyed a copy of the *Daily Worker* in the town's public library. Councillor Williams made his admission when the minutes of the Library Committee came up for consideration. A minute from the committee stated a copy of the newspaper was destroyed by a member of the Council, and the Committee decided that the Town Clerk write a letter to the Councillor expressing the Committee's regret because of his action in destroying the newspaper, the Council's property.

'I am the Councillor who was responsible for destroying this newspaper', said Councillor Williams. 'I deliberately destroyed it. I went to the library on December 12th, the day when that terrible massacre of Hungarians by the Russians in Budapest was at its height. I went round the newspaper stands and read all the papers. When I saw the *Daily Worker* with banner headlines 'Hungarian Fascists Defeated' it aroused my anger. I deliberately took it from the stand and after making a little comment to the people there at the time I tore it into pieces and told them: "I do this in protest against the Russian massacre of the Hungarian people". Councillor J. Bowen Griffith said the Library Committee were expressing regret not because Councillor Williams had destroyed the *Daily Worker* but because he had destroyed Council's property. That was the position as far as the Committee stood. Councillor W. Spanner said he entirely agreed with the findings of the Committee. It was not right and proper that any member of the Council or any member of the community should destroy any property belonging to the Committee. The Committee's decision was approved.

Later the Council discussed a notice of motion in the name of Councillor Howel Williams that the Council discontinue at once the purchase of the *Daily Worker* for the public library. Councillor Williams after mentioning that he did not belong to any political party said he had some regard for honest and truthful reporting. He regarded that the *Daily Worker* for quite some time was lacking those qualities of truthful reporting so much so that a correspondent of the newspaper had resigned. 'I do contend that the *Daily Worker* has forfeited all rights to respect and deserves nothing but our contempt', he said proposing his motion. . . . Councillor Comlyn Williams said that while he detested the newspaper as much as Councillor H. Williams, it was the principle of the matter he was after. He said: 'We must not lose the sense of principle however bitter our feelings may be over this terrible catastrophe in Hungary. Let the people who want to look at this newspaper do so. Do not let us stop something because the more you stop a thing the more dangerous it becomes'. Alderman Richard Davies, who said that he never read the newspaper and had no sympathy with its views, said they might detest the expressed views of the newspaper and the Party it represented, but the matter before them was a bigger issue. He thought it was the duty of the Library Committee to supply established national papers of all shades of opinion to give the public an opportunity of seeing the various shades of opinion. 'I understand that this newspaper is a national daily and we may detest the expressions it has and the party it represents' he said. Replying to the debate, Councillor Howel Williams maintained that the newspaper's propaganda was subtle and he was afraid that ordinary people who read it might fall for it with dire consequences. 'This newspaper is anti-British all along', he said. 'Without this malicious newspaper there would be a fresher and healthier place on the stands of our Library'.

Voting on the motion resulted in eleven voting in its favour and six against. So now the *Daily Worker* will not appear any more in Caernarvon's Library."[8]

A long series of reports which led to questions in Parliament and involved Birmingham Public Libraries, began just before Christmas 1956.

"Mr. V. H. Woods, Birmingham Chief Librarian, said today that the Customs had impounded as obscene a two volume edition of the complete works of M. Jean Genet, a contemporary French writer, which had been ordered for the library. Mr. Woods said: 'We are revising our French collection and this was one of the works which we ordered through Blackwells, the Oxford booksellers. I have not myself read any of the books in the collection, but in a review about two years ago, *The Times Literary Supplement* said that in the opinion of Sartre, who is a man of some standing, and in the opinion of many French critics, Genet was reckoned to be among the greatest of his contemporaries. We therefore felt that the work should be included in our collection. We have been told by Blackwells, however, that it has been impounded by the customs. They say we have a right to appeal, but subject to anything my Committee may say to the contrary I do not intend to make representations. My view is that censorship should be exercised by the Government and if they take the view that the books are unsuitable I shall not regard it as my duty to press for their return'. Mr. Meyrick Rees, Chairman of the public library committee, said the impounding of the books would be considered at the Committee's next meeting."[9]

But Councillor Rees added:

"I think the City Librarian and members of the Committee are capable of saying whether or not the book is suitable to place in the libraries. Filth as well as beauty is in the eyes of the beholder. I don't know what or who is responsible, but I should not be surprised if it was a law with whiskers on, made in the time of the first Elizabeth. We are living in 1956 and to impound a book which is freely read in France seems, to say the least, old-fashioned."[10]

The two volume edition was in the original French, not in English translation. In its leader of the 27th December 1956, *The Times* commented:

"The statement by Mr. V. H. Woods is disturbing news. . . . The episode raises once again the unending and unsatisfactory business of what is proper censorship. It is unending because the climate of taste steadily changes and what is regarded with repugnance by one generation comes to be a matter of interest, and in many cases even for admiration, in a later century. It is unsatisfactory because in Great Britain the whole law is in a most untidy and unsatisfactory state. The number of potential censors—or those who act for the real censors whoever they may be—is legion. The Courts, the Customs, the libraries are only some of those who have the power to say that, no matter what the writer's purpose or the reader's intention, such and such books shall not be made available. Because obscenity is incapable of definition the most cheap and nasty publications put on the market by hole-and-corner publishers, whose main purpose seems to be to peddle what is disgusting, can flourish scot-free. But work which is of social significance, produced by a publisher of repute, can be, and is, stopped in a number of ways. It would be crying for the moon to demand some really satisfactory solution to society's dilemma in this matter. The idea of an Index is rightly rejected. At the same time there must be some protection for society against the exploitation of mere salaciousness. The only answer is the constant challenging of each disputable exercise of censorship. Authority must be forced to stand and deliver justification. It must never be allowed to forget that, however deplorable works may be, unchecked suppression would be even more deplorable."[11]

On 8th January 1957, *The Times* reported that after a meeting of the Birmingham Public Libraries Committee, at which the seizure of the books was considered, the Chairman said he had no comment to make on any decisions reached:

"The books . . . were stopped on the way to the Birmingham Public Library. Mr. Denis Howell, Labour M.P. for All Saints, Birmingham, is to raise the matter in the House of Commons later this month. He is to ask who seized the books and on whose authority."[12]

Evan Hughes, writing in *Tribune* on 4th January 1957 criticized Woods' attitude to the seizure.

"So he does not intend to appeal against the decision. If he wishes to be logical, Mr. Woods should ask 'the Government' to go through all the books in his library and decide which ones are 'suitable'. Then we could have 'the Government' replacing the librarian—Mr. Woods could scarcely object and the result would hardly be more deplorable than to have a man who lives with books and by books accepting censorship without complaint. . . . What nonsense this ban is! It is not going to be corrupted because someone says in print the sort of things that people say every night in the local in a foreign language. It is far more likely to be damaged by a narrow-minded censorship and by the poor spirit of librarians unwilling to fight for the free circulation of a book they have chosen for their readers."[13]

Denis Howell, M.P. questioned by the *Birmingham Mail* said on 4th January, 1957:

"I feel that if an institution as important and as responsible as Birmingham Libraries Committee wishes to have these copies, then it is far more competent to take a decision than the Chancellor, Customs and Excise Officers, or whatever authority is responsible for this outrageous action."[14]

On 31st January Howell asked the Chancellor of the Exchequer:

"(1) What arrangements existed for the censorship of literary works being imported into this country: what standards were laid down for the guidance of those responsible; and
(2) in what circumstances two volumes of novels by Jean Genet had been prevented from entering the country by the Customs and Excise authorities; and if he will now facilitate their dispatch to the Birmingham Reference Library, who are the purchasers.

Mr. Enoch Powell (Financial Secretary, Treasury): 'The importation into the United Kingdom of indecent or obscene books is prohibited by (section 42 of) the Customs Consolidation Act, 1876 and the Commissioners of Customs and Excise are responsible for enforcement. Where books are seized under this provision, the importer may, within one month, claim that they are not liable to forfeiture; and if such a claim is made the Commissioners must have the issue determined by a Court. In the case referred to the importer was advised of his legal right but made no claim.'

Mr. Howell: 'Is it not farcical that these two books are readily available to French speaking scholars at the British Museum and the Library of Reading University. Why should the French speaking public of Birmingham be prevented from reading in the Birmingham Reference Library works which appear in those other places? Was it not time that this whole archaic business was reviewed by the Government, and the public treated as adults capable of censoring their own literary work? Should not the Government review the whole matter in the light of twentieth-century practice?'

Mr. Powell: 'If the importer of the books had shared the view of the Hon. member he would have exercised his rights of which he was informed, of making a claim and taking the matter to the courts.'

Mr. Howell: 'It may still be possible for the Birmingham City Council to exercise these rights. It ordered the books after a review of them in *The Times* (laughter). Why should the City of Birmingham Reference Library following a review of a good character in *The Times* be thwarted in this manner by the Treasury?'

Mr. Powell: 'If the City of Birmingham wishes to test this matter the Commissioners of Custom and Excise will be glad to arrange for importation for that purpose, so that it can be referred to the courts'."[15]

The *Birmingham Mail,* of 1st February 1957 reported that:

"A Birmingham City Corporation deputation consisting of the Chairman of the Public Libraries Committee (Councillor Meyrick Rees), the Town Clerk (Mr. J. F. Gregg), and the City Librarian (Mr. Victor Woods), has been to London and met the Deputy Chairman of the Board of Customs and Excise (Mr. A. D. Owen). Members of the deputation were able to read part of the works of Genet. On his return to Birmingham, Councillor Rees said that suggestions were to be made to the Public Libraries Committee when it meets on Monday."[16]

On 4th February *The Times* reported:

"Birmingham Public Libraries Committee will be recommended at their meeting tomorrow to take no action to recover a two-volume edition of the work of Jean Genet impounded by Customs and Excise Officers. After visiting the Customs and Excise department in London ... Mr. M. Rees, said today that he would recommend his Committee to take no action to recover the seized book. 'When I had the opportunity of reading translated passages from page after page of Genet's book I felt sick to the foundations of my being ... the theme was homosexuality. I am convinced that the Customs and Excise Department has rendered a public service in impounding such a book. I feel that the critics, however exalted, who have recommended this book are guilty of an offence against the public good'."[17]

The *Daily Mail* reported that:

"Whatever the Committee's decision Mr. Denis Howell, . . . is to press for a debate in the House on the censorship of imported books. He said yesterday: 'I am not concerned that the Chairman regards this work as pornographic and wants to drop the matter. I want to know who decides nationally that books should be banned. This book is already in the British Museum Library and Reading University—it is a farce that nobody else in Britain can read it'."[18]

The Birmingham Public Libraries Committee met on 4th February and it was stated afterwards that the case involving the seizure of the books was now closed and no further action would be taken by the Committee.[19]
The case was not closed, however, and it continued for another month and a half. Councillor Rees' actions were not wholly approved of by ex-Councillor Geoffrey Allen in his letter to the editor of the *Birmingham Evening Despatch,* 5th February 1957.

"Standing on one's head may be a suitable occupation for circus clowns but it is hardly a fitting one for the Chairman of a responsible Council committee. Only a few days ago, when discussing the arbitrary confiscation of Genet's works by the Customs Officials, my friend Councillor Meyrick Rees, chairman of our Public Library Committee, was full of fight for the right to read what we like and even declared that 'it was a pity that I hadn't sent a jolly letter to the Press'. Now, I find Councillor Rees has joined the book-burners and I find myself compelled to address such a letter as he suggested, albeit it will now invoke his disapproval rather than his support. Genet's works have been acclaimed by responsible literary critics, none of whom has been a Customs official: conversely, none of our Customs officers are, to the best of my knowledge, literary critics, although we have it on Councillor Rees' authority that the Library Committee abounds in 'geniuses' now to be over-ridden. But send the worthy chairman to London . . . and we find him dismissing Genet's works as 'filth' and commending the Customs authorities for their 'public duty'. If it were not tragic it would be frankly funny. If we are to ban all authors with mental or sexual abnormalities, then we shall find bare shelves in the city's public libraries. Even Shakespeare wrote love poems to a young man. If Genet is to be banned, why not Proust and Gide, or Jean-Paul Sartre? Why not invoke once again prohibitions against George Bernard Shaw, Henry Miller or Radclyffe Hall?
How are students of contemporary French literature now to study their subject? Are they supposed to emigrate? The works of Genet, published in French, were purely for use in the reference library, and were not available for public loan. Yet there are plenty of books in the city libraries with enough smut to satisfy the most salacious. If Birmingham is to maintain its reputation as one of the world's leading reference libraries, we must cease to consider undoubted works of literature as

scrawls on walls and pay respect to our duty as a mirror of contemporary world literature. You were right the first time, Councillor Rees."[20]

On 18th February in the House of Commons, Denis Howell again raised the subject of censorship of literary works imported into Great Britain, with particular reference to Genet's works, and a long debate ensued.[21] *The Times* published a summary of the debate on 19th February:

"Mr. Denis Howell . . . said the matter arose because of the seizure by the Customs and Excise. While there were conflicting views about Genet and his work, if any scholar was attempting to study contemporary French literature, Genet must be read. A critical analysis of Genet's works appeared in the *British Journal of Delinquency*—a review written by a Mr. John Croft, an official of the Home Office—which provided another good reason why this action should not have been taken. Since the matter was first raised there had been some change of face with the almost Gilbertian situation of the Birmingham town clerk, the city librarian, and the chairman of the libraries committee solemnly proceeding to London and being given translated passages from Genet—an objectionable practice, because it was impossible to judge any book by a few passages. They then decided that the book was unfit for anyone else in Birmingham to read. The Customs and Excise had abused their powers.

Mr. Fletcher said it shocked his conscience that the Customs and Excise could prohibit the book. He did not believe that Parliament under the Act of 1876 intended to give them power to ban works of scholarship.

Mr. Enoch Powell said that the offer of a test case in the Courts had not been accepted. After visiting London to read some translated passages, the chairman of the public libraries committee said: 'When I had the opportunity of reading translated passages from page after page of Genet's books, I felt sick to the foundations of my being'. It must be concluded that in this case the Customs and Excise had interpreted the law reasonably, and that generally speaking there was due opportunity for the public to be protected against an unreasonable administrative application of the law. The position at present was exactly that which was desiderated in a leading article in *The Times* on 27th December which put the very real difficulty, which was that there was a tremendous amount of literature which everyone would want to prevent from entering the country and that we did not want a stuffy and unduly narrow attitude to grow up and be enforced. 'The only answer' *The Times* said, 'is the constant challenging of each disputable exercise of censorship. Authority must be forced to stand and deliver justification'."[22]

The *Bookseller* of 23rd February gave a comprehensive resumé of the Genet affair,[23] while *Books and Bookmen* concluded:

"It is quite ludicrous that we who live in the mid-twentieth Century should be subject to laws of censorship which were made when Bowdler was considered a model literary man. Victorian prudery seems to be the only measure possessed by the teeming authorities in this country who have the power to suppress, seize, and burn books, on the grounds of indecency. .... It is only too apparent that our Governments live in the dream of Victorian England, for they are strangely sensitive to protests from small bodies of citizens who are as illiterate as they are bigoted. It cannot be denied that the establishment fulfils an absolutely negative function in its role as censor, and the time has come when a positive law—debated and agreed by all interested organizations—should replace the rule of busy bodies."[24]

The conclusion of the affair was noted in the *Birmingham Mail* on 13th March 1957.

"The works of the French writer, Jean Genet, will never appear on the shelves of Birmingham's Reference Library. An attempt to re-open the matter was made at yesterday's meeting of Birmingham City Council, when a move by Councillor Miss Sheila Wright and Councillor Len Wheeler inviting the Council to 'regret the action of the Committee in not proceeding with its arrangements for the two volumes of Jean Genet to be added to the Reference Library' was overwhelmingly defeated by a show of hands."[25]

At the meeting of the Beckenham Borough Council on Monday 28th January:

"A claim that by their decision not to buy a certain book, the Library Committee were deciding which books residents should read, was made . . . by Councillor C. M. Hamilton. . . . He said that the committee were in the position of deciding for residents what they should read and not read; what they should think and not think; and what attitude they should take to social problems. He was of the opinion that the Committee were over-stepping their prerogative. In the debate that followed Councillor G. I. White said he hoped that the Press would not mention the book's name 'because it would do more harm than good if it is brought to public notice'.
    The debate arose on a minute of the Library Committee which reported that they had decided not to purchase a book which was suggested by a reader. Councillor Hamilton said he contested the decision of the committee not to purchase the particular book. 'Any adult, if he takes any interest in life at all, is entitled to expect assistance from his local library . . . I do not intend to go into the problems that are involved in this book but this is the fourth time the Committee have thought for residents on very different subjects'. He then enumerated other occasions. . . . There was a book dealing with Nazi atrocities which the Committee decided not to take. Then there was *Labour,* the monthly publication of the TUC and another publication applying to a religious denomination, known as the Christadelphians. 'Now we have reached the stage . . . when we do not take a book that has been asked for by two residents at least and would probably be read by many more. As far as I can make out the only argument is that if people want to read that sort of book they can go out and buy it themselves'. . . . He was told by the Mayor (Councillor D. R. Knox-Johnston) that he could not move a reference back as under standing orders, the Committee had direct powers in matter like this.
    Alderman Parkin said the committee had been entrusted with powers of

censorship and the council should realize that this was a book written by a man who had been perverting youths, and had admitted unnatural practices. . . . Councillor Miss K. A. Moore, Chairman of the Committee, said that if Councillor Hamilton's views were taken to a logical conclusion the library would have every book that was published. All members of the Committee who had read the book reached the same conclusion and she was under the impression Councillor Hamilton had not read the book. Councillor Hamilton admitted that he had deliberately avoided reading the book because of the principle involved, not the subject matter."[26]

In Manchester a reader with a razor blade had been acting as an unofficial censor at the Central Library.

"Thousands of readers taking home books from the Central Library in Manchester have 'had the bedroom scenes spoilt for them', said Librarian Mr. James Green yesterday. Sixty books have been slashed apparently with a razor blade—and maybe more. So now Mr. Green and his assistants have set a trap for the phantom censor—the one man or woman among 20,000 borrowers of books. The officials believe that this Jack the Ripper of fiction has been at work for about a year. He appears to 'censor' about one book a week. In some of the mutilated books, page after page has been viciously slashed out. And the trap to catch the slasher? That's a secret, say officials."[27]

In Newcastle upon Tyne, a demand for censorship came from Councillor T. R. Burton.

"Books alleged by a city councillor to be 'pornographic and blasphemous' are appearing on the shelves of Newcastle public library. . . . He wants to see a censorship committee set up and will seek this by a request to the libraries committee. 'No one wants to dictate what reading matter should be available to adults . . . What I object to is that such books should be displayed where young people from the age of 16 may readily peruse them'. . . . Councillor J. Cox, vice-chairman of the Books and House Sub-Committee, said that no complaints about books had been brought to his Committee in the past two years of his service. 'The buying of books is left to the officials and we have had no reason to find fault with their choice in the past'. Councillor P. Boydell, vice-chairman of the Libraries Committee, said he could remember only one complaint of a book in 7 years. . . . The latest book which Councillor Burton thinks should be withdrawn from the library is described as 'squalid' in its own introduction. It has been regularly on loan during the past few months and there is a waiting list for it."[28]

Councillor Burton's suggestion was criticised in the Newcastle *Evening Chronicle*.

"Well, these are certainly serious charges, no wonder the old lady (Newcastle Central Library) is blushing so hard. But frankly, Councillor, we are inclined to take them with a tiniest pinch of salt. Surely things can't be as bad as all that? What we most dislike about the whole affair is your proposal for a censorship committee.

This seems to us a wrong-headed, dangerous suggestion. We have seen what happens when the self-appointed censors get to work. We have met the book banners and the book burners, the blue-pencillors and the busy Mrs. Grundies. We like none of them. We do not deny that there are works which should not fall into children's hands. . . . We also know that there are books that are unseemly even in the hands of adults. . . . And even if an occasional borderline case does slip through, this would be no excuse for the creation of a censorship committee. The cure, Councillor Burton, is worse than the disease."[29]

It had long been the practice in Sheffield Public Libraries to restrict the issue of valuable art books and medical books which might be mutilated or otherwise mis-used. Since 1936, regulations had also existed which stated that books on sexual hygiene and birth-control would be issued only on demand to those aged 21 or over after they had completed a special form and to those aged 18 to 20 provided they obtained the signature of a schoolmaster or other responsible person, and that these books were not to be issued in any circumstances to persons under 18 years of age. In later years, librarians had exercised discretion in applying these regulations but John Bebbington, City Librarian of Sheffield, was worried about these rules:

"Which in my opinion . . . create a somewhat ludicrous situation. We have had the spectacle on many occasions of a young married woman, her children with her, being informed that she cannot borrow a book on birth-control unless she obtained a signature of some responsible person such as a schoolmaster. It must be borne in mind, I think, that the situation has changed considerably since 1936. Sex education is much more freely given. In connection with books of this kind, I would suggest that they should continue to be available only on demand, and that requests should be dealt with in their discretion by the librarians in charge of each lending library, men and women of responsibility who could in case of any doubt seek my advice."[30]

On 10th October 1958, Bebbington submitted to his committee a report along these lines entitled *The selection and issue of certain classes of books*.

"(The committee) . . . accepted my proposals and the policy outlined has continued to the present time . . . a good deal of discretion is permitted to librarians, particularly in regard to the age of people to whom they issue books from this 'restricted' category. During the last few years, however, increased freedom of expression—starting I suppose with *Lady Chatterley's Lover*—has to some extent rendered decisions under this policy out of date. For some years before and after the report of 1958 it was the practice for my Committee to read books about which there had been complaints or to read books such as the *Tropics* before they were added to stock. This situation no longer applies and the decision about additions to stock and the segregation or otherwise of any kind of book is entirely my own. In my instruction to the staff, . . . I pointed out that no-one was permitted to place a book in the restricted stock without my permission, as clearly it was necessary for there to be uniformity of practice in the various Branch Libraries."[31]

Partly as a result of an approach from a conservation group which had a family planning section, Bebbington planned to raise the subject of restricted books with his Committee in September 1972, pointing out that attitudes had changed still further, that all books on contraception and sex education should be placed on the open shelves and equally that *Lady Chatterley's Lover* and other novels which had been put on restricted circulation for several years should also be placed on the open shelves, thus limiting restricted circulation to those books which were particularly liable to damage or other mis-use by readers.

In fact the Committee announced its decision in February 1973 and drastically reduced the number of novels and books on sex education kept in the 'restricted' category; although this category was not abolished completely with novels such as Henry Miller's *Tropics* and Selby's *Last Exit to Brooklyn* still being available only upon request.[32]

The autobiography of Lady Furness and her sister Gloria Vanderbilt, *Double Exposure,* was 'banned' from the Library at Leamington Spa, according to the *Daily Express,* 1st June 1959.

"A book that tells of an intimate friendship between the Duke of Windsor, then Prince of Wales, and Thelma Lady Furness, has been banned from the public library at Royal Leamington Spa. . . . 'It's in bad taste' said the library committee chairman, Councillor Norman Slater, who is a 53 year old ironmonger. He added: 'The throne doesn't want this sort of publicity. Books like these have only a notoriety value appealing to sensation-mongers. We don't want that kind of thing in Leamington'. A reader had asked for the book . . . to be bought for the Library. But the 12 man Committee all said 'No'. Explained Councillor Slater: 'It was the part dealing with an affair between the Duke and Lady Furness which led me to agree it should not be accepted. I don't regret the decision one bit. I feel the Duke and Duchess of Windsor are an old married couple by now. Surely it's an unkind gesture to drag up the past like this? . . . Please don't think we are setting ourselves up as censors. If we get a specific request we can always borrow a copy. But we definitely shan't put in on our shelves'. Another Committee member, 84-year-old Alderman Beaumont Fetherstone-Dilke, said 'I've been on the Committee for 25 years and we very rarely turn anything down. But critics, you know, were not favourable to this book'. Has he read it? 'No, but I might do now . . . I can't help feeling there are better books to spend our money on'.

Reviews on *Double Exposure* were read to the Committee by borough librarian H. Samuel Tallamy. In his opinion it was 'an utterly worthless piece of writing'."[33]

Tallamy, in his letter of 24th July 1972, wrote:

"My experience, based on the issue of the *Double Exposure* book, is that newspaper reports are mis-leading and often unfair. In the case of this book, the opposition came from me and not from members of the Committee, whose only part was to support my decision not to purchase the book which had had one hundred per cent damning reviews. The condemnation was concerned with its lack of quality and not in any way with the subject. The Press would not listen to explanations that the decision not to buy the book had nothing to do with the subject. I should add that we ordered the book in advance of publication and that it was possible to examine the book and confirm reviewers' hostility."[34]

In November 1959, Vladimir Nabokov's *Lolita* was published. This novel, like others known before publication to be controversial, led various sections of the Press to canvass public librarians to discover their attitudes to the book.

"Sheffield City Libraries Committee yesterday decided that the novel . . . will be banned from the shelves of its public libraries but may be obtained on application. Councillor J. Thorpe, chairman of the committee, said the novel would be on the 'restricted circulation' list. Eighty persons had put their names on the waiting list for the book."[35]

Similarly, in the West Riding County Libraries, the book was only to be available to adult borrowers.

"The West Riding is thus taking the same course as Sheffield, where the chairman of the Libraries Committee has described the novel as 'muck'. . . . In Leeds, the book has not been discussed by the Libraries Committee. Mr. F. G. B. Hutchings, Chief Librarian, said: 'If you go into any library in Leeds you will be able to reserve a copy of Lolita'."[36]

Other decisions were noticed:

"Bingley, Keighley, and Huddersfield Libraries Committees have already decided to allow *Lolita* on 'restricted circulation'. Alderman F. Sharp, chairman of Halifax's committee, said his members would make up their minds on Friday. He thought they would probably decide to make the book available on request. At Shipley a copy of *Lolita* has been added to the library, but, said the chief librarian, Miss J. Knott, there had been no special demand for it."[37]

In Glasgow, the book was to be available only on request:

"Councillor James McAteer, libraries convenor said yesterday: 'The book will not be placed on the open-access shelves where all and sundry can get it'. Said Mr. Charles W. Black, City Librarian, who had reported on the book to the Committee: '*Lolita* is not an obscene book—not according to modern standards at any rate. Branch librarians will ensure that the novel is not issued to immature minds or to persons who have not reached the years of discretion. The book has been published, and so far has not been banned. The fact that some people do not like it is no reason why others should not have an opportunity of reading it. Librarians are not censors of books nor are they the arbiters of public opinion. My advice to the committee was that the book should be available to the person who wants to read it and asks for it."[38]

This decision to keep *Lolita* on restricted access was a unique one for Glasgow. *The Times* of 5th December 1967, while discussing the case of Edinburgh Public Libraries and the novel *A Green Tree in Gedde* stated that:

"Glasgow's stock . . . contains just one novel that is available only on demand, *Lolita*. And that is a result of a specific decision by the Library Committee."[39]

In a letter of 12th November 1971, the City Librarian, C. W. Black wrote that to avoid undue publicity the decision was never minuted:

"The unusual decision taken with regard to this book was a compromise to satisfy a certain section of members who had misgivings about the advisability of the book being freely available. It was the only incident of its kind which I can recall and in view of our policy of no censorship, it is best forgotten."[40]

1. "Bill" for Reform of Obscene Libel Law is welcomed. *Bookseller,* 12th February 1955. pp.750-3
2. Alderman resigns over book. *Richmond and Twickenham Times,* 17th December 1955
3. Pin-up in Council Chamber. *Manchester Guardian,* 17th January 1956
4. Mares, Marie. No book censorship. *Books and Bookmen,* May 1956
5. Shoolbraid, Murray. Censorship in libraries. *Books and Bookmen,* July 1956
6. Guy, L. C. No book censorship. *Books and Bookmen,* September 1956
7. Move to ban Soviet paper from library fails. *West Lancashire Evening Gazette,* 8th November 1956
8. Councillor tore paper in library. *Caernarvon and Denbigh Herald,* 7th December 1956
9. Books seized as obscene. *The Times,* 24th December 1956
10. Demand for return of French novel. *Birmingham Post,* 24th December 1956
11. Literary contraband. *The Times,* 27th December 1956
12. Detained books. *The Times,* 8th January 1957
13. Hughes, Evan. Why ban these books? *Tribune,* 4th January 1957
14. M.P. asks about seized books. *Birmingham Mail,* 5th January 1957
15. Parliamentary Debates, Commons, vol. 563, 1956-57, cols. 1159-60
16. Two banned books: offer to the city. *Birmingham Mail,* 1st February 1957
17. Seizure of Genet's work. *The Times,* 4th February 1957
18. Customs 'right to seize this book'. *Daily Mail,* 4th February 1957
19. City will leave book impounded. *Birmingham Mail,* 5th February 1957

20. Allen, Geoffrey. 'Coun. Rees was right first time'. *Birmingham Evening Despatch,* 5th February 1957
21. Parliamentary Debates, Commons, vol. 565, 1956-57, cols. 166-176
22. Customs bar to Genet novels. *The Times,* 19th February 1957
23. Censorship by the Customs. *Bookseller,* 23rd February 1957. pp.920-2
24. Excisemen as censors. *Books and Bookmen,* March 1957
25. Not for city library shelves. *Birmingham Mail,* 13th March 1957
26. Book is banned from library. *Beckenham Advertiser,* 31st January 1957
27. The slashed novels. *Sunday Pictorial,* 12th May 1957
28. 'Dirt' books in library, says city councillor. *Newcastle Evening Chronicle,* 27th May 1957
29. Scrutiny. *Newcastle Evening Chronicle,* 28th May 1957
30. Bebbington, John. The selection and issue of certain classes of books. 10th October 1958 (Unpublished, held by Sheffield Public Libraries)
31. Letter from John Bebbington, City Librarian of Sheffield to the author, 1st August 1972 (Unpublished)
32. The wraps are taken off Lady Chatterley. *The Star,* 22nd February 1973
33. Royal Spa bars book about Royal Duke. *Daily Express,* 1st June 1959
34. Letter from H. S. Tallamy, Librarian and Curator, Leamington Spa to the author, 24th July 1972 (Unpublished)
35. 'Lolita' not for library shelves. *The Guardian,* 17th November 1959
36. Lolita gets 'adults only' tag in W.R. *Yorkshire Evening Post,* 17th November 1959
37. 'Lolita' on request at libraries. *The Guardian,* 17th November 1959
38. City puts 'Lolita' under the counter. *Scottish Daily Express,* 17th November 1959
39. Library books not on open shelf. *The Times,* 5th December 1967
40. Letter from C. W. Black, City Librarian of Glasgow to the author, 12th November 1971 (Unpublished)

CHAPTER 7

1960–1964

"MOTHER" of Bury St. Edmunds, wrote to the *Bury Free Press* on the 8th January 1960 asking:

> "If members of the Town Council's libraries committee are aware of certain types of novels, some of them really disgusting in their parade of sex and violence, which are available at the public library, especially among the brightly jacketed array of new books which have recently made their appearance. If not, then I suggest they should browse round and sort out a few of them for their week-end reading. They would get a shock. I am broadminded, but will not tolerate such degraded forms of writing, and I suggest there is need for a stricter supervision of municipal book buying. . . . This letter is intended as a warning to the public, especially those with teenagers, to be more selective in their choice of books. It is not in any way a criticism of our Borough Librarian and his staff who have done a first class job in building up a good lending department, and who show the public unfailing courtesy and helpfulness. . . . While I am not strictly in favour of any form of censorship in such matters, I would have thought it is the duty of any local authority to set a high tone, leaving the lower-minded section of the reading public to buy such books if they are so keen on them." [1]

The newspaper asked MOTHER to supply them with a list of the offending books, which she did, and one of their reporters borrowed the books from the Bury Lending Library.

> "Having read the books, I fully agree with your correspondent. There is an open parade of sex. . . . One novel in particular was absolutely disgusting. In fact, when I took it home I had to hide it from my teenage sons. And I felt rather embarrassed when I returned it to the library. Closer inspection of some of the books is most certainly needed."

The same issue was being discussed only a few weeks later in the *Kentish Mercury:*

"A drive to clear public library shelves of books that might adversely affect the minds of adolescents is to be launched in Lewisham. . . . an approach will be made to the library authorities to create a 'reserve list', where books will be available only if asked for, by schoolteacher Mr. Frank Norbury, . . . Mr. Norbury, unmarried, said, 'There ought to be a reserve list because there are works of art that are undeniably literature that, though fit for adults, are not fit for children. We do not allow our children to go into chemists and buy poisons for their bodies, and I think we should not allow them to go into libraries and get poisons for their minds'. . . . Another argument in favour of restricting some books to children, he says, is that teenagers have a rough time morally, and that it is possible for one incident in a book to unbalance them. While he realizes there can be no censorship, he believes a reserve list would get over this problem, because no book would be banned and, therefore, there could be (no) arguments over what should be excluded from libraries and what should be included."[2]

Books and Bookmen for August 1960 reported:

"When Ann Veronica by H. G. Wells was banned from the Manchester Public Libraries (1910) J. A. Hobson said, 'If the sun ever shone in Manchester, the Watch Committee would probably prosecute it for indecent exposure'. Even more recently, when I was shown around the Manchester Central Library it had the biggest collection of banned books I have ever seen. They were stored in a special section of the basement behind specially constructed iron bars. Many books that are in circulation at other public libraries all over the country were incarcerated here. Access to them was confined to very senior librarians who had to be convinced that the potential reader was incorruptible before allowing a book's release from the penitentiary."[3]

Certainly during the period when Charles Nowell was City Librarian of Manchester, the Manchester Central Library had two special collections of books which dealt with sex either in fact or fiction. The first collection, known as the 'K' collection comprised predominantly of fiction books belonging to the Central Lending Library which were available from this collection on request. This collection was disbanded after Charles Nowell's death. The second collection to which the *Books and Bookmen* comment probably refers still exists and is known as the 'C' collection, controlled now by the Social Sciences Library. Whilst this collection is maintained behind grilles in basement areas of the Central Library, the article is not strictly correct in that at the time it was written access was easily obtained by any member of the staff of the former Reference Library. Most of the books were issued for use in the Reference Library without special formality and there was only one book on the forensic aspects of a particular series of murders which was subject to specific instructions restricting its issue to members of the police and the legal profession.

Mrs. Ellen Morrison wrote in the *Catholic Times* of 14th October 1960:

> "I am glad to note that the matter of 'dirty' library books is coming out into the open. I have complained about certain books to the librarians, changed from one library to another, but with no result. One attendant informs me that the worse they are the better the public like them. I refuse to accept this, and to a certain extent the remedy is in our own hands. I have handed back my membership card giving my reason to the head librarian. . . . What we need here is a strong and vigorous censorship. The young are especially vulnerable, and to stop this pollution of young minds should be the concern of us all."[4]

On 2nd November 1960 the Jury at the Old Bailey decided that the Penguin Edition of *Lady Chatterley's Lover* by D. H. Lawrence was not an obscene article—a decision of tremendous importance in that it led to new freedom of expression in literature and in the arts generally. It was not the only factor which encouraged this new freedom of expression—the previous decade had seen a number of prosecutions for obscene libel, brought against reputable publishers, especially in 1954. These had encouraged the movement for reform of the law which led to the passing of the Obscene Publications Act, 1959. The case of *Lady Chatterley's Lover* was particularly significant as this was the first book to be the subject of a prosecution under Section 2 of the Act, i.e., involving trial of the publisher before a Jury.

On 2nd November 1960, the Press, both national and local, had a common front page story—the acquittal of Penguin Books Ltd. On 3rd November the Press offered a new slant on the case, namely the provision of *Lady Chatterley* by public libraries, and the point continued to receive attention in some newspapers until the end of 1963. Also on 3rd November 1960, K. A. Stockham, County Librarian of Nottinghamshire, issued a memorandum on *Lady Chatterley* to his Senior Staff throughout the service:

> "It is highly likely that during the next few weeks there will be a great many enquiries for this book. I am interested to have full details of this demand and I should be glad if you would send me a report on this matter written on Monday, 7th November. Will you please then send me further reports written on the following (3) Mondays. . . . In your reports I should like to have as much information as possible. For example, it will be interesting to learn the number of requests taken each day in each branch library, the type of person making the request, e.g., sex, age, old people, school children, etc.
>
> With regard to *Lady Chatterley's Lover,* my attitude is as follows. Now that the unexpurgated version is freely available for purchase, the County Library will buy copies. Although the book has been declared by a jury not to be obscene, it is advisable it should be issued to children only at the discretion of the Librarian. . . . All members of your staff should be told of the County Library policy in this

matter. Take particular care that junior assistants are advised how to deal with enquiries. . . ."[5]

On 18th November 1960 Stockham issued a further memorandum to his staff:

"Altogether 125 requests have so far been received for the book. Sixty-two of these have been made by women, mostly married and middle-aged, but in one case the book was requested by a girl of seventeen with the approval of her mother. Twenty-four requests have been made by men, and no details are given of the other thirty-nine requests. Two interesting conclusions can therefore be drawn:
(a) the demand has been small,
(b) the demand from women is much greater than from men.
Fifty copies of the book have been ordered—forty in the Heinemann edition and ten reinforced Penguins . . . ."[6]

Again on 3rd November, the Blackburn *Evening Telegraph* published the results of a survey of librarians in the east Lancashire area regarding their reactions to the book:

"Blackburn's Librarian (Mr. Walter Yeates), said no decision had yet been taken whether the book would be available at Blackburn library. But it will, in all probability be available at Accrington general library. Librarian Mr. G. C. Otter told the *Telegraph:* 'I have not read the book, but there is certain to be a demand for it, in view of the tremendous publicity'. Who decides whether to buy it? Mr. Otter said selection of books was normally up to the Librarian and when there was a doubt about anything the Libraries Committee Chairman was consulted. Inquiries about the novel have been pouring into Burnley Central Library steadily throughout the trial. 'People must have anticipated what the result would be', said the Borough Librarian, Mr. Richard Caul . . . 'But its readership will be restricted, and it will be available only on application'.
    Nelson and Clitheroe Libraries, it seems, will NOT be getting the book—but only because they do not handle paperbacks because of their flimsiness. . . . Colne Librarian, Mr. Peter Wightman thought there would be trouble about issuing of the book in certain libraries, but added: 'We will endeavour to get the book for our readers and will have it bound specially for library use, as in the case of other similar paper-backed books. Already we have had a large number of requests for it, and have had to refer would-be readers to a nearby bookseller'. . . . Bacup Librarian Mr. R. J. Benjamin, said he most certainly recommended the purchase of the book. If it were purchased, the procedure would be the same as with *Lolita*—the book would not be on the shelves, but would be available on request. One reason for not putting it on the shelves was that they had lost three copies of the expurgated version of the book in four years! The Chairman of Bacup Public Library Committee, Councillor John Crabtree, said he could not say whether the Committee would approve purchase. But as far as he could remember they had never turned down a recommendation by Mr. Benjamin. At Preston, Miss F. E. Cook, Lancashire County Librarian, said: 'We don't put paper-backed books on

our shelves unless there is a demand for them. If there is a request for this book it will be provided, but steps will be taken to see it is not issued to juveniles'. Dr. A. M. Korn, Preston Library Committee Chairman (said) . . . 'The Committee has always followed the recommendations of the Library Association in the past. Preston Library has never done any censoring on its own account'."[7]

On the same day the *Birmingham Evening Despatch* stated:

"The case of 'Lady Chatterley' will be considered by Birmingham's Libraries Committee at their meeting on Monday—but she seems almost certain to win. Mr. V. H. Woods, the Chief Librarian, said today: 'I shall mention the book at the meeting, but I can think of no reason why it should not go on the shelves of our libraries. We do, of course, exercise some restraint in the case of youngsters under the age of 16, so that there would be little danger of the book falling into the hands of young children'. A Committee member, Councillor A. B. Dark, said: 'It is not part of our job to sit as public censors when the book has already been passed as 'fit for human consumption' by the Courts. I have read extracts of the original book, and I must admit that some passages could be taken as pornography—if taken out of context. Certainly, I should not like any child of mine to read the book. I believe that, as the law becomes more liberal in these cases, it would be a good idea to introduce some sort of 'X Certificate' system for books as well as for films'."[8]

The Deputy City Librarian of Leeds, Mr. A. B. Craven, was reported by the *Yorkshire Evening News* on 3rd November, as saying:

"Fifty or sixty copies of *Lady Chatterley's Lover* will be bought by the Leeds Public Libraries Department. . . . 'We buy the numbers which we think will meet public demand, and in this case that is the sort of number that is likely to meet the demand'. . . . Alderman A. Adamson, Chairman of the Leeds Libraries and Arts Committee said: 'I am seeing the Chief Librarian, Mr. Hutchings today, to discuss the matter. In Leeds we have always taken the line that we don't censor any books, but I don't think we should overstock this particular one. The price of the book—3s. 6d.—is the price of a packet of cigarettes and therefore it will be easily available for people to buy if they wish to do so'."[9]

In Liverpool the book was to be bought but would not be available to persons under 21 without written application from their parents, teachers or in some cases, from a medical doctor. Liverpool's policy of buying two copies of each new book on publication applied to *Lady Chatterley's Lover*. When questioned on this by the *Liverpool Daily Post's* reporter, Dr. Chandler said: "The library's policy in duplication is determined by public demand which must demonstrate itself first."[10]

Brighton and Hove decided to buy the book. Jack Dove, Borough Librarian of Hove, said: "My Committee give me a very free hand, and now that the book has been cleared in court I cannot imagine their objecting to it".[11] Three months later however, the *Brighton and Hove*

Gazette of 10th February 1961, reported that a Hove Alderman was refused permission to read extracts from the unexpurgated version of *Lady Chatterley's Lover* at the Hove Borough Council Meeting on the previous day.

> "Alderman F. J. Miller, in seeking to ban copies of the book from Hove Public Library, asked the Mayor (Alderman Barry Funnell): 'You would not give permission for half a page of the book to be read?' The Mayor: 'No'. Alderman Miller: 'Well, that tells the story'. . . . Councillor Percy Earl moved that before a vote was taken on the notice of motion members should, by show of hands, indicate whether or not they had read the book. This suggestion was met by cries of 'Certainly not' and the Mayor declared: 'We cannot do that. It is inquiring into the private lives of members. It would be intolerable'. Alderman Miller: 'We have a nice, clean, well-behaved staff in our library. Is it fair that they should be in touch with this book?'. Councillor H. Lindsey-Lewis said the debate was a case of 'cultural schizophrenia! . . . Are we trying to force our opinions on 70,000 ratepayers? Are we going to tell them what they should read and what they should not read?'." [12]

Alderman Miller's move was defeated by sixteen votes to eleven.

In Bebington, Cheshire, the Rector, the Rev. A. G. Pouncy said that the libraries should wait at least a year before stocking the book. He commented:

> "If it is stocked, especially now, it is obvious that for one who will read it from literary motives, at least five will read it because of unhealthy curiosity, if not worse. I have not read the book, but judging from descriptions and extracts in the Press it is not a book which I should like my children to read, nor should I like it to be in my home. . . . I disagree entirely with the view that recognised moral standards can be forgotten, with approval, the moment one moves from the sphere of everyday human relationships into that of literary literature or other forms of art. If a story condones, or appears to condone, moral failure, that story is not a good story, whatever its author's name. If the Borough of Bebington insists on stocking the book in its libraries it should at least wait a year until some of the publicity for the book has been forgotten . . . . For the Christian, literary and philosophical considerations cannot be decisive; indeed he is committed to the standard the Apostle Paul sets *(sic)* in Philippians 4:8, 'Whatsoever things are true . . . honest . . . just . . . pure . . . lovely . . . of good report; if there by any virtue . . . think on these things. That is the word of God'. The Chairman of the Libraries Committee, Councillor W. Wedgewood, said that he saw no reason why Bebington Libraries should not stock the book." [13]

The Chairman of the Swansea Library Committee pointed out that the Committee had the power to decide on the purchase of books, but that it would be ill-advised not to accept the Chief Librarian's recommendation to purchase it. Leslie M. Rees, City Librarian, felt that his girl assistants should not be asked to issue the book unless they were asked for it by women in which case he hoped some of them would be prepared to do so. He also felt that assistants should be allowed to exercise discretion if asked for the book by a young person.[14]

The *Manchester Evening News* Postbag ran a number of letters discussing *Lady Chatterley's Lover*. Commenting on the decision of the Manchester and Oldham Libraries Committees to stock the book and not to act as censors and moralists, one writer asked:

"What I would like to know is this: what are the duties of Library Committees?"[15]

Councillor M. P. Pariser, Chairman of the Manchester Libraries Committee was asked to reply and wrote:

"We have a duty as custodians of ideas in all forms—books, records, newspapers, plays, lectures and music—to make those ideas available to the public. It would be quite wrong for us to be censors or arbiters of public taste. Only the public can decide. We cannot stop them misusing ideas or books. If the father of a 15-year-old girl does not want her to read *Lady C.* for instance, it is his responsibility to stop her buying the book or borrowing it from the Library."[15]

In some places however, it was decided *not* to stock the book in the public library. In Fleetwood, for instance:

"By a 14 to 3 vote, members of the Corporation Library Committee on Thursday night decided to ban the book after Councillor G. H. Platt had said that: 'It has the morals of the farmyard and gives a false picture of sex by glorifying fornication and adultery'. The question of the inclusion of the book, raised by letter by Councillor Platt at last month's meeting, had been deferred for a month. Councillor Platt said that he hoped the majority of members had taken the opportunity of reading the book and agreed with his comments that it was unhealthy and unbalanced. He obtained the views of a psychiatrist who confirmed his view that the book would have a considerable adverse effect on a growing mind. 'The question was raised last month whether this Council should set itself up as a censor of public morals . . . I think the answer to that lies in our duty to the community in general, and that we are expected to give protection in all matters of public welfare where we feel it necessary'. In banning the book from their libraries they would be acting in the same manner as when they refused to allow certain lurid paperbacks and postcards, considered to go beyond the reasonable margin of public taste, to be sold at their kiosks. . . . Councillor Platt went on: 'We all know that since the war public taste and morals have declined. Do we want to help that decline or show a courageous stand? If we refuse to face our responsibilities which, in this case, to my mind, could be a precedent, I am forced to wonder where it will all end'.

Councillor E. Williamson moved an amendment that the book should be obtained for issue to adults only. The finest legal brains in the country had tried the book and he didn't see that the Committee were in a position to try it again. . . .

Alderman J. P. Kennedy JP, opposing the amendment, said that if the book was considered sufficiently filthy and obscene to warrant it being banned for children, it was sufficiently so for adults. 'Dirt, or mud or filth is certainly going to leave a trail of trouble behind it . . . no matter whether it is read by adults or children'. . . . The amendment to include the book, available only to adults, was lost by a heavy majority, only three voting for it."[16]

In Beckenham, the Council decided not to make the book available in its libraries.

"This decision was denounced at the meeting as 'ignoring the law of the land' and 'illegal censorship'. Despite opposition, the Council accepted a Library Committee decision not to purchase the book. In their report, the Committee stated that they had had eleven requests for the book, but, after special consideration, they had voted against buying it. Councillor J. Lloyd-Eley (Labour) opening the debate, urged that the Council should reject the Libraries Committee's decision and buy the book. . . . In refusing to buy the book . . . the Committee were 'adopting an ostrich-like attitude. This book has already been afforded a decision in its favour by a jury and, to my mind, it is quite improper for a committee of this council to say that it does not agree with that decision'. The refusal of the Committee to buy the book, he continued, raised several very important issues. Not the least of these was the fact that the Committee were saying they did not agree with a legal decision. Secondly, there was the fact that there had been a number of requests for the book, and the people had a right to expect a proper service from the library. 'It seems that this committee seek to impose their own censorship, which the law of the land does not uphold'. His third point was that as the book was available at most book shops it was really nonsense for this Committee to think it can be the guardian of public morals."[17]

Councillor Lloyd-Eley's proposal was defeated by 14 votes to 13.

In Wimbledon, there was considerable opposition to *Lady Chatterley* and the Borough Council rejected the librarian's proposal to purchase copies.

"Alderman Sir Cyril Black said that he had read the book out of public duty and he thought it more serious 'to poison the soul than to poison the body'. Sir Cyril went on to describe 'the appalling slide in moral values' that had taken place over recent years and said that his voice would be raised against any suggestion by the library to take in books of that sort. Alderman N. S. Clarke described the book as 'an insult to womanhood' adding that he was surprised that an organized body of women had not set out to ban it. He described the court case as a 'lamentable piece of British justice' and said that he would not have the book in his own home. 'If I see it there, I shall burn it', he said."[18]

A similar decision was taken at Widnes in Lancashire. A 'Widnes Mother' wrote in the *Widnes Weekly News* on 16th December 1960:

"A person who writes certain words in a public convenience is often described as mentally unsound. Yet a person who writes the same words in a novel is described by certain people as a genius. Thank goodness, this book, *Lady Chatterley's Lover* will not be in our library to debase the fair name of English literature. The people of Widnes are not sheep, to be brainwashed into a belief that filth is art. Now that Christmas is so near, it is a joy to see parents and children in a local store, buying those well-loved classics, *David Copperfield, Lorna Doone, Little Women* etc. Widnes can be proud of the literary senses of its residents." [19]

At the November Meeting the Nottingham City Libraries Committee decided that twelve of its members be asked to read the book to decide whether or not it should be purchased. [20]

The Nottingham Evening Post, 20th December, reported the committee's decision of the previous day that copies be purchased for the library service.

"But it is certain that the decision will be challenged at the next ordinary meeting of the Council. . . . At the last Committee meeting, members were not in agreement that the book should be obtainable from a library and their decision was held over . . .". [21]

On 2nd January 1961 when the matter was raised in the City Council it was resolved that the Libraries Committee be requested not to implement its decision of 19th December to purchase copies of the book. The voting was very close—16 for and 15 against.

"In Nottingham last year there were 15 unmarried mothers under the age of 16, Alderman Ernest Purser, Chairman of the Health Committee informed the City Council in moving the resolution. 'This is a problem we in Nottingham have to face. There were seven up to February last year and the final figure was 15. The previous year there was one. Is a man with any sense of decency prepared to sit down, and not find his blood rising at this figure. You and I both have some responsibility to prevent this. . . . We can stand firm and lead the world on moral government, even if we have not got the dollars'. . . . Alderman Purser said he made no apology for not having read the book. 'I know when the fire is hot, and I know I shall not be foolish enough to put my hand into it to try it. What we are faced with is in which direction does the book go in essence? Does it seek to fortify our best moral instincts? Does it help improve us to the highest? Those are the things people have to ask themselves in relation to this literature. . . . We are weakening the moral stamina of our people by allowing them to read such things. This is not a drawing room matter'. . . . Alderman Cox declared: 'Alderman Purser and I are not starting a new career as missionaries, but it is a matter of moral rearmament against the forces of evil, and that is where we take our stand. . . . If, in debate in this chamber members attempted to use some of the language found in this book, knowing you as I do, my Lord Mayor, you would not just ask them to leave the Chamber. You would come down fully robed and throw them through the nearest window and earn the thanks of Nottingham'. 'What is going to be the position of our magistrates? . . . if they get a case, brought by the police, for using obscene language in the street, they just cannot inflict a penalty on them if they give just one answer—that they were only using the language read in a book supplied by Nottingham Public Libraries. If I read this book aloud in the bus queue, a charge would be taken against me for using obscene language. It is an open gateway to any sexual maniac to write a more filthy book, but that is impossible, but to write another. It is an open gateway to more of this kind of thing. . . . It can be said people will buy the book if they are not allowed to have it from the libraries. Well, let them . . . I fail to see how we are going to justify ourselves if we allow this 'poison' to be given over free from the Corporation and let them take it *ad lib*. The poisoning of the soul of young people is far bigger a crime than the poisoning of the body'. He appealed to every man and woman to follow the lead of Long Eaton and Sutton-in-Ashfield and keep it out of the libraries. Mr. H. W. Peck asked members to remember that in the eighteenth century men had two or three mistresses and no one bothered about it. 'The whole point indeed in this debate is that anyone who imagines that just knowing the good old Anglo-Saxon four-letter words that we all perfectly well know and use from time to time, has any effect on people's behaviour is quite ignorant of the workings of people's minds. I am perfectly well aware of the words "murder" "knife" and "heart" but the knowledge does not in the least degree inspire me to plunge a dagger in the bosom of the Lord Mayor—or members of the opposition'. Young people now seemed to know all the words 'from the cradle up' and, Mr. Peck contended, did not seem any the worse for it and had a healthier view than in the days of 'furtiveness, snigger and mumbo-jumbo'. 'If this book comes before a young person ignorant of the words it is incomprehensible rigmarole . . . . If they do know the words they must have learned them somewhere else'. Mr. R. D. Neal said he felt it was a matter of deep regret that the matter had to be debated so openly and be publicised out of all proportion and quite unwarranted to a mere 3s. 6d. novel. He said that he had read the book to carry out his duty as a member of the Libraries Committee to give an opinion on it and he gave his opinion against it. 'I am not ashamed to say that in my opinion this is a very disgusting book. It is a book which I think should not be found in the home or in the possession of any well-thinking man, woman, boy or girl'." [22]

The same newspaper reported on another page, that regardless of the decision of the Council, the unexpurgated copy of *Lady Chatterley's Lover* would still be available in Nottingham Central Library.

"Yesterday's full meeting of the Council . . . does not affect the fact that an unexpurgated copy has been in the Central Library for thirty years, and will remain there. The City Library claims to have the best collection of first edition D. H. Lawrence works in the country in its section for students of his life. Anyone who says he is studying Lawrence can see the book on request, said the City Librarian Mr. F. C. Tighe, today. He said: 'I don't think anybody but a genuine student would bother to go to those lengths. But there is nothing to stop anybody saying they want to see the book. We do not ask for any evidence that the person is a student Anyway, we regard our original copy of *Lady Chatterley* as being very low on the list of valuables in the Lawrence collection', he added. The Library's unexpurgated copy is the Paris edition of 1931.

The Chairman of the Libraries Committee, Councillor Brian Morley, told the *Post* today that he thought members would accept yesterday's decision by the council that the book should not appear in libraries. He said: 'I have not yet discussed the matter with the City Librarian, but I expect the decision will be formally reported to the Committee at its next meeting on January 16th. I anticipate that we will accept the Council's decision. I cannot see that we can do anything else'."[23]

The Nottingham Council's decision was followed by a number of letters to both the Nottingham and national papers. John G. Simpson of Ilkeston, wrote to the *Guardian-Journal* on the 6th January 1961:

"Reading the report of the debate, it would appear to justify the conclusion that many members of the Council are prone to wholly untenable and unjustifiable exaggerations. It may be true that the morals of people generally give rise to genuine concern; but surely this is in no way due to a book that, far from being immoral or obscene, seeks to elevate a healthy sex-consciousness as opposed to the cheap tawdry and grossly sensual attitudes of our present dispensers of the public palate. I hope I may be forgiven if I express a weariness of reading and hearing condemnations of *Lady C* from people who have never read the book; they render it a colossal injustice. It is more to the point to remind readers that the twelve members of the jury not only listened to the evidence and the defence and prosecuting counsel's pleas, but had actually read the book. To imply by a pious vote that this British jury were misled in their decision is surely a body-blow to the concepts of British justice."[24]

In Cardiganshire the decision not to buy the book was taken by the County Librarian, and not by the Library Committee.

"At a meeting of Cardiganshire Joint Library Committee on Friday he stated that the main reason he had for rejecting the book, and others of its kind, stemmed from a sense of moral responsibility for the young people. 'We have a special responsibility . . . to safeguard our young people against immoral suggestions, and crooked attitudes towards institutions which form the very basis of our civilisation. We have a right to expect authors to respect moral standards in forming the main themes of their novels.' . . . Mr. Edwards pointed out that the decisions of other librarians had been 'most conflicting'. It revealed only too glaringly the dilemma of the profession when confronted with difficult moral problems. Some libraries, in an effort to avoid embarrassment to female assistants, decided that only male members of the staff should deal with requests for the book. . . . The Librarian's action was confirmed by the Committee."[25]

On 30th August 1963 *The Guardian* reported a statement in the *Nottingham Public Libraries Annual Report:*

"The Libraries Committee has taken much satisfaction from the lack of demand for novels with frequent references to the sex act complete with four-letter words not commonly used in general conversation." [26]

It also noted similar reactions from the D. H. Lawrence country:

"Mr. Kenneth Stockham, Nottinghamshire County Librarian, said: 'It is interesting that our library report for Eastwood and Kirby—the home of Lawrence—adds that *Lady Chatterley* often sits serenely on the library shelves'." [26]

A somewhat different view of the *Nottingham Public Libraries Annual Report* appeared on the same day in the *Oldham Evening Chronicle and Standard*.

"It would be nice to think that the worthies of the Nottingham Libraries Committee are unique in being glad to have unread books on their shelves. Alas, they are all too typical. Many public libraries buy controversial books, tuck them away in dark corners, and generally take steps to prevent readers knowing they exist. They usually end up being read by all the councillors, who then agree among themselves that such books would have a bad influence on lesser mortals who read them. Yet few councillors seem to become raving lechers as a result of their dutiful reading—in much the same way that Watch Committee councillors, who dutifully sit through spicy films before banning them, seem to remain remarkably uncorrupted by the ordeal." [27]

Liaison, the newsletter section of the *Library Association Record,* December 1960, reported:

"The Librarian and the staff of the Yeovil Public Library have begun a major search among the stock of 30,000 volumes with the object of marking all books which contain no references to 'violent or objectionable' sex with a white spot on the spines. Asked why a white spot was chosen, the Librarian, Mr. E. Batty said: 'It *is* a sign of purity. There is no censorship involved. The idea is simply to save certain people embarrassment'." [28]

This action was taken after the Yeovil Library and Museums Committee had received complaints from some readers that some of the books they had taken home "were not what they wished to read and not the sort they would like their daughters to see".

"One woman member told the Committee the first few pages of one book she had taken home 'made her hair stand on end'. The Librarian said today: 'There were complaints that many books in the library were sexy or violent. The Committee asked me to keep a careful eye on the position and see that books like that were not bought. As a logical corollary I thought we ought to help people—they are mostly members of women's organizations and elderly folk—to pick out harmless and innocuous love-stories. We are therefore going through all new editions since the beginning of September and those that come into that category are being marked with a white spot. So far we have found fewer than a dozen but that doesn't mean the others are all violent and sexy. We have been very discriminating in our choice'."[29]

The use of white spots received a fair amount of comment in the Press, some of it rather scathing and the procedure was soon discontinued—certainly it was no longer in operation in 1964.

At the Library Association Annual Conference at Hastings, on 22nd September 1961, Bernard Williams, Lecturer in Philosophy at University College, London, spoke on censorship and reading. Williams made the point that it was only governmental control or something amounting to that, which could render a work completely unavailable to the public. The point was significant:

"Since the word 'censorship' is quite often applied to such things as the refusal of local library committees to have works of certain types in their libraries. The word is perhaps rightly applied in respect of the intentions of such bodies; their intentions are no doubt, like those of governmental censors, to prevent the public reading what is thought to be no good for them."[30]

Early in January 1962, both Blackburn Library Committee and Somerset County Libraries Sub-Committee received complaints that certain books in their libraries were obscene. In Blackburn the complaint came from the Knights of St. Columba, a fraternal order of Catholic men, and arose after one of their members had read a passage from a modern novel at their December Council Meeting. Investigating the complaint:

"Members of the Library Committee are now reading the books before recommending whether any action should be taken. . . . The next step by the Library Committee will be to decide whether the books mentioned are, in fact, obscene. Some members are expected to point to the danger of censorship in a public lending library."[31]

In Somerset the complaint came from a county councillor, Mr. Archie Clark, who held up a small blue book at the Somerset County Council's meeting. Mr. Clark declared:

"It was blue in more ways than one. . . . It was shocking, blasphemous, sexual, and sensual . . . and he had borrowed it from Somerset's Mobile Library Service. 'How it passed the censor I don't know', said Mr. Clark. He wanted to know who was responsible for sending it out."[32]

Clark would not reveal the name of the book. The Chairman of the Education Committee told him that if he would give her the name of the book she would refer it to the County Librarian. The Chairman of the Library Sub-Committee said there was no censorship in Somerset's County Libraries.

In February 1962, it was the turn of Lancashire County Libraries. A local Vicar who at one time had been a policeman and a member of the Vice Squad, refused to return a book he had borrowed from his local Library:

> " 'I shall not return the book no matter what the library people may do to me. If they decide to prosecute, let them get on with it'. .... 'The Chatterley case is frightening the authorities. They know they cannot get convictions. I shall send the book to the Bishop of Woolwich, who defended 'Lady Chatterley' to show him the harm he has done'."[33]

Alderman Leonard Ball, Chairman of the County's Library Committee said that people could not start to take the law into their own hands. Florence Cook, the County Librarian, said:

> "I intend to read the book myself. There is no question of it being withdrawn. My job is to provide books for the public—not to take them away."[33]

The book, *Dark Seas Running* by George Morrill had sold 5,000 copies, according to its publishers Secker and Warburg. They were surprised to hear of the Vicar's complaint, as this was the only one they had heard of. The Vicar, the Rev. Edward Ward then wrote to the *Liverpool Daily Post* explaining his action and stating that the reason he had not complained to the Library Committee was that he felt that the Committee would have discreetly withdrawn the book:

> "This book, however, is not just a local or county matter, it must be in many more libraries, is on sale in many bookshops, and is now to be put into paperback circulation. There is, too, the question of moral standards and if these are to be judged by the decision on *Lady Chatterley's Lover* (the book I complain of contains one of the worst words in that novel) then I believe the whole question of the law on obscene literature must be reviewed. Only public opinion can bring this to pass, and if the publicity which has been given to this case may help in some little way towards this end I have no regrets."[34]

At the 1969 Joint Conference of the Library Association of Ireland and the Northern Ireland Branch of the Library Association, Councillo A. N. Johnston, Chairman of the Antrim County Library Committee gave a talk entitled "Achieving standards in Public Libraries". Part o his talk was concerned with book selection policy in Antrim Count Library.

"In general terms I believe that an efficient library should offer freely, particularly to the youth of today, the accumulated knowledge and experience of the human race. The Library Act established that every library authority must provide an 'efficient and comprehensive' service for all. For the average ratepayers' representative that immediately poses a problem. What is meant by 'efficient and comprehensive'? Some Councillors I have heard, talk about having 'too many novels and not enough good books', whatever that may mean, and others complain about pornographic literature.

If it is ever desired to stimulate interest and controversy in library affairs I can recommend a sure and certain method. When I first entered the County Council a few years ago one of the first Committees on which I served was that of the Library. I was soon in hot water—I used a very naughty word which has emotional overtones with rather too much abandon, and immediately had a hornets' nest around my ears. The word was 'pornography'. No one appreciates more than I do that we must adjust ourselves to the changing standards of public taste and tolerance and, whilst I recognize that it is not our function to censor, nevertheless it is the duty of councillors to exercise some control over the selection of our book purchases and in so doing perform a dual role. First of all we protect our librarian against unfair and uniformed attacks and at the same time discharge our responsibility to the general ratepaying public we represent by closely scrutinising the money we spend on their behalf, in such a way that it neither offends nor is repugnant to them. Librarians may be idealists but councillors must always be realists.

When the question of book purchase control was first considered there were many reasons which prompted the Antrim Committee to examine close supervision. Some members observed that novels are in the entertainment category and should not be provided free for purely entertainment purposes. They consider these to be a social need similar to the cinema, T.V., etc., and expressed the view that the cost should therefore be borne by those with this particular taste. I personally was not influenced by these arguments as I have always considered that the criterion of a good library indicates a healthy balance between fiction and non-fiction issues. I am certain that an enlightened and sophisticated community is always reflected in the usage of the non-fiction section available.

A further reason for purchase control was complaints from parents that their adolescent children were obtaining objectionable literature from the library shelves and surreptitiously reading same and in some cases circulating information about titles around their contemporaries. In addition, cases have been known where requests were received from inmates of certain institutions and sometimes requests have been for as many as six titles with homosexual or similar themes and in this context I am not referring to serious books on these subjects.

We approached this problem by electing a Book-Selection Committee which was divided into four groups each with a reading membership of three, together with a standby member. Doubtful or suspect books were referred by the librarian to this committee which in turn placed them in one or other of the following categories:

(a) Books that should not be purchased;
(b) Books that should not appear on the public shelves but are available on special request;
(c) Copies may appear on public shelves but reasonable steps must be taken to ensure that the book is not issued to persons under the age of 16;

(d) Books that are not objectionable.

A majority decision is acceptable, but in the event of each group member indicating a different category, then this book is referred to a second or third group until a majority decision is reached. Since the introduction of this selection procedure the pattern of grouping has been as follows: (a) 6%; (b) 12%; (c) 55%; (d) 27%. I need not remind you that these figures reflect only the very small proportion of books which the librarian referred to the Book Selection Sub-Committee. It may be of interest that there never has been a shortage of reading members to serve on these groups and indeed it is not unknown for manoeuvring to take place by a Committee member to get himself elected.''[35]

The first British edition of Henry Miller's novel *Tropic of Cancer* was published by John Calder on 4th April 1963. The *Sunday Pictorial* contacted a number of librarians shortly before publication date to ask them what attitude they were taking to this novel. Bernard McElwaine reported the replies of a number of librarians on 31st March, five days before publication:

" 'My younger assistants will not be asked to handle it, and anyone requesting it will be sent a circular letter telling them exactly what sort of book it is', said Mr. Leslie Rees, Swansea's Chief Librarian.

'It won't be available except on application, to ensure that teenagers don't get hold of it', said Mr. Bill Best Harris, Chief Librarian at Plymouth. 'We have ordered only one copy in case it is banned—which seems likely'.

Leeds has ordered thirty copies but, as if to highlight the absurdity of literary censorship, the City Librarian disclosed that they have had a copy for the last 18 months. It was ordered by mistake and was accidentally passed by customs when it arrived from America. 'It has been safely locked up—but my staff have read it', Mr. F. Hutchins said.

Rather more barriers have been erected in Liverpool. An official said: 'Adolescents wishing to borrow the book will be called upon to produce evidence, signed by parents or teacher or some other responsible adult, that they have permission to read it'.

The County Librarian in the West Riding, Mr. William Murison, came out boldly 'We have ordered two copies. It should never have been banned'.

In Newcastle . . . 'I haven't seen it, so I can't say about restriction', said Mr. W Tynemouth, the City's assistant librarian.

Another Librarian who has not read the book is Mr. E. Clarke, Durham County Head Librarian. 'But I know what is in it—perversion', he said. 'It is a safe bet that if we get *Tropic of Cancer* it will be restricted to genuine students'. He didn't say of what.

Manchester's Chief Librarian, Mr. D. I. Colley, reckons they will order between fifty and sixty copies. 'There will be no restrictions', he said. 'We as a Library should not set ourselves up as censors'.

One copy will be bought by the Edinburgh Library—for reference only. 'Later we may place it on the restricted list, to be lent out on special requests only', the City Librarian explained.

Bold Belfast have ordered two copies—but 'definitely not to be on the open shelves'.

Glasgow said: 'We have not heard of it up here'."[36]

Press reports of decisions by other libraries were to appear frequently over the next four months and spasmodically afterwards. In Leamington Spa, where the Library Committee voted against purchasing the novel:

"Councillor B. Fetherstone-Dilke, an 87-year-old member of the Committee, told the *Courier:* 'I don't think it was fit for the public library. If people want these sort of books they can go and buy them for themselves'."[37]

In Cardiff the book was bought but was available only on request.

"Councillor David Purnell (Chairman) said any suggestion to put the book on the shelves would have been treated with severity. By making it available on demand, the Committee were covering themselves as custodians of the public."[38]

In Bristol, the book was bought but kept off the open shelves.[39] Hampstead [40] and Chelsea[41] bought the book and kept it off the open shelves while the Chief Librarian of Stockport[42] decided against stocking the book.

Replying on 16th May 1963 to a letter he had received, Kenneth Stockham, then County Librarian, stated the book selection policy of Nottinghamshire County Library:

"1. Book selection is not the concern of the County Library Committee. All book selection is the responsibility of the County Librarian, with the one exception that books costing more than five pounds have to have the approval of the Chairman of the Committee.
2. The final decision of purchase of any book is mine.
3. When considering the purchase of a controversial book, the overriding consideration is literary merit. For example, it is quite clear to me that James Baldwin's recent novel is a real contribution to modern literature. This view is also borne out by a reading of reviews in important journals. However much a librarian may dislike this book and the subject it deals with, it seems to me that no librarian can even consider not purchasing a novel which *The Times Literary Supplement* felt merited a full page review.
4. So far as I know all novels . . . are placed on the open shelves and not kept in librarians' offices. For example, there has never been any question of *Lady Chatterley's Lover* not being freely available on branch library shelves.

5. The new Henry Miller is a particularly difficult case. In Nottinghamshire we have purchased ten copies at the moment and each region has a considerable waiting list. What we are not doing, as I understand the cities of Cambridge and Nottingham have decided to, is buying a copy of this book and keeping it in the Reference Library for consultation. This seems to be quite absurd, but I am still pondering on whether or not this book should eventually find its place on the open Library shelves."[43]

In May, 1963, the Council of the Library Association adopted the following statement on censorship for use in the event of public controversy involving librarians or the Library Association:

"The function of a library service is to provide, so far as resources allow, all books, periodicals, etc., other than the trivial, in which its readers claim legitimate interest. In determining what is a legitimate interest the librarian can safely rely upon one guide only—the law of the land. If the publication of such material has not incurred penalties under the law it should not be excluded from libraries on any moral, political, religious or racial ground alone, to satisfy any sectional interest. The public are entitled to rely upon libraries for access to information and enlightenment upon every field of human experience and activity. Those who provide library services should not restrict this access except by standards which are endorsed by law."[44]

This statement was most useful in that many librarians used it as the basis of their replies to readers who complained about various types of book. It helped to clarify and strengthen the librarian's position in relation to the various cases which have arisen since 1963.

Action, the Union Movement's weekly publication, was not selected for the reading room of the Malden and Coombe (Surrey) Central Library though not without opposition from some members of the Council. The Chairman of the Library Committee, Councillor F. A. W. Selley, reported that his Committee had to be selective as there was a large number of periodicals from which the Committee had to choose. The Committee had already refused to accept a complimentary copy of *Action.* Councillor Mrs. M. E. Buck, a member of the Library Committee said:

"This is published by the British Union of Fascists, and I think it is wrong to put it in the Library to sow its disgusting seeds of political thought. Fascism is only round the corner, ready to rear its ugly head."[45]

But Councillor F. D. Williams said that to ban one political periodical while accepting others in the Library was quite wrong:

"Censorship is not a function that we should exercise. However obnoxious we believe the policy of that party to be, to ban this publication would be quite wrong."

And Alderman H. Arbon-Collins felt that it was not the Council's duty to try to impose its own tastes upon individuals:

> "This is not a court of morals—it is a council. The borough residents have a perfect right to read what they want."

In September 1963, the Bristol Public Libraries Committee refused to accept the Anarchist newspaper *Freedom* for display in the Central Library reading room. They then received a letter from one of the local anarchist leaders which stated that action might be taken against the Library if the decision was not reversed:

> "I am not satisfied with the decision, and in view of the fact that no reason was given, I can only assume that this is another case of political discrimination against libertarian ideas. It is an apt reflection on Council democracy that you should consider your electors too weak to read this newspaper without being 'corrupted' by it. Freedom of the press is a myth unless accompanied by the freedom to read. In the event of receiving no satisfaction, part of the responsibility for any subsequent action will rest with the Libraries Committee."[46]

The Committee decided to note the letter and inform the local police.

Novels of 'an unsavoury and nasty nature' were discussed by the Libraries Committee of Heston and Isleworth Borough Council at the October 1963 meeting:

> "Councillor P. B. Renk told the Committee he had just read *Another Country* by the American Negro writer, James Baldwin. 'It is a rattling good book and I thoroughly enjoyed it, but it is most unsavoury and nasty. . . . Is this sort of book on the library shelves, available to young men and women?' Mr. Cunnington (the Librarian) said the type of book Councillor Renk referred to was at the libraries, but it was not on the shelves. 'People who want to read a book like this can get it on application. . . . We do try to limit the borrowing of books which we feel are a little doubtful'. . . . Councillor A. A. Beck said he hesitated to suggest book censorship because it 'would be difficult to know where to stop'. What would disturb some people might not influence others, and they could not lay down hard and fast rules. If the book was really bad it wouldn't sell'."

The Committee agreed to leave matters unchanged but would reconsider the situation if it 'grew acute'.[47]

Ealing Public Libraries' report for 1963 stated that professional librarians were becoming increasingly disturbed by the falling standard of morality and good taste in current fiction:

> "The dilemma is not easy to solve, especially when advance claims of literary merit are made for what so often turns out to be salacious rubbish. . . . Nevertheless, there is initially a high demand for them on publication, often from readers unaware of

what they are asking for. This is rapidly sated and issues fall to a level which reflects all to clearly the true value of the books in question. Local censorship is repugnant to most of us, and where it has been tried, as in America, the results have usually been disastrous. Salvation lies perhaps, in the fact that book funds are not unlimited and the librarian must do his best with the amount available. Thus, censorship apart, it is good economic sense to buy the more worthwhile books first. Happily, there are enough of these to contain those in the other category within fairly narrow limits."[48]

Norman E. Binns, the Borough Librarian of Ealing commenting on his annual report to the *Middlesex County Times*:

"When the Court ruled in favour of *Lady Chatterley's Lover*—a book to which I had no personal objection—some of us were afraid that this might open the gates to a flood of more dubious books where 'four-letter words' were used mainly with an eye on sales. What my report says is that this is now happening and that is a pity. When I speak of 'salacious rubbish' I am expressing a personal opinion, to which, surely, I am entitled, but I am not alone in this. Most of my colleagues feel this way and to judge by their comment to me so do many of our readers in Ealing. Any Chief Librarian should know his job and this usually includes day to day book selection. If he buys this sort of book, he is liable to upset people who object to it; if he doesn't, others will decry him as a self-appointed censor on morals. I neither wish nor would presume to act in this capacity. My task is to spend a limited amount of public money to the greatest public advantage."[49]

Binns' comments were noticed by the *Daily Express* on 20th November 1963 (the paper published a brief quotation from his report without further comment),[50] and by the *West London Observer* on the 22nd November 1963. An editorial in the *West London Observer* says:

". . . The report places the blame squarely where it lies, when it refers to claims of literary merit. A much higher and more responsible standard of literary criticism is needed: book reviewing calls for wise and mature judgement, not for the verbal antics of the half-baked who slavishly conform to what they believe to be fashionable and in line with the fads and foibles of fevered advocates of a 'new morality'. There is no such thing as a new morality; as Lord Shawcross has remarked: 'This so-called new morality is too often the old immorality condoned'."[51]

The Editor of the *Rochdale Observer* published a letter he had received in December 1963 from a reader who was concerned as he believed that this country was being inundated by pornography published in the United States. The reader had discovered one such book available for loan in the Rochdale Public Library and, on complaining to the library staff, had been told that as the book was freely available in bookshops there was no reason why it should not be available in the library. Unable to accept such an answer, he appealed in his letter for a public protest to stop the Libraries Committee from buying books of this nature and to demand the withdrawal of all such books from the library stock. With this letter, the Editor also printed the Council's reply, which simply consisted of the text of the Library Association's statement on censorship published earlier in the year, with a note that this statement had been approved for use by the Rochdale Council.[52]

In February 1964, the Weston-super-Mare Libraries Committee decided that the Borough Librarian should not have to shoulder the sole responsibility of rejecting books which he considered 'doubtful'. The Committee decided that if he received at least six written requests for a book that he thought was 'doubtful' he had to refer it to a sub-committee for a decision as to whether the book would be bought. Councillor V. J. Hutton raised the matter by saying:

" 'Recently our Librarian has been refusing to buy a book for which he has had requests. I do not intend to name it, but it is not *Fanny Hill*. It is what one could call a story consisting mostly of unadulaterated smut. While I agree he was right not to waste our money on this type of book, it is not for him or me to tell 45,000 people in Weston what they should or should not read. For the Librarian, I feel the responsibility is a little too much and we should take some of it from his shoulders, without actually interfering too much with his book selection and rejection. . . . It would be much better for the Librarian to be able to say, 'my Committee will not allow me to buy this book', rather than accept on his own responsibility something with which we might disagree'.

The Chairman, Alderman Mrs. M. J. Grey, said there was nothing at present to prevent the Librarian coming to the Committee and seeking their advice. It was up to a Local Authority to see that books of a certain type were not available in a public library. The Librarian, Mr. G. P. Rye, said there would always be books on the shelves to which some people would object. No one was going to overcome that problem. He did not feel strongly about the proposal now made, as he had endeavoured to serve the town and the Committee to the best of his ability with a selection of books for the money that was provided. 'I have no objection to this resolution if you wish to accept it. I just try to carry out my job'.

Councillor Hutton said it would not be taking away any of Mr. Rye's privileges. It would be relieving him of a little responsibility. When a member said Mr. Rye was a responsible officer, trained to his job and able to consult his Chairman or the Committee when in doubt, Councillor Hutton replied: 'I am not implying any lack of confidence in him'. He said it was not just a case of deciding about what might be called 'immoral' books. There might be requests say, for a technical book costing 10 or 15 guineas, and the Librarian might wonder whether it was worth spending that much money."[53]

On 3rd April 1964, the *Sevenoaks Chronicle* reported:

"Sevenoaks U.D.C. is sticking to its decision to ban religious publications from the reading room of the public library, although efforts were made at last week's meeting to have the ban removed. Councillor John Buckwell (said): 'Sevenoaks was the only town to ban religious publications from its Library'. Councillor Paul Hayden, Chairman of the Library Committee said the reason for the ban was that the periodicals were not used. 'People who, like myself, want religious papers buy them', he told members. 'Many libraries would like to do the same as us, but have not got the courage to do so'. Sir John Dunlop said the Council had a unique record for attendance at Church services and they could hardly be thought of as not religious. Councillor Hayden said the Library was there to provide a service and if no use was made of religious publications there was no point in 'stuffing them down people's throats'."[54]

On the 19th June 1964, the *Tonbridge Free Press* published the second of two letters from the Reverend L. A. Fereday, a local Baptist Minister, who was not in favour of the Sevenoaks Council's ban:

"For the Chairman of the Library Committee to say, 'that anyone who wants a religious periodical goes out and buys them' is a boomerang argument. It could be used of the gardening papers, the womens magazines, *The Times Educational Supplement* and other specialist papers now provided by his Committee. Few among us can afford to buy more than one religious paper and we welcomed the privilege afforded us of reading the other denominational journals and informing ourselves of what the other churches were thinking and doing. ... And one consequence of this ban is that a great international newspaper, *The Christian Science Monitor,* because it is also a religious paper, can no longer be seen at the Library."[55]

At the August meeting of the Sevenoaks Urban District Council the Clerk reported that he had received a number of letters from people on the subject of religious magazines and newspapers, asking that the Council should reconsider their decision regarding the purchase of religious periodicals for the Library:

"The Council decided to adhere to their original decision. But they also agreed that when the review of the list of periodicals, magazines and newspapers takes place in October, 'further consideration be given to the question'."[56]

This 'further consideration' led to a change in policy, for on the 28th January 1965, the *Baptist Times* reported:

"A ban on religious newspapers in the Reading Room of the Sevenoaks Public Library has been lifted after public protest, initiated by action from the Sevenoaks Baptist Church. Six of the leading newspapers will now be available to readers and the *Baptist Times* will be one of them."[57]

A number of newspapers reported on the annual conference of the Association of Assistant Librarians, held in Durham on the 11th and 12th of April 1964. *The Northern Echo* of the 13th April 1964 reported that:

> "Mr. T. S. Broadhurst, Deputy Librarian at Liverpool University, compared the effects of erotica on a company director and a coal-man, and said they could be the same. He described as 'infuriatingly priggish' a statement attributed to Mr. N. St. John Stevas, the critic and broadcaster, that, perverts excepted, educated people did not read pornography, since their taste for reading was fully formed and they found it dull and uninteresting.
>
> Had the Roman Catholic Church the right to impose on its members censorship of birth-control books? Yes, said Mr. T. E. Callander, Croydon Borough Librarian—but only on its members. 'This Church is right to instruct its members not to read books on the subject and to put every legitimate obstacle in the way of their doing so. But I deny the right of a church to impose this kind of censorship on people who are not its adherents and I deny the right of any group to impose its rule on the community at large'. Of adolescents and unsuitable books, Mr. Callander said: 'My practice is to apply no censorship to my stock, but a section is segregated on private shelves. My staff issue segregated books without question, but children have to bring a note from a parent specifically asking for a 'naughty' book to be issued to a child. My staff uses discretion in steering 'old ladies' away from segregated stock'." [58]

T. E. Callander was quoted again in the *Croydon Advertiser,* on 17th April 1964:

> "Saying that he tried to avoid press discussion of censorship in relation to Croydon Public Libraries, he added: 'The London evening papers are very fond of a sexy story and one or other will generally ring up when a saucy book is in the news and ask if it is in our stock. I answer, 'Yes' or 'No' and decline to comment. So far I have not made any headlines'. Mr. Callander said he had asked his Libraries Committee to give a decision on whether a book on anti-semitism should be stocked. The Committee had decided it should not. Mr. Callander felt that a book on such a subject would 'pollute the Library shelves' and went on: 'Probably as a Librarian I was wrong. As a man and a citizen I know I was right'. There were other censorship problems, apart from sex. He found it difficult to make a decision about astrology. He said: 'The Public Library should not be a party to the dissemination of superstition'." [59]

On 18th April 1964 the *Yorkshire Evening Post* reported an address by Godfrey Thompson, then City Librarian of Leeds, to a meeting of the School Library Association in Leeds on the 17th April. Mr. Thompson was discussing:

> "The opponents of 'the freedom of each person to read what he chooses'. . . . The guise in which these 'opponents of liberty' came was always a moral one, he said.

'They want to protect us all from books and ideas which will contaminate us and they, and they alone must be the judges of what we read. We in public libraries have met these people for many years, and there is a temptation for us to treat them too lightly. We can write them off as cranks or we can laugh at the sort of dirty mind that gets such satisfaction at finding a moral reason to search for filth. If we stand firm and oppose these attacks on 'the right to read' we may seem to put ourselves in the wrong. But there is a very important matter of principle at stake. The laws of this country are specifically designed to protect citizens against corruption and it is up to Parliament to alter the legislation or it is up to the Courts to alter the interpretation if called upon to do so', he said. This was not a matter for small self-appointed local tribunals."[60]

In January 1964 the Sheffield Police made simultaneous raids on 14 book shops in Sheffield, seizing 48 novels and 906 magazines which they claimed were obscene. Amongst the novels seized were *Cain's Book* by Alexander Trocchi, published by John Calder (Publishers) Ltd., who decided to intervene at the hearing on the 1st February 1964 to deny that the publication was obscene.

"It is the intention of the publishers to lead evidence on the issue generally and call evidence before you of the literary merit of this particular work which already has received extremely good notices and reviews from the literary critics of this country and abroad."[61]

One of the witnesses called for the defence at the hearing on the 14th April was the City Librarian of Sheffield, John Bebbington, who said,

"I think it is a book of quite serious intent. I do not think it is capable of depraving or corrupting."[62]

John Bebbington added that there were 20 copies of *Cain's Book* in Sheffield City Libraries, kept in a reserved category available only for adults. The novel was held to be obscene by the Sheffield magistrates and the publishers immediately announced that they would appeal against this ruling. The magistrates ordered the copy seized from a Sheffield bookseller to be forfeited and destroyed. On 16th April the *Daily Herald* pointed out that this order applied only to the booksellers copy and not to the copies in the City Libraries. When Bebbington was asked about this he said that no decision about the books had been taken and that the Sheffield Libraries Sub-Committee was waiting for advice from the Town Clerk.[63] Councillor John Thorpe, Chairman of the Libraries Sub-Committee said that:

"A national decision on this type of thing is wanted. This sort of thing—taking action against an individual—is wasting time and a lot of money."[64]

The *Daily Herald* reported on 17th April 1964, however, that:

> "People who have borrowed *Cain's Book* by Alexander Trocchi from Sheffield Public Library are being asked to return it immediately—whether they have finished reading it or not. The Library's copies of the book are being withdrawn."[65]

This decision to withdraw copies of the book in circulation was the result of the Town Clerk's advice to the City Librarian.[66] At the same time copies of the book were withdrawn from the shelves of Mexborough Public Library by the Librarian, Frank Parry.[67]

John Calder's appeal before the High Court at the beginning of December 1964 was dismissed.[68] The minutes of the Sheffield Public Libraries Sub-Committee of 8th December 1964, read:

> "The City Librarian referred to the decision of the Sheffield Magistrates' Court ordering the forfeiture of *Cain's Book* by Alexander Trocchi and reminded the Committee that, on the advice of the Town Clerk, the twenty copies of the book in the City Libraries stock had been withdrawn from circulation pending the results of any appeals that might be made against the Court's decision. He stated that an appeal had now been made in the High Court by John Calder (Publishers) Ltd, the publishers of the book, against the decision of the Sheffield City Justices and this had been dismissed. The Committee noted this information and agreed that the twenty copies of the book be placed in storage."[69]

There the books still remain. They have not been made available because the magistrate's decision and the Town Clerk's advice both still stand in Sheffield.

The *North London Press*, 18th September 1964, poked literary fun at the Librarian:

> "Browsing among books, shelf after shelf, volume upon volume, thousands and thousands of soothing, mellowing, hallowing repositories of wisdom and knowledge; what more peaceful occupation, what more gentlemanly way of life than the librarian's? But wait. Deep within the reverenced recesses of the public library, in rooms marked 'Private' where panelled walls, old leather and tangible silence contemplate the academic navel of the community, there beats a pulse at variance with the ordered calm, there mists an eye more glassy than dewy, there floats a spot before the eye more devious than any decimal, there wrestles a conscience in convolutions unknown to Cumberland or Karati.
>
> Who is this man of letters, disorientated by Western judo, schizophrenic with legal conundrums, febrile in the conflict of a highbrow and a low dissipation of literary excitement? He is the librarian, that emperor of calm, that benign purveyor of ordered knowledge, who trembles on the brink of abysmal social error, who hovers in the up-currents of moral rectitude. He is debating with himself, which books are fit to be put on the shelves, which to be kept under the counter and which to be locked away until applied for, in triplicate, by a mature, responsible,

ratepaying citizen certified sane and morally worthy and backed by three ministers in holy orders, two justices of the peace and a retired judge of the Indian High Court.

With a supreme effort of will, our librarian is projecting himself simultaneously into the minds of the man on the Clapham omnibus, the adolescent school girl, the precocious school boy, the easily-led housemaid, the impressionable housewife, and a host of other figures of legal fiction. He is also embodying the book critic, sub-divided into high-brow, middle-brow and low-brow, and sub-sub-divided according to moral fibre and amoral pithlessness. Book selecting is a tough job. Like sitting on a watch committee, it calls for qualities of character not given to most of the citizenry, an ability to discern what is or might be corrupting without being corrupted, a subtlety of intellect denied the simple literalist who thinks that a word, a phrase, a sentence, means what it says and says what it means and no more. The Obscene Publications Act has put librarians into the position of libel lawyers. It's not what the passage says, nor even what it means, but what it might be held to mean."[70]

1. Shockers in the Bury public library. *Bury Free Press* (Suffolk), 8th January 1960
2. M.P. and Schoolteacher head drive to clean up libraries. *Kentish Mercury,* 19th February 1960
3. Prudish Manchester. *Books and Bookmen,* vol. 5, no. 11, August 1960. p.3
4. Dirty Books. *Catholic Times,* 14th October 1960
5. Nottinghamshire County Library: Memorandum, 3rd November 1960
6. Nottinghamshire County Library: Memorandum, 18th November 1960
7. Lady C: on the shelves, or under the counter? *Blackburn Evening Telegraph,* 3rd November 1960
8. City Libraries expected to stock Lady C. *Birmingham Evening Despatch,* 3rd November 1960
9. 50 or 60 *Lady C's* for Leeds Library. *Yorkshire Evening News,* 3rd November 1960
10. But the Lady's not for general reading in Liverpool Libraries. *Liverpool Daily Post,* 3rd November 1960
11. *Lady C* available soon at libraries? *Brighton Gazette,* 4th November 1960
12. Refused permission to read *Lady C* extracts. *Brighton Gazette,* 10th February 1961
13. Lady Chatterley protest by Rector. *Birkenhead News,* 5th November 1960
14. *Lady C* will be library request book. *South Wales Evening Post,* 9th November 1960
15. Who uses blue pencil on public books. *Manchester Evening News,* 10th November 1960
16. Committee ban on *Lady Chatterley's Lover. Fleetwood Chronicle,* 15th December 1960
17. Will not be in libraries. *Beckenham Advertiser,* 22nd December 1960
18. No *Lady C* for Wimbledon library shelves. *Wimbledon Borough News,* 23rd December 1960
19. Widnes people 'not sheep'. *Widnes Weekly News,* 16th December 1960
20. Letter from K. A. Stockham, County Librarian of Nottinghamshire to Philip M. Whiteman, Head of Department, Department of Librarianship, Manchester College of Commerce, 17th November 1960.(Unpublished)

21. *Lady C* for city libraries. *Nottingham Evening Post*, 20th December 1960
22. The lady is not for reading. *Nottingham Evening News*, 3rd January 1961
23. Council ban, but *Lady C* still there. *Nottingham Evening News*, 3rd January 1961
24. Simpson, John G. False conception of values. (Nottingham) *Guardian–Journal*, 6th January 1961
25. County Libraries bans that book. *Western Telegraph*, 12th January 1961
26. Lawrence country cuts *Lady C. The Guardian*, 30th August 1963
27. Editorial. *Oldham Evening Chronicle and Standard*, 30th August 1963
28. 'Briefly'. *Liaison*, December 1960. p.95
29. Letter from K. Lloyd Plumridge, Borough Librarian of Yeovil, to Michael J. Cooke, Liaison and Training Officer, College of Librarianship, Wales, 5th July 1972. (Unpublished, copy held by the author.)
30. Library Association. Proceedings, papers and summaries of discussions at the Hastings Conference, 18th to 22nd September 1961. pp.64-74
31. Blackburn 'Knights' hit out at two library books. *Blackburn Evening Telegraph*, 4th January 1962
32. Library's blue book shocks councillor. *Western Daily Press*, 9th January 1962
33. Chatterley word so he keeps library book. *Sunday Express*, 4th February 1962
34. Ward, Edward. The book from Huyton Library. *Liverpool Daily Post*, 8th February 1962
35. Johnston, A. N. Achieving standards in public libraries. *An Leabharlann*, vol. 27, no. 3, September 1969. pp.114-118
36. Blush. *Sunday Pictorial*, 31st March 1963
37. Book banned by library. *Leamington Spa Courier*, 5th April 1963
38. Book under the counter at the public library. *South Wales Echo*, 10th April 1963
39. Tropic stays off the shelves. *Western Daily Press*, 11th April 1963
40. Tropic too hot for Smith's. *Hampstead News*, 12th April 1963
41. Tropic: unmoved. *West London Press*, 12th April 1963
42. Tropic of Cancer. *Stockport Express*, 11th April 1963
43. Letter from K. A. Stockham, County Librarian of Nottinghamshire, to Miss J. Hall-Carter, Student Librarian, Manchester School of Librarianship, 16th May 1963. (Unpublished, held by Nottinghamshire County Libraries.)
44. Censorship: L.A. Statement. *Liaison*, May 1963. p.31
45. Library ban Union Movement. *Wimbledon Borough News*, 5th July 1963
46. The angry anarchist threatens library. *Western Daily Press*, 12th October 1963
47. They have a word for novels that are 'unsatisfactory'. *Richmond and Twickenham Times*, 19th October 1963
48. Ealing, London Borough of. The Ealing Library Service. 1962–1963
49. The censored library service. *Middlesex County Times*, 16th November 1963
50. Quote. *Daily Express*, 20th November 1963
51. Dirty books. *West London Observer*, 22nd November 1963
52. Bolton, J. R. Pornographic books. *Rochdale Observer*, 14th December 1963
53. Library Sub-Committee decision on doubtful books is recommended. *Weston Mercury*, 21st June 1964
54. Library ban remains. *Sevenoaks Chronicle*, 3rd April 1964
55. Fereday, L. A. Letters to the Editor. *Tonbridge Free Press*, 19th June 1964
56. Religious papers ban. *Tonbridge Free Press*, 28th August 1964
57. Ban lifted. *Baptist Times*, 28th January 1965

58. The quiet men. *The Northern Echo*, 13th April 1964
59. 'Segregation' safeguard at libraries. *Croydon Advertiser*, 17th April 1964
60. 'Freedom to read what we choose'. *Yorkshire Evening Post*, 18th April 1964
61. 954 books on trial for obscenity. *Sheffield Telegraph*, 2nd February 1964
62. Publisher defends 'Cain's Book'. *The Times*, 15th April 1964
63. 'Cain' stays in library. *Daily Herald*, 16th April 1964
64. Allsop speaks up for novel. *The Star*, 15th April 1964
65. 'Cain' called in by library. *Daily Herald*, 17th April 1964
66. Letter from John Bebbington, City Librarian of Sheffield, to the author, 12th November 1971. (Unpublished)
67. Library withdraws 'obscene' novel. *The Star*, 16th April 1964
68. Drugs book is obscene, says the High Court. *Sheffield Telegraph*, 11th December 1964
69. Sheffield City Council. Minutes of Libraries Sub-Committee, 8th December 1964
70. Editorial. *North London Press*, 18th September 1964

CHAPTER 8

The Enid Blyton Affair

No single author has caused more controversy among librarians, literary critics, teachers and other educationalists and parents during the last thirty years, than Enid Blyton. How is it that the books of this tremendously popular writer for children should have given rise to accusations of censorship against librarians in Australia, New Zealand and the United Kingdom?

Enid Blyton was born in the late 1890's and was educated privately. Although an accomplished musician she decided to make teaching her career and studied for three years at a Froebel Institute. Later she became involved in theorectical education, becoming the editor of a number of educational journals. Although she published her first book, a collection of her own verses for children, in 1923, it was not until the mid 1930s that she was writing children's stories on any scale. She became well known through the publication of the successful young children's weekly magazine *Sunny Stories* which she wrote and edited from cover to cover.[1] For the next thirty-five years, she wrote at a tremendous rate, producing nearly four hundred books which were translated into over thirty different languages. At one time during this period seventeen different British publishers were involved in the publication of her books. Some three quarters of a million pounds were spent each year on copies of her works. An attempt to keep a count of the numbers of copies of her books sold, failed when the figure reached seventy-five million and was still increasing by five million copies each year. She wrote an average of one book a month throughout her career and according to her literary agent George Greenfield she employed neither a ghost writer nor a secretary, and she would complete a *Famous Five* book in a week of solid writing.[2]

According to George Greenfield:

"No other children's author writing in English has had the fantastic appeal that she had. . . . Hundreds and thousands of children first learned to enjoy reading through Noddy or the Faraway Tree and have grown up into book reading adults. . . . She was a superb technician. Trained under the Froebel system she had taught young children for several years and knew by training and instinct how to keep the attention of a child. . . . She knew instinctively that many children need a simple but firm and well regulated code of behaviour in their everyday lives and in her books goodness is always rewarded and arrogance and deceit punished. The characters are always consistent and never complex."[2]

Greenfield's comments were valid to a great extent but they concealed the factors underlying the problems faced by librarians in connection with her works. Certainly many young children read and enjoyed Enid Blyton's stories, but although they may not have been their first introduction to reading, they quickly passed to books by other authors in which the characters were not always "consistent", and were sometimes very complex indeed. Enid Blyton has rarely presented a problem to the keen and intelligent reader. Her works represented a simple stage in their reading development. Roland Earl, Headmaster of a junior boys' school in Surrey stated:

"Getting children to read is one of the most important and difficult jobs of the primary teacher. A boy who likes reading is no trouble. He will devour everything from The Swift to Gulliver's Travels, from the ubiquitous Enid Blyton to the expensive encyclopaedia, from jampot labels to Jennings."[3]

George Greenfield, quoted above, continued:

"It is easy to sneer at the Enid Blyton stories with their soft padded bourgeois backgrounds and their simple vocabulary. Great success often brings its own backlash and in recent years there have been occasional headlines when yet another librarian banned her books from the children's shelves of their libraries for a variety of strange reasons:
They inculcated snobbish values.
The simple events and simple language in which they were described did not sufficiently stretch the young readers imagination and vocabulary.
Moral concepts were too neatly encapsulated, with good always triumphing and vice being punished.
Life was not really like that, the librarians would claim. The final complaint was that Enid Blyton's books were too popular; if they were kept off the shelves, the children would have to read faute de mieux stories by less popular but, in the opinion of the librarians, more worthy writers."

Appearing with this article was one by a children's librarian, Constance Martin, in which she likened Enid Blyton's enormous appeal to tobacco—acceptable in limited quantities. In illustration she quoted an intelligent young teacher who had read nothing else as a child but Enid Blyton and now did not read at all. She continued:

"It is the lack of stimulation to a young mind coupled with enormous popularity which makes a Blyton book—or any other of similar standards by another author—one to be avoided by anyone concerned with the buying of children's books who has a true interest of a child at heart.

Certainly Miss Blyton knew what children liked; hidden treasure, underground passages, pets, secret societies, and she gave it to them in easy-to-read dialogue peppered with exclamation marks and few unknown or difficult words. There is nothing to make a child look around him with heightened perception, nothing to take him beyond himself, to help him to experience the feelings of others, to stretch his imagination. . . . Every subject Enid Blyton explores has been more subtly done by someone else, with a finer use of words, and more original imagination and certainly with more admirable heroes; for let's face it The Secret Seven and the Famous Five of her most popular series are pretty nasty creatures on the whole, sniggering and quarrelsome, whilst we are told that 'dear little funny Noddy' (in the first Noddy book taken up at random) found great enjoyment in the prospect of tying his victim behind his car in order to drag him along the road to the police station. That is another of Enid Blyton's short-comings: she tells us that something is good, or exciting, or creepy, instead of letting the events speak for themselves, so that the mature reader remains totally unconvinced. Perhaps that is why many children soon outgrow the Blyton cult leaving the backward or culturally deprived child to wallow in a sticky morass of Blytonese which may give a temporary delight without the smallest impetus to struggle out of it and beyond. Surely there are comics, T.V. advertisements and films enough of this calibre in the modern child's environment without re-inforcement from the public or school library. While there is so much excellent material being published for children at every level it hardly seems to be a skilled librarians job to spend money on the fourth rate."[4]

Enid Blyton once said that she liked "to take a child by the hand when he is three and walk with him all his childhood days". Brian Doyle commented:

"I think it is true to say that she did just that with a great many young readers. A diet of nothing but Blyton would of course be unthinkable. A child cannot eat cakes and sweets all the time, otherwise he gets indigestion to say the least. He needs a few solids too to balance his diet. The same goes for his reading. But one excellent point about Blyton's works is that they form a very good 'jumping-off' place and get children into the all important reading habit. She is easy to read and that is what a young child wants when he is just starting out into the print jungle. Mayne, Pearce, Ransome, Garner . . . can come later. I once heard Blyton criticised as being too easy to read! That is nonsense of course. A writer writes first and foremost with the object of being read and understood and enjoyed. And Enid Blyton, despite her critics, certainly achieved her object. Ask anyone who has been a child during the past thirty years."[5]

Brian Doyle's comments are valid as far as the intelligent child is concerned. Certainly the teachers and the librarians quoted were not worried about them. Their concern was with the less intelligent child who may, indeed, walk hand in hand with Enid Blyton through their entire childhood.

The periodical *Where* carried a short, **light**-hearted paragraph asking how parents coped with children 'hooked on Miss Blyton'. The Publishers were taken aback by the strong reactions this paragraph brought from the press and in letters from subscribers and also from others who read the press comments. Thirteen correspondents were firmly pro-Blyton, whilst seven were unenthusiastic but believed she did no harm and six were firmly anti-Blyton. This latter group included the only teachers and librarians who had written, and also two individual parents who confiscated Blytons on sight. The Editor of *Where* then asked Edward Blishen, journalist, broadcaster and editor of the *Oxford Book of Poetry for children* to write about Enid Blyton. He, like many other writers about Miss Blyton, concentrated mainly on the Noddy books:

> "It is the essence of the Noddy stories that a reader's imagination is not roused. Instead it is positively damped. . . . But the dreariest and the most anti-imaginative characteristics of these stories lies in their language. Adjectives with which the pages are peppered include 'lovely', 'nice', 'dear' and 'little' (often together— Noddy having a 'dear little home' and 'dear little car' and even wearing 'dear little trousers and shoes') 'cosy', 'peculiar' (usually 'most peculiar') 'funny'. Bad things are commonly 'horrid' or 'dreadful'. Emphasis created by the use of the word 'very', often repeated, so that an event is 'very, very good' or 'very, very sad', and 'bad' characters are 'very, very stupid'. This is not children's language, but rather the language used when talking to children by ill-informed aunts who supposed children must be wrapped in verbal wool. The enfeeblement of vocabulary is consistent, unrelieved anywhere by a single sharp and even mildly exciting usage. Add to this a slack exclamatoriness—'just look at them!' 'oh dear' 'oh dear me!' 'Isn't it a lovely garage!'; and a constant use of what I must call diddums-language: 'the little red and yellow car sleeps there, at night, as cosy as can be'; add a story element that is most often resolved by little nursery tellings off ('what he wants is a good spanking!') or indeed by actual spankings; and the total effect is of a bland exhaustion of fantasy, in which the dominant atmosphere is that of a curiously prim nursery, the whole being dressed in language that is mostly diddums-plus-dear-me-plus-naughty-naughty. The heights of euphoria are achieved when Noddy exclaims 'aren't people nice' . . . ."[6]

Edward Blishen considered the phenomenon of her enormous popularity:

> "My own view is that, given the present state of things—that is, primarily of book selling and book buying—it would be astonishing if there were not an Enid Blyton

The manner in which books for children are most commonly chosen and bought, hurried and unadvised, must have made it possible for someone to dominate the field, simply by representing the ultimate economy of choice. Miss Blyton's name is known where the name of no other children's writer whatever is known. Vast forces of publicity have been at work on her, and Noddy's behalf. As many readers writing to *Where* have pointed out her popularity with both parents and children is largely based on her sheer availability. I think myself that with children her popularity is also founded on two qualities of her writing; she is undemanding, using a small vocabulary and a small basic set of narrative elements; and her voice bumbles in the ear like that of some universal mum, a lowest common denominator of mummishness, alternatively cosy and cross. The over simple apparatus of reward and punishments on which so many of her stories are based, the head patting praise or the telling off or spanking, alas, appeals to juvenile puritanism. At the same time, because the stories are undemanding, and because they rest on a simple code, they offer a certain security: which is increased, of course, by the endlessness of the opus. You can always go on and on, through all the titles.

The rage of many of Miss Blyton's defenders, I suspect, arises because they themselves find her bland insipid world, with its strict nursery basis, a comforting one. The attack on her they identify with all critical attacks on what is safe and successful. I have more sympathy with the opponents of her work, because in the very nature of things she must be felt by intelligent parents and librarians to be a challenge as nobody else is. There are worse writers for children, but none so pervasive. But some, I feel, lose their sense of humour and balance as thoroughly as their shriller antagonists. I cannot think that it is sensible actually to 'outlaw' the Noddy books or to decry them to children on the grounds (very shaky ones) that Miss Blyton's books are ill-spelt. It is up to any parent or teacher or librarian to take such steps as he thinks reasonable to protect children against whatever seems to him unsuitable for them; yet there is an important sense in which children cannot be protected, and perhaps ought not to be. Censorship is a nasty business, and not strictly controllable in its effects.''

In August 1964, the *Daily Express* reported that Canberra (Australia) Public Libraries had banished ''Noddy'', ''Biggles'' and ''Willaim''. '''Better books are available for children', says the librarian''.[7] The linking in the context of book selection of Enid Blyton, Richmal Crompton and Captain W. E. Johns, all of them prolific, popular and formularized, occurred in New Zealand, Australia and in the United Kingdom. The *Bookseller* reported on the Australian case:

> ''Rejection of Enid Blyton's 'Noddy' books by the Canberra Public Library and some other libraries in Australia has been taken up not only at Parliamentry but at Prime Ministerial level . . . .''[8]

The report stated that the Canberra Library had dropped ''William'' and ''Biggles'', because they did not ''stimulate the imagination or extend the knowledge'' of children, and the *Bookseller* quoted from two letters which readers had written to *The Guardian* on this subject. Mr.

Lawrence Golding of Hove, in a letter of 31st August 1964, declared that from Enid Blyton's books he had:

"Extracted the moral principles which form the very foundations of our nation."

and claimed that:

"The action of these libraries symbolises the rejection of that rich gift, the British Heritage, bestowed upon our colonies."[9]

Another reader, Michael Hill, agreed with him in his letter[10] of 2nd September 1964:

A more serious letter appeared in the *Bookseller* from Daniel Haye, Borough Librarian of Whitehaven:

"The report quoted in your issue of 5th September that Australian libraries have rejected Enid Blyton and dropped 'William' and 'Biggles' would be funny if it were not an attitude that finds sympathy in some libraries in this country. . . . No sensible person would say that the 'Noddy'—'William'—'Biggles' trio should be supplied in vast quantities, but on the other hand any child who wants to read about them should be able to do so if he so desires. How many of those who would ban Noddy and Co. do so out of blind prejudice and how many out of any real study of children's reading."[11]

The place of Enid Blyton in British public libraries had received attention years earlier when Eileen H. Colwell, then Children's Librarian of Hendon Public Libraries, gave a paper before the Brighton Conference of the Library Association on the 10th June 1947 entitled "Twenty eventful years in Children's Books". Concluding her resume, she said:

"Finally, no survey of the books of the last twenty years would be complete without mention of the three most popular authors of today, W. E. Johns, Richmal Crompton and Enid Blyton. Captain John's 'Biggles' has his many fans amongst the adventurous boys and girls of today, but I do not suppose that his books will have any lasting fame for they are topical and his heroes are of the kind who will inevitably be superseded by still more up-to-date supermen. Miss Crompton's 'William' is the eternally naughty boy, well-meaning but always in hot water, whose adventures have already lasted over twenty years. William's character does not date, but his slang and the environment of his adventures do . . . Will he survive when no new titles appear to keep his memory green? Whatever the verdict of posterity, our children—and grown-ups—are none the worse for the many laughs William has given them in these depressing times.

What about Enid Blyton? She is the most prolific writer of the day and possibly the most versatile. School stories, plays and rhymes, nature tales, easy reading books about toys, wildly improbable adventure stories, all flow from her pen at terrific speed. Out they all come, 'like cotton from a reel' to use her own expression, and as soon as one book is completed she starts on the next. Her name is known everywhere where there are children, her organized publicity is extensive, the children ask continually for her stories. Copies of the 'latest Blyton' roll off the press by the hundred while, unnoticed in the clamour, Alice, Mole and Rat and the Little Tin Soldier wait patiently for their chance to make themselves known to a new generation of children. But which will survive the verdict of the years—the latest Enid Blyton or *The Wind in the Willows?* I venture to predict that Enid Blyton's stories, although they meet a popular need, are ephemeral, for their characters are puppets. There is no depth or sense of the true values of life in her stories. They are so easy to read that they defeat their own purpose, for they are as easily forgotten as read. The demand is always for the *latest* Enid Blyton, the early ones have not become treasured friends. The criterion of popularity is not enough, and a book that is too easy to read and does not challenge a child's mind will not endure. As Dr. Johnson says, 'A child likes to stretch and stimulate his little mind'."[12]

On the 6th April 1963 the *Daily Herald* reported:

"The famous Noddy Stories by Enid Blyton have been 'barred' from the children's section of seven public libraries. So have the tales by Richmal Crompton—creator of 'Just William' and Captain W. E. Johns, whose hero is 'Biggles'. The man who banned them is Mr. William Taylor, Borough Librarian of St. Pancras, London.

Says Mr. Taylor: 'They are not actually on the banned list—we just don't buy them . . . they are badly written and do not stimulate a child's imagination'. His other charges are:

Enid Blyton is not approved of by leading educationalists.

Captain Johns' attitude to coloured people reflects an outmoded Kipling approach.

Richmal Crompton's books are not normally asked for by youngsters. The only people who want them are nostalgic adults who feel that, because they loved William, their children must too.

Said 72-year-old Miss Crompton last night 'I think the Librarian is quite justified in choosing educational books for children, though. I don't claim that William is written for any other purpose than entertainment'." [13]

This was followed three days later by a letter to the *Daily Herald* from Mrs. H. L. Cummings of Brighton:

"All my children have enjoyed the books by Enid Blyton, Captain Johns and Richmal Crompton . . . they preferred them to 'children's classics' because they have compelling stories. Books like these encouraged my children to read for themselves when quite young. As a result they progressed at an early age to adult classics." [14]

Mr. S. Jodrell of Brixton, in his letter to the *Surveyor* a few days later wrote:

"One acknowledges that a library has to be selective in stocking its shelves with only a limited amount of money to spend. On the other hand there is a tendency for librarians to be somewhat heavy-handed when they assume the role of Censor. I expect most children are like myself and read to be entertained. Is not this tendency to be high-brow over children's books rather childish? In this day and age children do not have to look far to find ample material to feed their imaginations and extend their horizons. Relaxation with Noddy might be counted a better occupation." [15]

In his column "Books and Bookmen", in *British Books,* June 1963, "Ferdinand" commented on the situation:

"To a fifty-year-old like me, the Noddy Books do seem a trifle non-venturesome, but then that seems to apply to most of the children's books of today, and I suspect that what Mr. Taylor is troubled about is that Enid Blyton's books are popular, and must therefore be bad books compared with books that are not so popular. Captain W. E. Johns comes under the same ban, with the added criticism that Biggles represents ideas about the English which are no longer English. What I would like to know is, on what scientific grounds does Mr. Taylor base his criticisms, except his own perception? And if he bases it on his own perception and that of other adults, is he not perhaps using criteria that are not valid for his particular purpose? . . Before we can foster discrimination and good taste, surely we must foster that act and habit of reading and I can personally see no great harm in either Miss Blyton or Captain Johns, so long as it is realized they are writing for a particular audience at particular stage of development. Mr. Taylor could be right, but he can't know that he is right, unless he has positive proof that these authors he has banned have a harmful rather than beneficial effect."[16]

In his letter of the 8th November 1971 Mr. Taylor clarified the position:

"At no time did I censor her books; I merely decided, in the early 1950's, that as we had only a limited amount of money to spend on children's books, this should be devoted to providing, and duplicating where necessary, the best in children's literature. This meant there was no money left over to buy mediocre children's fiction, such as that written by Miss Blyton, Captain Johns, Eric Leyland, etc. Consequently these books were not replaced as they wore out and very quickly the St. Pancras Children's Libraries ceased to stock them. This situation existed for several years until some time in 1963 when the *Daily Express* received a complaint from the parent of a potential reader of Enid Blyton and the affair blew up into a national nine-days wonder. . . . The Libraries and Arts Committee had a long discussion about the policy, which had not previously been considered by them, and they decided that in future the Children's Libraries should stock a small number of books by these authors and this instruction was put into effect. . . . I would repeat, however, that in my view this affair has nothing whatever to do with censorship."[17]

Early in February 1964, the press devoted much space to another library which was reported to have banned Enid Blyton's books. The Nottingham City Libraries were involved this time and there appears to have been an element of sensationalism and some mis-reporting by the press.

Miss M. I. McKie, Tutor Librarian at the Loughborough College of Education, who was supervisor of work with young people in Nottingham City Libraries at the time, provided the following details about children's book selection in Nottingham City Libraries. While she was in charge of children's work, she did not feel that she should influence the branch librarians in their selection of children's books to any great extent, because she took the view that as professionals, the branch librarians should do their own selection in the light of their local situations. A weekly book selection meeting was held at which a collection of newly published books provided by a local bookseller was available for the librarians to examine. By the time Miss McKie became supervisor of work with young people the booksellers had stopped sending books by Enid Blyton and other prolific authors because they knew the chances were that these books would not be selected by the librarians.

Miss McKie emphasised there was no definite rejection of Enid Blyton by Nottingham City Libraries as a whole. Some branch librarians had quite large collections of her books, particularly those branches serving the poorer areas of the city. There was a collection of Enid Blyton books in the central children's collection during Miss McKie's time there. There were other branch librarians however, who because of their local situations and the limited amount of money available to them for children's books, had decided not to buy any more titles by Enid Blyton or replacement copies of those books which were wearing out.

According to David Gerard, who was Deputy City Librarian of Nottingham in 1964, a child had asked for books by Enid Blyton at the Woolaton Branch Library and was told by a member of staff that the library did not buy her books. While this was true of the Woolaton Branch, it was not true of all other branches in the system. The child had returned home and informed his father who was a newspaper reporter, and the story soon appeared in most of the national newspapers and the local Nottingham papers.

Adrian Clancy, reporting in the *Daily Mail* under the headlines "Noddy banned from library shelves" stated:

"Nearly all Enid Blyton's children's books, including the adventures of Noddy and Big Ears, have been banned from a city's libraries. Nottingham Librarian Mr. Francis Tighe said yesterday that the books did 'not have a sufficiently wide vocabulary'. The characters, he said 'tended to be caricatures'.... Miss Blyton, ... said of the ban 'what rubbish, this has happened because the books are so frightfully popular. The children keep clamouring for them and the librarians get angry and try to take it out on me. They want to foist some high-falutin' books on them. I think Noddy, Big Ears and Plod the Policeman will get on very nicely despite this ban'."[18]

The reporter of the *Daily Express* John Weaver, interviewed K. A. Stockham, County Librarian of Nottinghamshire, who was quoted as saying 'we find that nowadays there are a lot more books for children with better educational value'.[19] Within a day or two Mr. Stockham was interviewed for radio and television:

"I was interviewed for a piece that went out on *Woman's Hour* on radio and also was interviewed on a television programme. ... Subsequently, commercial television approached me to see if I would be prepared to appear in one of their programmes and be questioned by Enid Blyton herself. The idea of the programme was that the author was to be in an attacking position and I was to be a public officer on the defence. The idea never came to fruition, because Enid Blyton was in no way interested."[20]

The *Daily Mirror* quoted F. C. Tighe:

"This is not a ban on Miss Blyton's books. It is simply that we have limited fund and there are hundreds of children's books which we cannot afford. We are no renewing the Blyton books when they wear out because we feel that they ar limited in vocabulary. They appeal only to the seven-to-eight age group. We feel we should spend our money on books of wider appeal. After all anyone who wants a Noddy book can find one in almost any bookshop."[21]

Enid Blyton's husband, Surgeon Kenneth Waters was also quoted in the same article:

"These librarians don't like books being popular. They try to force the classics onto the children, but the children will not read them."

The controversy then spread to local papers in a number of towns and cities up and down the country. The *Northampton Chronicle and Echo* quoted D. H. Halliday, Chief Librarian of Northampton, as saying:

"I have a great deal of sympathy with the Nottingham Librarian's point of view. Reading only Enid Blyton can stultify a child's imagination. Children who are quite capable of reading more advanced books often seem to come down to Enid Blyton."

And the *Echo* continued:

"In Northamptonshire, at least, Miss Blyton's characters, or caricatures, can find asylum. Her books are freely available at libraries in town and county, not because the librarians think they have any special merits, but because they 'would not think of censoring the reading habits of anyone' . . . the trouble . . . is that Miss Blyton's books are attractive in a way which makes them almost habit-forming. The dangers of this were pointed out quite recently in a survey carried out by the University of North Wales.[23] They found that at about the age when children leave primary schools to go to secondary schools those who had read only one author, not necessarily Enid Blyton, often stopped reading voluntarily altogether. Mrs. Margery Fisher . . . who reads a thousand to fifteen hundred children's books a year in the course of preparing her monthly magazine *Growing Point* said, 'Enid Blyton's vocabulary is exceptionally boring, but at the same time, she has this enormous power of invention which makes her situations very attractive. A great deal of her popularity is possibly pure habit. Children must have something which gives them an expanding vocabulary—there is a great deal to be said for removing the Enid Blyton-type book from their sights. During the last ten years . . . the number of books which were not absolutely first-class literature, but nevertheless very good, had increased enormously'. She felt that many good writers had been completely overlooked because of the addiction to Enid Blyton."[22]

The results of the survey carried out by the University College of North Wales were given in a paper by I. Leng at the Library Association Annual Conference at Llandudno in 1962.

"What do they find that makes reading of abiding value to them? The two following cases may help us find an answer. Both are boys whom we first meet when they enter standard V in their primary school. They are both of only moderate ability, and at the beginning of next year they will both find themselves in the secondary modern school. Both are members of the public library.

The first begins the year by borrowing Enid Blyton's *Mystery of the Hidden House.* Three months later he is reading Enid Blyton's *Lucky story book;* three months later still, it is Blyton's *Sunny story book,* and at the end of the year he is back where he began, with Enid Blyton's *Mystery of the Hidden House.* In all he borrowed 74 books in the year, 38 of them by Blyton. The following year he borrowed none at all. No doubt he enjoyed his reading, but it got him nowhere, so he gave up. And he was wise to do so I suggest. Others, less wise or less fortunate, fail to break the habit, but obsessively continue looking for they know not what, reading ever more futilely, until at last they come into our adult libraries, voracious readers of nothing but the trivial.

Look, by way of contrast, at the second boy. He begins the year in much the same way, with Enid Blyton's *Mystery of Tally-Ho Cottage.* In the following five weeks he runs through ten books by Enid Blyton in a row, and then moves on to other tales of mystery and adventure by John Kennet, F. W. Dixon, Eric Leyland and others, reading altogether 43 books in the year, and finishing with *Biggles takes the case,* by W. E. Johns. The following year he rejoined the library and took out a further 27 books.

The first boy's reading was static or regressive, a childish pastime which, he came to feel, could be of little value to him as he grew. The second boy stumbled on the secret of progressive reading; his reading grew with him, and played a part in the process of his growth. That was its true importance for him, and that is why he continued to read. To seem worthwhile to both himself and us, a child's reading must keep pace with, and make some contribution to, his growth."[23]

The *Burnley Express* reported that the Nottingham City Librarian had decided to ban Noddy and Big Ears because their vocabulary was not sufficiently wide for young readers.

"He well may be right. But we feel he is acting as a literary critic rather than a librarian when he takes his opinion to such lengths. A librarian's job is to bring books to the people—and people to the books. To achieve this double object, he may often have to forget his own tastes and prejudices, cultivated by long training, and be content merely to awaken a popular interest in reading, in the hope that discrimination will follow. . . . We feel that the Burnley Borough Librarian is on sounder lines when he says that, although Enid Blyton's books may be very simple, they help to get children into the libraries, where they will soon find something more valuable and interesting."[24]

The *Star* quoted John Bebbington, City Librarian of Sheffield, as saying that:

"We cater for children from a very early age, and I intend to take no action to remove the Blyton books from our shelves. They are not so popular that they are read to the exclusion of countless hundreds of other books and the limited vocabulary bears no significance to children at an early stage of reading development."[25]

The *Liverpool Echo* reported Dr. G. Chandler, then City Librarian of Liverpool as saying:

"We never ban a book from the shelves if the public want it."[26]

There was a considerable response to the Nottingham City Librarian's reported actions, both in reader's letters to the press and press comment, and in the many letters addressed to Mr. Tighe himself. Headed 'The Censor', the leader of the *Daily Mail* asked:

"By what right does the Nottingham Librarian set himself up as critic and censor and ban Enid Blyton's books? Any such decision should surely be made, if at all, by the people's representatives and not be dictated by one man. Enid Blyton's simple stories may not suit everyone's taste, but they are clean and decent. She has been writing for children for at least thirty years, and presumably knows more about what they like than the high-and-mighty librarian. If his action is accepted what is to stop others from deciding that any author is unacceptable? This is not to be tolerated."[27]

Not unnaturally the widespread reporting of the affair had disturbed the Nottingham City Libraries Committee, who asked Mr. Tighe to draw up a report on the controversy. This was submitted to the Libraries Committee on 19th February 1964. After receiving the report, the Chairman of the Libraries Committee, Mr. Brian Morley said that the Committee had unanimously supported the City Librarian's policy. Mr. Tighe had told the Committee that two thousand six hundred children's books were published every year and no more than one thousand six hundred could be bought for the City's children's libraries. Therefore a considerable degree of selection was needed. The Chairman concluded:

"We feel and re-affirm that the City Librarian and his staff are buying the best books available for the children."[28]

Much of the correspondence in the press and to the City Librarian, was hostile. One example of the many letters was that by Alan Donn to the Nottingham *Evening Post:*

"Although as a child I was not an enthusiastic reader of Enid Blyton's books I must protest, nevertheless, at the arbitrary decision and high-handed manner of the Nottingham Librarian in the banning of her works. I certainly contest his right to dictate what is good for our children. I, for one, hope that the protest grows and that he is made to realise that the children read for enjoyment."[29]

Similar sentiments were expressed in many of the other letters.

There were however, letters agreeing with Tighe's actions. Mrs. D. M. Trollope, wrote to the Nottingham *Evening Post:*

> "In reply to Mr. Alan Donn's letter . . . contesting the City Librarian's right to 'dictate what is good for our children', surely that is one of the main purposes of a librarian. As a person responsible for the education and intelligence of our children, the librarian, like the teacher, has a duty to help and direct the choice of the reading material of his borrowers, whether they be children or adults. With a limited book fund surely it is the responsibility of the librarian to choose between books of poor or little literary value and those by which a child would benefit. There are many children's books these days of a similar subject matter to those of Enid Blyton which are of a higher standard, both from a literary and an educational point of view. There will always be a difference of opinion between those who believe that the librarian is there solely to provide any book that a reader may desire; and those who know that the librarian has a responsibility both to the public and to the higher educational standard of the country. Who better to benefit from this than the child, the citizen of tomorrow?"[30]

In replies to correspondence on the matter F. C. Tighe echoed the attitudes of many librarians to this problem[31]:

> "The whole work of a librarian is selection, because we could not possibly hope to represent every book published in our libraries, and our duty is to provide first rate material. Blyton books are not first rate and it is as simple as that. I see no reason to change my views since we first decided no longer to include this material for children round about 1955. We select some twelve hundred children's books each year, which surely gives a wide range of choice for every age group."
>
> "I think it a dangerous proposition that what is popular is therefore good, for if this is applied to adult fiction, one can quickly see examples of books which are popular and yet are fifth rate and even vicious. An interesting thing is that the support in the press has crystallised the figure of Noddy and this unthinking defence of an image seems to me to be a dangerous thing. If authorities in the educational field, the BBC, children's book critics and children's librarians frown on Blyton, is it not therefore a possibility that from their experience of children and their knowledge of children's books that they may be right."
>
> "Librarians, so far as children's books are concerned, have been in no small measure responsible for the rising standards of children's books in the past few years, and one can only hope that children will use the public libraries where they will get guidance from librarians on books which they will find interesting to read and which will help them in learning use of the language."
>
> "The newspapers were wrong in their report of 'banning' of Blyton books. It is difficult to avoid personal prejudices in the matter of selection of material for the libraries, but we try to be balanced and sensible in our judgment, and while I agree that Enid Blyton books have the merit of being easy to read, they do tend to be repetitive and there are other books which are better in helping children both to read and have their imagination stimulated. The Blyton books are easily available

through commercial channels if parents feel their children must have Blyton books, but our own book funds are limited and we have to use the money to the best advantage and hence the need to exercise a degree of selection."[31]

In 1964, W. A. Taylor, Borough Librarian of St. Pancras was appointed to the position of City Librarian of Birmingham. A reporter of the *Birmingham Evening Mail,* no doubt remembering the earlier controversy over Enid Blyton in St. Pancras Borough Libraries spoke to Mr. Taylor.

"Mr. Taylor . . . said today that children's libraries there (St. Pancras) did not contain books by Enid Blyton, or 'Biggles' or 'William' books. This he said was part of a policy of improving the standard of books in children's libraries which he would be discussing with Birmingham Library Committee when he took up his new post in the new year. 'I want to make it clear, however, that this is a policy of direction and not rejection', he said. 'There is not a great deal of money to spend in libraries, and by the time the worthwhile books—the classics and so on—have been bought in heavy duplication none would be left over to buy these other books'. Mr. Taylor said it was a constructive approach to the problem of how to make the best use of children's libraries 'where we no longer have the queues we used to have before the war'. It was a question of improving the standard of selection in the children's libraries . . . Mr. Taylor said that it should be made clear that these were his own views and not decided policies at Birmingham Public Library. He would be recommending his policies to the Library Committee for approval."[32]

This newspaper report gave rise to critical comment from readers and this time from Enid Blyton herself. Mrs. Ann Jones writing about under-privileged children in a letter to the *Birmingham Evening Mail* suggested that:

"If some of these children can be enabled to discover that reading is a pleasure, then something rather wonderful has been achieved. Enid Blyton with her 'good story' and comparatively simple vocabulary is very good for this purpose. I should have thought that our libraries ought to provide for ALL Birmingham children and not just for the more literate minority with others frozen out."[33]

There were other letters along similar lines.

Mr. Taylor's reported comments had reached the Birmingham Libraries Committee, and on 3rd November John Lewis, the municipal reporter for *The Birmingham Post* wrote that:

"'Biggles', 'Just William' and 'Noddy' were never in real danger after all. The ugly rumours that they were about to be banished from the shelves of Birmingham Libraries were due to a mis-understanding. The full explanation was given last night by the Chairman of the City's Library Committee, Councillor George Jonas, after the threat to the three fictional heroes had been raised in Committee. . . .

Councillor Jonas treated the rumours with the seriousness they deserved. 'In view of the real concern and suspicions among young readers that certain types of children's books are no longer to appear in Birmingham Libraries, I can assure them (and those adults who have expressed alarm) that there has been a misunderstanding', he said. The new Librarian meant to convey that the policy he had discussed in interviews described only what was happening in St. Pancras. 'There is no question of any recommendation being made by him to this Committee that these books be taken out of Birmingham Library System and I have his authority for saying so', Councillor Jonas added. 'I understand Mr. Taylor was saying that there was today a far better choice of good children's books than in the days when 'Noddy' and 'Biggles' were the standard fare and it was necessary to keep a proper sense of proportion about books like 'William'. We are already doing that in Birmingham' he said and added jokingly 'besides which I like Noddy'."[34]

The following day Enid Blyton wrote to the same newspaper.

". . . on behalf of the children I do thank all the readers of the *Evening Mail* who rallied to the defence of Noddy when they thought that he might no longer live on their library shelves."

The main body of the letter was about Noddy himself, but Miss Blyton concludes:

"The main purpose of the Noddy books is to introduce young children to reading and, I hope, to make them love it and quickly go on to more advanced books."[35]

In May 1966 the Blyton controversy again found its way into both local and national papers, when it was reported that the Librarian of Sittingbourne, Kent, Kenneth Chatfield was not issuing 'Noddy' books to children.

"A Sittingbourne woman's ten-year-old daughter had her request for an Enid Blyton book turned down at the library. Now Mr. Chatfield has admitted that he does not keep any books by Enid Blyton in stock. 'They are just too trivial' he claims. 'They demand nothing from children. It is not a case of them being unsuitable'. . . . Told of the complaint, Councillor Mrs. Margaret Boulding, Chairman of Sittingbourne Council's Library Committee, said the librarian had jurisdiction over the selection of books for the library. 'If there is a popular demand for books then he should see that they are put on the shelves', she added. The Library Committee, she said, tried to encourage children to read other kinds of material beside bedtime type stories. Usually people bought this type of book if they wanted it. She continued 'these books are so cheap nowadays we cannot really afford money for this type of reading'. The library tried to provide something a little more educational because, after all, this was the function of libraries, Councillor Mrs. Boulding said. 'I certainly would not have thought any parent would have been looking in the children's libraries for that sort of airy-fairy reading'."[36]

In the view of the *Daily Express* commentator:

> "What is not in doubt at all, however, is that a librarian is acting with extraordinary arrogance when he bans the Blyton books, Noddy and the rest. They are wholesome, harmless, and beloved by children. Librarians are servants of the public. Not dictators of its tastes."[37]

Along with the *Daily Express,* the *Daily Mirror* and the *Sun,* the *Daily Mail* made much of the various Blyton controversies. Following the Sittingbourne ban, it looked at other libraries in Kent and discovered that Blyton had been banned not only at Sittingbourne, but also at Herne Bay, Deal and Sandwich.

> "An official at Deal public library said: 'It is the policy of the Kent County Library not to stock Enid Blyton books'. John Pagett, the librarian at Herne Bay, said: 'They are not really suitable . . .'. The Broadstairs Librarian, John Walters, said: 'I feel that Miss Blyton's books do not meet the standard of literature that we require for children. We have a few and we do not intend to bring in any more."

The article[38] also quoted Olive Jones, children's editor for Methuen's, publishers of a number of Miss Blyton's books. She said:

> "Miss Blyton is helping more slow readers than any other author. Librarians like to think every child is an intellectual reader wanting high quality, but a great many children are slow readers and the librarians must face the facts."

In September 1968 the *Daily Mail* returned to the attack. Diana Norman, in an article asked:

> "When are British public libraries going to end their censorship of the writer who ranks alongside names like Stalin and Lenin in the world's best sellers. When in fact are they going to give a fair deal to Enid Blyton?"

Then under the sub-heading 'Censorship' she continued:

> "Many, maybe most, of the public libraries in this country as well as Australia and New Zealand do not stock her books. Some have openly banned them. Others tacitly do not buy them. There is not a single Enid Blyton book stocked in any public library in Hertfordshire, for instance. . . . But shouldn't it worry us? For children who cannot afford them the libraries decision is a virtual censorship. The Library Association says 'the job of the public libraries is to educate and entertain. In the children's departments we put a heavier stress on education. It is thought that Miss Blyton does not present enough of a challenge to children'. Enid Blyton is a phase which all children should be allowed to enter and then gently steered out of. The most highbrow of women can relapse into Georgette Heyer sometimes, the most intellectual of men indulge in thrillers. Then why not allow children to relax

into the safety and comfort of a woman who knows better than anyone else how to please them?"[39]

'All things Blyton beautiful', Nicholas Tucker's article in *The Times Literary Supplement* of 16th April 1970 added one or two new points:

> "The phenomenal success of Enid Blyton has always rather vexed teachers and librarians. It is made more difficult to argue for a strong literary taste among children towards the best writing, reflected in awards like the Carnegie, Newbery and Caldecott medals, if so many readers still insist upon turning to books that are so demonstrably bad . . . there were stories of young library goers not returning their Blyton books to the desk unless able to make a lightning exchange with another incoming addict. One little girl, who was unable to find a partner in this literary black market, actually ended up taking out the same Blyton book three times running, rather than release such a trump card unrewarded."[40]

In November 1962, Adam Sykes had interviewed Enid Blyton for *Time and Tide,* and his article concluded:

> "The test of children's books is whether adults enjoy them as well. Such has been the case with the classics, as A. A. Milne, Beatrix Potter and Kenneth Grahame. Some of Enid Blyton's books, like *The Children of Cherry Tree Farm* have adult appeal; others, like Noddy, have less. If the amount of letters received from parents is any true indication, Miss Blyton may well be encouraged. Already a generation reared on her books is growing up; the test will be whether it reads them to its own children. But whether it does or not, in output and wide spread popularity Miss Blyton has, and has had, no equal."[41]

Although Enid Blyton died on 28th November 1968, the controversy over her books continues. In 1971, a member of the Nottinghamshire County Libraries Committee complained that her grandchildren were not able to obtain Enid Blyton books from one of the County branch libraries, and insisted on a statement being provided by the County Librarian for the Committee. Previous to this statement, Kenneth Stockham had ensured that:

> "In all the statements that were made to newspapers, etc, both Children's Librarians and I maintained a consistent line, that there was no ban on Enid Blyton's books, but that they were not selected in large numbers."[42]

However, his report, entitled *Book Selection for Children* was submitted to the County Libraries Committee on 2nd July 1971, and was accepted. The statement described the County Libraries children's book-selection process in which a copy of each title published costing more than twelve pence, was purchased and from these books the staff carefully selected about half the titles for addition to stock in larger numbers. He continued:

> "It is therefore clear that there are many authors, of whose books no further copies are purchased. In the case of Enid Blyton, the number of additional copies purchased has usually been limited. In an article entitled "All things Blyton Beautiful' Nicholas Tucker wrote that she produced 'books that are so demonstrably bad'. This view is widely held by teachers and librarians, some of whom go so far as to regard the reading of many of her books as positively harmful. Before the Second World War, Miss Blyton's early works were quite well reviewed and subsequently were to be found in public libraries. But later when she was producing more than one book each week, as well as bringing out a fortnightly magazine, her standards dropped to a low level. . . . During the years when Enid Blyton's books sank to a mediocre level, the number of good books available increased and librarians were anxious to buy these books, in which authors used language skilfully to entertain, and stimulated the imagination so that children learnt more about themselves and the world around them. With limited public funds at their disposal, Nottinghamshire Children's librarians have always been concerned to buy the best books to suit all ages and all kinds of reading ability."[43]

Nottinghamshire's views were and are still shared by most other librarians, though some take the attitude that as their funds are so limited, they should buy only the best and these do not include Enid Blyton's books.

The same attitude was taken by the Wiltshire and Hertfordshire County Libraries. In November 1971 the *Swindon Evening Advertiser* reported that the Devizes Library no longer stocked books by Enid Blyton or Angela Brazil on the grounds that "Enid with her limited vocabulary and Angela with her colonial, snobbish values" were no longer considered worthwhile.[44] The news that Hertfordshire were no longer to stock Enid Blyton's books was revealed by the London *Evening News* in March 1973. The decision was taken despite a "Save Noddy" plea by some parents, because "Enid Blyton just did not stand up in the face of stiff opposition from the newer, more sophisticated books on the market."[45]

No doubt this issue will recur in the press from time to time. Enid Blyton's popularity still appears to be considerable, despite there being no new titles. Certainly there are often almost as many books by Enid Blyton for sale in local bookshops as there are books by all other children's authors combined.

1. Doyle, Brian. Blyton and Biggles. *Books and Bookmen,* vol. 14, no. 8. May 1969. pp.24-26
2. Greenfield, George. Phenomenon. National Book League. *Books,* no. 2, Winter 1970. pp.24-25

3. Behind the lines. *Bookseller,* 20th August 1960. p.1022
4. Martin, Constance. South Sea Bubble. National Book League. *Books,* no. 2, Winter 1970. pp.26-27
5. Doyle, Brian. Blyton and Biggles. *Op cit.,* see note 1
6. Blishen, Edward. Who's afraid of Enid Blyton? *Where.* July 1967. pp.28-29. Also *The Guardian,* 7th July 1967
7. Last chapter. *Daily Express,* 13th August 1964
8. Australian Libraries reject Enid Blyton. *Bookseller,* 5th September 1964
9. Golding, Laurance. Banning Blyton. *The Guardian,* 31st August 1964
10. Hill, Michael. Banning Blyton. *The Guardian,* 2nd September 1964
11. Hay, Daniel. Noddy and Co. *Bookseller,* 12th September 1964
12. Colwell, Eileen H. Twenty eventful years in Children's Books. Papers and Summaries of Discussions at the Brighton Conference of the Library Association, 9th to 13th June 1947. pp.55-59
13. Noddy and Biggles banned by libraries. *Daily Herald,* 6th April 1963
14. Cummings, Mrs. H. L. Compelling. *Daily Herald,* 9th April 1963
15. Jodrell, S. Noddy censored. *Surveyor,* 13th April 1963
16. 'Ferdinand'. Books and bookmen. *British Books,* June 1963. p.32
17. Letter from W. A. Taylor, City Librarian of Birmingham, to the author, 8th November 1971. (Unpublished)
18. Clancy, Adrian. Noddy banned from library shelves. *Daily Mail,* 6th February 1964
19. Weaver, John. Little Noddy's simple words get him banned. *Daily Express,* 6th February 1964
20. Letter from K. A. Stockham, County Librarian of Nottinghamshire, to the author, 1st August 1972. (Unpublished)
21. City turns out Noddy and friends. *Daily Mirror,* 6th February 1964
22. Noddy stays put in Northants. *Chronicle and Echo,* 6th February 1964
23. Leng, I. Children's reading. Proceedings, Papers and Summaries of Discussions at the Llandudno Conference, 25th to 28th September 1962. pp.111-116
24. Books on the blacklist. *Burnley Express,* 12th February 1964
25. We won't ban popular 'Noddy', says Sheffield. *The Star,* 6th February 1964
26. No ban on Noddy. *Liverpool Echo,* 21st February 1964
27. The Censor. *Daily Mail,* 7th February 1964
28. No reprieve for banned Noddy. *Sheffield Telegraph,* 20th February 1964
29. Donn, Alan. Children's books. *Nottingham Evening Post,* 11th February 1964
30. Trollope, Mrs. D. M. Librarian's duty to help and direct book choice. *Nottingham Evening Post,* 19th February 1964
31. Extracts from letters by F. C. Tighe, . . . apropos the 'Blyton Case'. (Unpublished, held by Nottingham Public Libraries)
32. New City Librarian aims to 'direct' children's reading. *Birmingham Evening Mail,* 24th October 1964
33. Jones, Mrs. A. Blyton encourages children to find pleasure in reading. *Birmingham Evening Mail,* 27th October 1964
34. Lewis, John. Noddy and Co. to stay. *Birmingham Post,* 3rd November 1964
35. Blyton, Enid. So nice to hear the news about Noddy. *Birmingham Evening Mail,* 4th November 1964
36. 'Noddy' books banned by town library. *East Kent Gazette,* 19th May 1966

37. Veto on Noddy. *Daily Express,* 21st May 1966
38. More libraries ban Noddy books. *Daily Mail,* 26th May 1966
39. Norman, Diana. Let's bring Noddy back from exile! *Daily Mail,* 14th September 1968
40. Tucker, Nicholas. All things Blyton beautiful. *The Times Literary Supplement,* 16th April 1970. p.422
41. Sykes, Adam. The books that children love. *Time and Tide,* 22nd-29th November 1962. pp.21-23
42. Letter from K. A. Stockham to the author, *op cit.* See note 20
43. Stockham, K. Book selection for children (a report for the Nottinghamshire County Libraries Committee), 2nd July 1971. (Unpublished, held by Nottinghamshire County Libraries.)
44. Greer-in-Blyton-out. (Swindon) *Evening Advertiser,* 29th November 1971
45. County Library puts a ban on Noddy books. *Evening News,* 14th March 1973

CHAPTER 9

1965–1969

Following the Enid Blyton affair at the end of 1964 Birmingham Public Libraries were concerned in three other cases early in 1965.

The first of these, whilst not unique, was an unusual one for it showed a City Council standing up for its rights under national law against the rulings of a local magistrate.

"Four books confiscated by a Birmingham Magistrate as obscene will remain available to adult borrowers at the City's 28 public libraries. One of the books, the *Carpet-Baggers* is on the library shelves in a restricted category, and the other three, *Kama Sutra, The Perfumed Garden* and *The Tropic of Capricorn,* are kept 'under the counter' and issued only on request to adults. Last week the Birmingham Stipendiary, Mr. John Milward, ordered copies of all four, seized by police in a bookshop raid, to be confiscated under the Obscene Publications Act. But last night Birmingham Library Committee decided by a 15 to 2 vote to retain the books in public libraries with the existing safeguards which prevent their issue to junior borrowers. Mr. George Jonas, the Committee Chairman said: 'We are prepared to take the risk, negligible though we believe it to be, of proceedings being brought against us. If they are we will defend and seek to show that these books do not tend to deprave or corrupt, and that it is in the public interest we should continue to issue them'. The Committee, he said, regarded the seizure of the books and the order of their destruction as 'a matter of considerable importance to all of us who are concerned with the freedom of expression and the right to publish'.

Mr. Jonas, who is a solicitor, said that the Magistrate heard no arguments, defence or witnesses because the case was brought under Section 3 of the Act. Under Section 2 the case would have been one for a Jury, properly directed by a High Court Judge, and the books, if found illegal, would have been immediately removed from the Birmingham Libraries. ... Mr. Anthony Beaumont-Dark, Conservative spokesman on the Committee, said: 'If the police wish to prosecute us I will be delighted; in fact, I invite the Chief Constable to prosecute us. This case strikes me as confirmation of the classic assertion that the law is an ass'."[1]

Mr. Jonas was reported as saying:

> "It is the function of the Libraries Committee to provide the public with the means of access to books and literature, some good, some bad, some great and some not so great . . . the Committee has tried to discharge this function to the best of its ability by making available as many different types of books as possible, without acting as a censorship body, but insisting on safeguards."[2]

Two weeks later the Home Secretary was asked in a written Parliamentary question:

> "If he will introduce legislation to prevent public libraries stocking books which booksellers have been prevented from selling and of which their stocks have been confiscated. Mr. George Thomas: My right honourable friend is not convinced that such legislation is necessary or would be practicable."[3]

The Daily Telegraph of 11th May 1965 reported that the police had warned booksellers in Birmingham the day before that they would be prosecuted if they continued to sell the novel *The Carpet-Baggers*. A Libraries Committee spokesman told *The Daily Telegraph* that if the Committee was prosecuted the city would fight the case.[4] No attempt was made to prosecute the Libraries Committee or to stop the Birmingham Public Libraries displaying the book. It continued to be displayed and is still available today.[5]

The second case in which Birmingham featured involved the *Daily Worker*.

> "A decision taken this week to ban the Communist *Daily Worker* from Birmingham Reference Library sparked off a row. Mr. William Dunn, Secretary of Birmingham Communist Party, described the decision as 'a most undemocratic action which should be reversed as soon as possible'. The City Librarian, Mr. William Taylor, said that the committee's decision—on a suggestion from the public that the paper should be included—was 'not a case of anti-*Daily Worker*'. There were already, he said, a dozen or more copies of the *Daily Worker* in various branch libraries."[6]

In the case involving Birmingham and *The Carpet-Baggers,* Mr. Jonas had declared that it was not the Committee's function to exercise censorship but had insisted that there should be certain safeguards. Birmingham received publicity for the third time, when *British Books,* April 1965, reported on one of these safeguards:

> "X Books mark for Birmingham.—A secret mark to distinguish books considered unsuitable for children under 16 years of age is being used by all the . . . libraries controlled by the Birmingham Libraries Department."[7]

The system to which *British Books* referred, had in fact begun as early as 1930. The following is an extract from the City Librarian's Minutes (information and instructions to staff), Number 27, of 1930; under the heading "Books unsuitable for Young People":

> "Books in the lending libraries which are unsuitable for unrestricted circulation must be marked in ink with a black asterisk at the top right hand corner of the date label and the book card. Junior assistants must not issue any books so marked but must refer it to the Librarian or senior assistant who must exercise discretion as to whether or not it is desirable to issue the book to the borrower who has selected it. No book so marked is to be issued to a child."[8]

A system based on this instruction still operates in the reorganised Birmingham Public Libraries today, although increasingly fewer books receive a star:

> "The Deputy City Librarian has drawn to his attention all books which may justify a star. This may occur when the books are first displayed at the Book Purchase Department, or subsequently if a reader complains. His decision is notified by Routine Instruction (weekly staff Instruction sheets), under two categories (a) starred, and (b) starred and kept off the public shelves.
>
> Books so listed are marked by a star on fly-leaf, book card and catalogue card. A staff index of all such books is kept by all Branch Libraries to facilitate starring second or subsequent copies of books. A public index is kept of books kept off the public shelves. Books starred may be fiction or certain non-fiction, usually sex instruction or childbirth books."[9]

On 21st May 1965, D. I. Colley, City Librarian of Manchester, received a letter which included a definite demand for censorship in the children's library:

> "Whilst glancing through my seven-year-old daughter's library books yesterday, I was horrified to read the following lines:
> 'After a few moments she saw the floor was covered with clotted blood, in which were mirrored the bodies of several dead women, hanging on hooks around the walls. Bluebeard had married and murdered one after another'.
> Anyone with any experience of young children will realize that the horror of that particular extract will remain with the child long after the other stories have faded from their memories, and I should like to know who authorised such a book to be placed in the young children's section of the public library. The book in question is *Blue Beard, and other Fairy Tales of Charles Perrault*, page 32.
> One expects the highest possible standard of books in the public libraries and the greatest care possible to be taken in the choosing of books for the children's section. Would you please ensure that this book, and any others like it, are removed without delay from the shelves of the children's libraries?"[10]

Colley defended the library's provision of the book:

". . . I am surprised that you object to your daughter reading the fairy tales of Charles Perrault. For centuries . . . these stories have been read and enjoyed by countless children and, as far as I am aware, have harmed none of them. The element of the horrific is present in a great many fairy stories—there are no better examples than the tales collected by the Brothers Grimm. There is, however, no reason to believe that the horrific has an injurious effect on the child's mind. Bertrand Russell writes on this very question 'stories such as Blue Beard and Jack the Giant Killer do not involve any knowledge of cruelty whatever. To the child they are purely fantastic and he never connects them with the real world in any way'.

Harvey Darton in his *Children's Books in England* . . . declares that 'the adult disapproval of fairy tales is a manifestation, in England, of a deep rooted sin complex'.

Jeanne Cappe in *Coutes bleus, livres roses,* says . . . 'let us leave the children to penetrate into the kingdom of fiction. . . . They will only be the better for it. They will only be fitter to become men'.

Certain 19th century moralists were opposed to this point of view but as a father of four daughters myself I have always allowed them a free rein in their reading and I assure you they are none the worse for it.

If you wish to read further on this subject may I recommend you to consult *Tales out of School* by Geoffrey Trease which includes the quotations cited above and many others. I think you may then well agree with me that Perrault is not harmful reading for children."[11]

W. J. Murison, the County Librarian of the West Riding of Yorkshire was interviewed by the *Yorkshire Post* about a number of complaints received in his libraries.

" 'Over-emphasis on sexual matters in many modern books was causing concern to an increasing number of readers. . . . More and more people are thinking that a lot of books are becoming too obscene. Two written complaints arrived on my desk today, the third in a few weeks. Usually we get about three a year. People are talking more and more about their desire to get rid of obscene literature. I think things have gone over the mark'. There was no doubt that during the war and immediately after it there was a quite justifiable turn towards a realistic approach to literature, and franker descriptions of motives and behaviour. 'This was quite reasonable, but now it has come to such a state that the public are naturally reacting against it. This is reflected by the number of people writing or complaining verbally to us—progressive, open-minded people, not prudes. They are from all walks of life, from gentle elderly housewives to forthright miners'. . . . It was a library's job to provide books and other literature in which a reader could take a legitimate interest. There was only one infallible way of determining what was legitimate interest, and that was the law of the land. 'If a book has not been penalized by the law it would seem inappropriate for us to exclude it on any moral, political, religious or racial grounds. We don't want to become moral censors. All branch librarians had instructions to protect young people by not issuing them with books considered unsuitable . . .'."[12]

Murison commented further on this subject in his annual report for the year 1964-1965.

"Financial resources, adequacy in coverage, the number of titles to be added, these are not all that have to be considered in selecting books for addition to the library; and presumably the (Department of Education and Science) Circular 4/65 (Public Libraries and Museums Act 1964. 29th March 1965) deliberately avoided an excursion into assessing what is good and what is bad literature to avoid any implication of censorship, present or to come. But all book selection is acceptance or rejection. The study of the large output of the British, American and foreign presses has been a huge job in the past year and it was patently impossible to examine every book in detail individually.

The guiding principle of the County Library's book selection may be compared to the long walk in the country. First, there is a satisfying experience of walking across clean moors which may be equated with the joy of reading good fiction or non-fiction for relaxation. Secondly, if there is a hill or a rock face to be climbed in order to achieve some view, this may represent the books which have to be read for examination or general study purposes, solid work but with a valued end-product. But, of course, if this long walk is uncharted (and modern publishing is venturesome) and leads through some bog it will be no surprise if someone slips in the dirt.

The first two experiences are pleasant, satisfying, even profitable, and worth repeating many times. So it is that books of worth are bought in large numbers and those of dubious value are either avoided or bought in very limited number. The pity is that the ever-increasing frankness among authors suggests that many do not always appear to recognise the subtleties of liberty and licence, prudery and propriety, or, worse still, some do not recognise good taste in what is worth saying or what is best left unsaid."[13]

On 15th October 1965, under the heading 'Censor to end filth in books, suggests Librarian' the *Liverpool Daily Post* reported comments made by Eric Luke, the County Librarian of Denbighshire, in his Annual Report for 1964-1965:

"The quality of many modern day novels comes in for scathing criticism. . . . He says he notes with considerable trepidation the increasing number of books relying on sex and sadism as their *raison d'etre*.[14]

If some measure of censorship is considered necessary for the stage and cinema . . . then there is equally as strong a case for some censorship of the printed word. Some of the rubbish being printed today is nothing less than unadulterated filth and someone must do something about it."[15]

In June of the following year, Luke was ready to do something about it:

"Shocked and disgusted by the growing number of novels which rely on sex and sadism as their main selling attraction, Mr. Eric Luke, Denbighshire County

Librarian, is prepared to lead a crusade against objectionable books. Next week he is to move a resolution at the annual conference of Welsh library authorities at Llandudno calling for urgent Government action to control publication of books of a pornographic nature. At county headquarters in Ruthin . . . Mr. Luke yesterday produced the evidence to support his campaign—a collection of 300 books withdrawn from the open shelves because of complaints by readers. As we talked three more were handed in. 'There has always been a certain amount of traffic in pornography . . . but since *Lady Chatterley* was cleared in the courts, the flood gates opened, and such books, and even worse, are pouring on to the market. But no one seems to care, or to do anything about it'. The difficulty, he said, was that many people did not realize the kind of book they were taking home, and were then alarmed in case it fell into the hands of other members of the family, particularly children and young people. There was a real danger of corrupting influence from such books. ... As a result of Parliamentary reform and court decisions, publications which, less than a decade ago, would have been regarded by most people as wholly objectionable, were now freely available mass produced commodities. Mr. Luke suggested the Government should take action to arrest this avalanche of degrading filth. He said that if some measure of censorship was considered necessary for the stage and cinema, there was equally a strong case for censorship of the printed word. 'I am no puritanical prude, . . . I spent six years in the Army during the war and I thought nothing really could shock me. But some of the material being published now is sickening. I hope to get support at the Llandudno Conference to pursue this campaign. We are being exorted to Keep Wales Tidy by preventing litter. It is now equally, if not more important to keep Wales clean in another sense by arresting the spread of literature that tends to lower moral standards'." [16]

Support for Luke's campaign from other librarians in Wales was reported within a few days:

"Mr. D. G. Williams, Glamorgan's County Librarian, said last night that Mr. Luke would get support at next week's Conference. 'I am with him all the way when he talks about this pornographic literature and I feel sure that Mr. Luke will win the day at the Conference'. . . . Mr. Williams called for a remodelling of the Obscene Publications Act and unless this happened he did not feel that the Government could act. 'What it needs is a change in legislation. In a time when there is a general laxity in all things these shocking novels make me wonder', he said." [17]

Backing Luke's claim that obscene and pornographic literature was on the increase, T. Elwyn Griffiths, Chairman of the Wales and Monmouthshire Branch of the Library Association, said:

" 'In many cases the sexual matter concerned has no bearing on the actual story itself, as is the case in *Lady Chatterley,* but is *(sic)* of pornographic nature'. Mr. Griffiths, who is County Librarian for Caernarvonshire, said he had often withdrawn books from the shelves after complaints by readers. . . . 'We are not being puritanical, but you can get too much of a good thing and it becomes sickening. The difficulty from the standpoint of a county librarian like myself is to be able to vet these books before they reach the shelves. Adding to our stock some thousands of books in a year, and with the present shortage of qualified staff, it is virtually impossible to do so. We have, therefore, to rely on readers to draw our attention to such books. The policy here is that, having had my attention drawn to a book of that nature, I then vet it personally. Provided there is some virtue in what the reader has said regarding the unsuitability of the book, I then withdraw it from the shelves, but it is still available to readers on request'."[18]

At the 33rd Conference of Library Authorities in Wales and Monmouthshire held in Llandudno on 8th, 9th and 10th June 1966, Luke proposed the following motion:

"That this Conference views with grave concern the alarming increase in publications relying on sex and sadism as their *raison d'etre* and requests the Government as a matter of urgency to control the publication of books of a pornographic nature."

The motion was seconded by Alun Edwards, Librarian of the Cardiganshire Joint Library and an amendment was proposed by E. D. Pollard, and seconded by Alderman G. V. Davies. This effectively altered the motion to read:

"That this Conference views with grave concern the alarming increase in publications having sex and sadism as their *raison d'etre* and urges the Publishers Association to use its influence with its members, on whose good taste and sense of social responsibility public libraries have so far relied, to control the publication of such books."

There was considerable discussion following and Luke accepted the wording of the amendment. By a large majority, delegates approved the Pollard amendment and the Honorary Secretaries were asked to take the necessary action and forward copies to the Wales and Monmouthshire Branch of the Library Association, the Library Association, the Welsh Office, the Press Council, the Publishers Association and all local Authorities in Wales and Monmouthshire.[19]

The resolution was forwarded to the Publishers Association on 20th June and copies sent as directed.[20] Only two replies were received, from the Publishers Association itself and from the Press Council—there was no response from any local authority or the Welsh Office.[21][22] P. C. L. Phelan, Assistant Secretary of the Publishers Association, replied on 22nd July 1966 that he had placed the resolution before his Council at its recent meeting, and the terms of the resolution would be made known to his members. At the same time he pointed out that the P.A. was a trade association and not a disciplinary body, and accordingly exercised no editorial control over what its members published in their books.[23] The Press Council simply acknowledged receipt.[24]

The resolution appeared on the agenda of at least two library authorities, however. The Pontypool *Free Press* reported on the 22nd July 1966:

> "Monmouthshire county libraries sub-committee is concerned about the alarming increase in publications having sex and sadism as the sole reason for their existence. The committee are to recommend Monmouthshire Education Committee to raise the issue with the County Council's Association and urge the Publishers Association to use their influence to control such publications. A county spokesman said: 'Some members were appalled at some of the publications placed in front of children in certain general stores and supermarkets. They felt in some respects that liberty has become licence . . . the library committee can do a lot to inculcate a taste for literature, but it has no direct powers to reduce the flow of trashy publications'."[25]

A week later there was a brief discussion in the Newport Libraries Committee about whether public libraries should exercise censorship, but no decision was arrived at.[26]

The resolution adopted by the 33rd Conference of Library Authorities in Wales and Monmouthshire and the subsequent discussion in certain library authorities, particularly Monmouthshire, gave rise to comment in the House of Commons in a rather indirect way. Under the 10 minute rule, John Cordle, M.P. for Bournemouth East and Christchurch, begged to move:

> "That leave be given to bring in a Bill to prescribe pornographic publications. . . . Only last week I was interested to see that Monmouthshire County Libraries Committee have been concerned with this flood of sex and sadism and is urging the county council's education committee to raise the matter with the County Council's Association, in the hope of gaining support from other local authorities. I believe that they are rightly concerned about the effect upon young children. . . . My Bill would propose to set up a statutory body with power to control and stamp out this unsavoury exploitation. It would be composed of local authority and educational representatives, representatives of the Publishers Association and of the retail trades. It could demand the withdrawal of books and records the covers of which depicted scenes which bore no resemblance to the story in the book or the music on the record. It could also require the withdrawal of books and records the covers or sleeves of which might fulfil this first condition, but which, nevertheless, offended public taste and which might have a depraving or corrupting influence on young people who could not help seeing the cover on public display.
>
> I abhor restrictive and oppressive legislation, but, where the trade refuses to put its own house in order, I believe that Parliament must step in to protect those who cannot protect themselves. . . . If publishers continue to fan the growing unhealthy interest in sex and sadism, then the gusts of lust which sweep our country today can

bring in its wake an indictment which will shame this House, and the British people in years to come."[27]

Cordle felt that while the problem had been confined to Soho and similar areas in big cities it was tolerable, but now that this type of material was being openly displayed everywhere, the problem had become much more urgent. He described the clientele of the Soho type bookshops as 'largely male, middle-aged, and psychologically mixed up'. The Bill was ordered to be printed and its second reading was fixed for 9th December 1966. This was deferred to 20th January 1967, but in fact the Bill did not achieve a second reading at all and there was no further mention of it in Hansard.[28]

In the Denbighshire County Libraries annual report for 1965/1966 Luke repeated his warnings of the previous year. He noted that complaints by readers had never been so numerous.[29] Support for Luke and his crusade came not only from Welsh librarians but also from the Denbighshire Federation of Women's Institutes. At its annual meeting on the 3rd November 1966, Mrs. C. J. Luke, the wife of the County Librarian, supported a resolution from the Llanbedr Dyffryn Clwyd Women's Institute which called on the meeting to deplore the circulation of books with an unpleasant or pornographic content and asking members to assist librarians in the identification and withdrawal of such books:

> " 'Librarians', she said, 'needed all the help they could get to combat the moral danger of such books falling into the hands of innocent young people whose education had not been completed. Publishers,' she added, 'were in business to make money and a few of them were not over scrupulous. There are people who will condemn us for trying to sit (sic) ourselves up as judges, but the public libraries are maintained through the rates and taxes we all pay and the books they contain should appeal to the majority and not to the sadistically minded minority'. Mrs. A. H. Voster . . . who proposed the resolution, said that it was not directed at works of high literary merit nor against serious books which were based on unpleasant subjects. It was aimed, she said, against pornographic passages included in inferior works just to titilate the reader. . . . 'If you see a bood (sic) of the sort I have referred to in your local library it is your duty to point it out to the staff who will read and discuss it and, if they consider it unsuitable, remove it from the shelves. . . . Pornographic and sadistic books had little effect on normal healthy minds but they had an evil effect on the minds of the unbalanced and unhappy'."[30]

In February 1966 the Labour controlled Libraries Sub-Committee of Sheffield was accused of censorship by a Sheffield Liberal Party official because it would not allow the *Liberal News* to be provided in the City's reading rooms. For over five years the Liberal Party had been trying to persuade the Libraries Sub-Committee to include the *Liberal News* among the newspapers available to the public. In 1965 their request was referred to the Libraries Sub-Committee but the display of the paper was not approved. Graham Oxley, the Party's Press Officer, who had personally checked the newspapers available in the Central Library's Reading Room and found papers representing other Political parties said:

> "There is very obviously political bias behind this decision. . . . After all, the reading rooms are there for public use, and many members of the Liberal Party are among the ratepayers who help to provide those facilities. This is not democracy. It is censorship by the Labour-controlled Libraries Committee."[31]

Alderman John Thorpe, Chairman of the Sheffield Libraries Sub-Committee, refuted Oxley's allegations:

> "Mr. Oxley states the Liberal Party as a responsible political party has just as much right as any other to have its literature available for the public to read. . . . In a letter to the City Librarian dated 7th December 1965, the honorary secretary of the Sheffield Liberal Party stated: 'This weekly paper is quite independent and is not published by the Liberal Party. The Committee had considered the periodical entirely on its merits as a newspaper and made their decision accordingly."[32]

On 18th Februray 1966, the Editor of *The Star* commented on Oxley's charge:

> "Sheffield's Labour Group have been accused of political censorship. It is a charge that must be answered, for at this moment it is one of the ugliest charges that can be made. The Labour-controlled Libraries Committee is the target because of its persistent refusal to allow a Liberal newspaper to be made available in the city's reading rooms. . . . In fact, there is probably no censorship involved: the leaders of Sheffield City Council may have their own mysterious ways when it comes to making decisions, and their own mysterious ways of announcing them, but opposition is something they have never run away from. Our own complaint against them has been that rather than shirk facing opposing points of view they have never shown the slightest sign of being influenced by them. That is not censorship. . . . Nevertheless, there is a case to answer."[33]

The Times, 7th February 1967, reported that a new case under the Obscene Publications Act was to be heard in the spring:

> "With expert witnesses queueing to get into the box; it could cause as profound repercusions in the book-selling world as the Chatterley affair. . . . In December (1966) the Marlborough Street Magistrate, Mr. Leo Gradwell, made an order for the forfeiture and destruction of three copies of the book after a private action by Sir Cyril Black, M.P. for Wimbledon. And now the Director of Public Prosecutions has changed his mind about the book. Last year he was sent an advance copy and decided not to prosecute when the book first appeared."[34]

The book was *Last Exit to Brooklyn* by the American author, Hubert Selby, Jnr. published by the firm of Calder and Boyars, Ltd.:

"Mrs. Boyars said it is all a plot by a group of people 'whose mentality is nineteenth century, and who would have attacked Dickens if he had been alive. Zola's *La Terre* was attacked on exactly the same grounds. If these people win, it will mean we will never again live the sort of life we think we ought to live'.

Meanwhile librarians around the country yesterday made their dispositions to deal with the decision to prosecute. In Kensington Central Library the book was still on restricted issue. That means it was not on the public shelves, but was available for 'anyone within reason' who asked for it. . . . Manchester libraries prudently removed the book from their shelves as soon as Sir Cyril Black brought his private prosecution. On principle they buy most novels that are reviewed in the serious newspapers and weeklies, because they assume the books must have some literary merit to get themselves reviewed in such august columns. And down in Sudbury, Suffolk, among the barley and the sugar beet, there was an interminable pause while they searched their files to see if they had the book on their shelves. Eventually it turned out that they did not have it, and that so far they have had few if any requests for it. They expect shortly to be avalanched for requests as a result of the case."[34]

In Sir Cyril Black's own constituency, Wimbledon, the book had already been withdrawn from the Library on the orders of the Chairman of the Merton Library Committee, Councillor Mrs. I. A. Derriman. This order was given when it became known that Sir Cyril Black was taking private action against the book:

"*Last Exit to Brooklyn* has never been on the open shelves at the Merton libraries but has been available to borrowers on application. It has been withdrawn from circulation pending the result of the Bow Street action. The responsibility for this decision is entirely mine as chairman of the libraries committee. A library authority has discretion in the selection of books at all times and it seemed wise to withdraw this one until the present case is decided."[35]

At the Central Criminal Court on the 2nd November 1967, Calder and Boyars Ltd., was found guilty under Section 2 of the Obscene Publications Act, 1959, of publishing an obscene article and was fined £100, plus costs.[36] The following day the *Birmingham Evening Mail* reported that:

"Birmingham Public Libraries were today urgently calling in copies of a book about violence, sex and drug-taking which were still out on loan to readers. . . . Immediately after the judgement, Alderman A. Beaumont Dark, Chairman of Birmingham Libraries Committee, . . . withdrew from circulation all other copies—about 30—in the libraries. . . . Alderman Beaumont Dark said: 'We bought this book, quite properly, as it was looked upon as a work of some literary merit. But because of its nature, it was not on the general shelves, because we did not want it to get into impressionable hands. It was available on demand to people over 18. Immediately the judgement was known, I asked for all copies to be placed under the librarian's control and for them to be no longer issued'. . . . Alderman Beaumont Dark said he read the book before it went out to the city libraries. 'I found it unpleasant and disturbing but the fact is that life is sometimes unpleasant and disturbing. I do not think the author intended to write a pornographic book and I think it is of some literary merit. But we are not censors—nor do we set ourselves up as such. We are obeying the law's decision. If the book continued to be on issue, I and the Committee could be prosecuted for publishing obscene material and sent to prison. None of us want that.''[37]

On 31st August 1968, however, the Court of Appeal allowed with costs, the appeal of Calder and Boyars, Ltd., against its conviction in November 1967, for publishing 'an obscene article' in the novel *Last Exit to Brooklyn*.[38] The book was thus no longer banned and appeared again in the bookshops. Many librarians, knowing that an appeal was in the offing, had not discarded their copies but had held them in reserve until the final judgement was known. The appeal having been allowed, librarians simply put their copies back into circulation.

In April 1966 the Government of Northern Ireland issued *The Public Library Service in Northern Ireland*,[39] the report of a committee under the chairmanship of Dr. J. S. Hawnt, which had examined the state of public library provision in the province. This report, usually known as the Hawnt Report, dealt specifically with the subject of offensive books—unlike the Roberts Report on libraries in England and Wales[40] and earlier reports on libraries in various parts of the United Kingdom. Section XII, paragraph 78 stated:

> "*Offensive books.* We have had representations made to us regarding the number of offensive and obscene books of no literary merit now being published, and we commend the efforts of librarians and committees to spend public money with discretion and to restrict the circulation of such books. These books may be condemned by due process of law."[41]

The Hawnt Report was debated in the Senate of the Northern Ireland Parliament on Tuesday 11th October 1966, when Dr. P. F. McGill begged to move that the report be taken into consideration. During a considerable speech he spent some time on Paragraph 78.

> "I say that here is a subject on which the Committee might well have expanded much more than it has done. . . . Again, I speak on this matter . . . with some knowledge when I mention that I have seen in public libraries books to which I have had to draw the attention of the librarian in charge. Need I say that my approach was always received with interest and was immediately acted upon? All I said was:

'I do not consider this a book that ought to be in this library for young people. Will you please have it referred to the county librarian', and the book vanished forthwith; I do not know what action was afterwards taken. I think it is wrong that members of the public using a library which young people are also using should have to come by chance as it were, upon offensive books. . . . The rats which have their being in the sewers of the great cities are cleaner things than the people who write some of the material which is circulating in, I do not say all public libraries but some libraries, public and private. . . . I think that a librarian, and particularly the committee in charge of the library service of an entire county, should exercise an unremitting vigilance and a very keen scrutiny of all titles coming into the library. . . .

Some effort must be made to put an end to this demoralisation of the young and, perhaps, the not so young. . . . An outstanding public service will be done if the public libraries set an example in ridding their shelves of anything which wears the taint of that which it ought not to wear."[42]

Not all the members of the Senate agreed with Dr. McGill, however.

When the Hawnt Report was debated in the Northern Ireland House of Commons on the 8th November, paragraph 78 was first mentioned by Miss S. Murnaghan, member for Queen's University:

"May I now take the opportunity to comment on a statement of policy which was recently made by the city librarian in connection with the supply of pornographic literature in the public library? I should like to endorse Mr. Crawley's statement that he was not going to have pornographic literature appearing on the open shelves in the library. I think even the most liberal among us . . . will agree that a reader should be able to go along, request the literature that he desires and that that can be obtained. I want to take this opportunity to endorse the view of the librarian that pornographic literature or questionable literature should not appear on open shelves just to be picked up at random by people who may be looking for something completely different. There is a vast difference between censorship in putting some forms of literature completely out of court and refusing to deal with them at all and on the other hand regulating the supply in a way which takes into account the possible deterioration of morals in the community. We have to take into account the effect there might be on a young person reading material to which he might not be able to build a resistance . . . ."[43]

Miss Murnaghan was referring to a recent policy statement by the City Librarian of Belfast regarding the supply of pornographic literature in the public library. On the 8th September 1966 Belfast Corporation Libraries Committee announced that it was to tighten its control on 'undesirable books' available in its library system:

"This decision was taken today after the committee heard that many parents were complaining about the availability of sex books on open shelves. The City Librarian, Mr. Ivan (sic. i.e., Ivor) Crawley, said: 'A high percentage of books coming to Belfast's libraries from publishers is salacious filth . . . we are not advocating censorship, but I think the matter should be taken up at national level."[44]

The next day the *Belfast Telegraph* announced that a row was brewing over the decision of Belfast Libraries Committee to tighten its control:

"The Belfast Centre of Irish P.E.N. is to seek a meeting with the city librarian, Mr. Ivan *(sic.)* Crawley, to clarify what the Committee has in mind. Said P.E.N. Chairman, Mr. William Carters: 'We see tremendous danger in any form of censorship, even if it is put forward under the name of selection'.

The Committee decided to keep a closer eye on the books available on the open shelves after Councillor Stephen McKearney had reported many parents had complained to him about the easy access to doubtful sex books at city libraries. As yet, no decision has been taken about what selection procedure will come into operation. Mr. Crawley said: 'It is likely a reading panel will have to be established. I will also have to discuss with my staff the best ways of implemeting the decision of the committee'. It is understood doubtful books will be taken off the open shelves—but that they will still be available to readers on request. Said Mr. Crawley: 'We are not censoring any books. The aim of the committee is to ensure that if anybody is offended by a book then he or she will have gone to a certain amount of trouble to be offended'. . . . Mr. Carter added: 'We recognize the library committee has a duty to the public about what type of books is available, but we are opposed to any form of censorship. We say adults should know what is good for them, rather than be told what is good and what is bad. Standards are constantly changing. What was not acceptable 10 years ago may be acceptable now. Sometimes library committees do not change with public attitude'. . . . Local novelist Mr. Leith is against censorship. He said: 'The Committee's decision is a retrograde step. By making it more difficult to obtain certain books, it is interfering with the rights of the individual. Let us hope the committee keep the public in touch with developments. It is our right to know what selection procedure is being operated'."[45]

These articles generated a certain amount of correspondence in the local newspapers. On the 15th September 1966 the *Belfast Telegraph* published a letter from Philip M. Whiteman, then Deputy Director of the School of Library Studies at Queen's University, Belfast:

"Book selection is a central task of the Librarian. It is an imperfect art and librarians are unfortunately vulnerable, in that while their attempts to observe objective standards may be based on factors like literary quality, authority, and factual accuracy, they are constantly under pressure from those whose judgment of books is based on a subjective view of their supposed good or bad effect on those who may read them. Library committees exist to administer library services, but they do not infrequently take upon themselves the function of the courts of law, as regards books which they consider objectionable. Objectionable to whom? To quote D. H. Lawrence: 'What is pornography to one man is the laughter of genius to another'. By what authority, legal or otherwise, does a public library committee presume to decide what books are unsuitable for reading by adult members of the community?

One can hardly feel happy about the suggestion that 'a proportion of books should be withheld from the open shelves and be available on request only'. This practice already exists in some public libraries, including Belfast. Not only does it restrict the choice of a reader who picks up his books by browsing at the shelves—it also puts the reader requiring a restricted book in the intolerable position of having to ask at the counter for it, in the full knowledge that his request classifies him as one who seeks to delve into the collection of what committee has in effect labelled 'dirty books'. Furthermore, the practice of hiding books away, in fact, draws the attention of those whose interests are in pornography, to the existence of a segregated but accessible gold mine. One of the strongest arguments against all censorship is that it invariably arouses interest, not always a healthy interest, in the publications proscribed.

The real issue is whether a book should be provided at all, and the only proper course for library authorities to take is the one suggested by the Library Association in its policy statement of 1963 . . . ."[46]

Patricia O'Connor of Belfast wrote:

"Editors, publishers and those responsible for the selection of T.V. and radio material scream in agony at the sound of the word 'censor'. I suspect this is a guilty conscience. In any real understanding of the word, all these people are censors. They decide what and how material shall be communicated, and what withheld. Of course, they have to select and reject! I am not arguing. I am not even asking for their qualifications to do the job. But Mr. Crawley has a job to do, too.

What I do argue is that those who ask the question 'Who can we trust to select what we should read or watch?' are ignoring the fact. We are trusting all kinds of people all the time. The question should be: 'Are those we trust showing a sense of responsibility to society as a whole?' It is logical to argue that a society's culture is for the individuals in it to decide separately, and their behaviour an equally personal affair. It is stupid to argue that culture is purely a matter of choice, but that behaviour must be controlled by laws. That impossible demand is responsible for many of our present troubles."[47]

Peter McKeown, of Belfast 14, wrote in a more light-hearted vein.

"You reported the City Librarian, Mr. Crawley, as saying that 'a high percentage of books coming to Belfast's libraries from publishers is salacious filth'. Perhaps this is his entry for the idiotic generalisation of the year competition. May I attempt to stop him taking first prize, though I doubt it is possible to match his masterly use of the banal exaggeration, by saying: 'A high proportion of the City Librarian's statements to the Press is inaccurate, hollow-minded and quaintly phrased rubbish'. . . . Your report also indicates that a remark by Mr. Stephen McKearney, a Libraries Committee member, that many complaints by parents about 'sex books' in libraries was the main reason for the Corporation's decision to tighten control on 'undesirable books'.

How many parents complained? About which books? With what justification? Groucho Marx, asked his views on sex, said: 'I think it's here to stay'. Perhaps Mr. Kearney *(sic)* would agree that Groucho had a point. If so, it follows that in novels purporting to reflect 'life', sex will quite often be written about. This is not only right but inevitable. What is amusing is Mr. McKearney wanting to 'protect' us from it. If people, including young folk, want to read books which treat of sex, surely this is its own justification for letting them, unless perhaps it can be proved that this is harmful. And where is such proof?"[48]

On the 18th September Crawley's own letter to the *Belfast Telegraph* was published.

"I agree that no person should be in favour of censorship. This does not mean that they should favour scatalogical or salacious books, but that they recognise that the means of supressing them, namely censorship, is a far worse evil. Having said this, we must recognise that the printed word is still a powerful way of disseminating ideas and influencing people. If this is so, then we must accept that it can have a baneful as well as a benign influence and therefore reject the naive remark that 'reading salacious books does no harm'.

We must recognise, too, that during the last few years publishers are prepared to accept material they would have rejected previously, and it is difficult not to connect this with the fact that the police lost one or two prosecutions for obscene libel which perhaps should not have been instigated in the first place. This has made them reluctant to bring others—a fact which was noted by some publishers, who immediately published a spate of questionable material which proved immensely popular to sections of the public and lucrative to the publishers. It is not difficult to see the reason why other reputable publishers followed suit. They are in a business to make profits and authors are workmen who like to be paid.

Therefore, I contend that artistic and literary merit is no longer the main reason the book is printed, if indeed it ever was. Far more books than one cares to think about are written in the form they are, and on topics they contain, not because they are valuable social commentaries but because they sell. Now, although censorship is not the answer, someone going into a public library might stand a very good chance of picking a book from the shelves which he might find offensive. Surely the realistic approach is to expect any adult who wants to read these novels to elect to read them, thus ensuring that if a reader does read an unpleasant book he has chosen to do so. By not displaying this material on the public shelves, the system adopted in the Belfast City Libraries is designed to do this. We must get rid of the ideas that readers browse and by chance alight on the right book. This almost never happens. Readers are almost invariably looking for books by specified authors in a special genre."[49]

"Lucian" an anonymous contributor (now known to be John R. Broom, Deputy County Librarian of Caithness)[50] to *S.L.A. News* (the official journal of the Scottish Library Association) August-September 1966, attacked two librarians and their systems in his column "Ex-Libris". The first Librarian he criticised was I. A. Crawley, City

Librarian of Belfast who, "Lucian" stated, was reported as proposing that books of a "doubtful" character should no longer be catalogued and should be supplied on request only. Lucian's article continued:

> "There are far too many censors in Holy Ireland already without a leading librarian adding himself to their number. . . . I regret to say that the situation in the capital of unholy Scotland is not much better. In the Central Fiction Department of Edinburgh Public Libraries 'doubtful' works, though catalogued, are forthwith relegated to the 'Annexe', which is actually a small cubicle adjacent to the Department. . . . The other day I wanted to read Alan Sharp's widely praised novel *Green Tree in Gedde.* The assistant, having searched for it in the aforementioned annexe, returned to report it was on loan. When I asked her to reserve it for me, she replied that this could not be done as it was 'under two years old'. It follows that the only way a reader at Edinburgh's Central can obtain a recent novel which has been consigned to the annexe is to ask personally for it on every visit. What possible defence can be offered of this deplorable policy."[51]

The *Scottish Daily Express* asked the City Librarian C. S. Minto about this issue. He replied:

> "I don't make comments on anonymous articles. The thing is inaccurate. And if he wants information he can ask for it."[52]

The next report on the matter came almost a year later from *The Glasgow Herald,* 10th August 1967.

> "Some bookshops in Edinburgh are sold out of copies of the prize winning Scottish novel *A Green Tree in Gedde* which is banned from the open shelves in Edinburgh Central Library. . . . Copies of the novel are kept by Edinburgh Central Library in its fiction annexe from which it can be borrowed on demand. Mr. C. S. Minto, Edinburgh city librarian, said yesterday there had been complaints about the book and they considered it better to make it available only to readers who particularly asked for it. This seemed to cause no great hardship."[53]

The Edinburgh Public Libraries and Museums Committee, at its meeting on 16th November 1967 had before it:

> "A motion by Councillor Fox regarding the preparation by the City Librarian and Curator of a report giving the history and background of the reasons for placing certain books in an annexe and not on the open shelves of the library.
>
>   The report submitted by the City Librarian and Curator indicated that since the introduction of the open-access system, Libraries generally had adopted the 'annexe' as an instrument of administration. It had always been recognized that all libraries would require to have the facility of making some books available only on request. The main reason for this was the protection of stock from theft, defacement or mutilation. The annexe was also used for books which were only used occasionally and for extra copies of books subject to seasonal or other fluctuation of demand. The annexe was also used for books which gave offence to

numbers of the library's users. .... So far as fiction was concerned the annexe included novels which had been proceeded against in the Courts but not banned, as well as novels of a 'strong meat' character. There were also included novels which had been accepted on the basis of favourable review of literary merit but which might later be complained about by the public. The placing of these books in the annexe allowed them to continue to be available on request. In many cases consignment to the annexe shelves was the only means of ensuring that books of this type remained available.

The Libraries Sub-Committee, on the casting vote of the Convener, had recommended that no alteration be made in the existing arrangements. At this meeting Councillor McLaughlin, seconded by Dr. Inglis, moved approval of the Sub-Committee's recommendation that no alteration be made in the existing arrangements.

Councillor Fox, seconded by Councillor Irvine, moved, as an amendment, that in future non-fiction works be 'annexed' only for reasons of possible theft, defacement or mutilation, or that they were only occasionally used books and, in the case of works of fiction, no book should be 'annexed' because it had been the object of subjective criticism by members of the public.

On a division the motion (that recommended that no alteration be made in the existing arrangements) was carried by six votes to five and the Committee resolved accordingly.[54]

Councillor Fox's amendment was thus defeated. At the meeting Dr. W. B. Inglis said:

"Edinburgh's public libraries had never been puritanical. They had given their readers the widest possible range of choice. Moving the motion for the retention of 'annexing' books about which complaints are received, the chairman of the committee, Councillor Robert McLaughlin, said the last thing the Committee wanted to do was to head for censorship, but the system was good and had operated well in the past."[55]

John R. Broom ("Lucian") wrote to *The Scotsman* a week later:

"The Edinburgh City Librarian is incorrect when he states in his report to the Libraries and Museums Committee that 'since the introduction of the open access system, libraries generally have adopted the annexe as a system of administration', nor has it 'always been recognised that all libraries would require to have the facility of making some books available only on request'. On the contrary, as a former librarian myself, I can say with confidence the vast majority of British librarians are strongly opposed to any attempts to restrict the availability of books on moral grounds. Even among the few library systems which do still operate some form of censorship, I doubt very much if any have such a formidable list of annexed titles as Edinburgh."[56]

Broom then went on to list a number of titles in the annexe including Radclyffe Hall's *The Well of Loneliness*.

"Certainly Edinburgh must surely enjoy the unenviable distinction of being the only library in the world which continues to keep the last-named celebrated classic under lock and key. And yet, we have Dr. W. B. Inglis claiming that 'Edinburgh Public Libraries have never been puritanical!' Councillor Robert McLaughlin's statement that 'the system is good and has worked well in the past' is ludicrous. Since a book cannot be reserved in Edinburgh until it is two years old, it follows that borrowers wishing to read a new novel which has been annexed must ask for it personally on every visit on the off-chance that it will be in. Is this really Councillor McLaughlin's conception of a good, efficient working system? . . . It is to be hoped that the town council will revise the library committee's regretable decision to continue the present, deplorable policy which is bringing the library profession in general, and Edinburgh in particular, into such ridicule and contempt."

On 7th December the report of the Edinburgh Public Libraries and Museums Committee was submitted to Council. Once again Councillor Fox moved his amendment to the Committee's resolution, but:

"The Corporation decided by a majority tonight to continue to allow the city librarian to decide which works of fiction should not be on the open shelves . . . Councillor Fox's move was defeated by 36 votes to 19."[57]

In his letter to the author on the 23rd November 1971, J. W. Cockburn, City Librarian and Curator of Edinburgh, wrote:

"The policy with regard to fiction is probably more enlightened now than it was in 1967, and it is becoming noticeable as the years pass that the books which were regarded as 'advanced' then are often looked on as quite innocuous today. Certain fiction books, however, are still annexed, e.g. *Ulysses* (because it is a recommended reader at the University and copies in the past have disappeared from the open shelves). When readers complain about certain novels which we feel ought not to be withdrawn from the open shelves, we quote to them the statement on censorship published in the Annual Report of 1963 published by the Library Association. We find this most useful."[58]

J. Alan Howe, the present City Librarian of Edinburgh, outlined the current situation in Edinburgh Public Libraries in his letter of 9th January 1975.[59] Referring to the Minute of 1967 he wrote:

"In fairness to Edinburgh, I think I should point out that the general liberalising of public attitudes since that date has permitted us in fact to adhere to the spirit of the defeated amendment . . . . Subjective complaints from members of the public are dealt with politely but firmly and in the case of fiction, all titles in stock are now displayed on the open shelves."

Mr. Dennis Knight, a solicitor's clerk and a witness at a Brighton court case told the Magistrates that books seized by police from a

Brighton book shop and ruled to be obscene were available on the shelves of the Brighton Public Library.[60] This was no isolated occurrence, similar evidence having been given in a number of other cases, in which police had seized material from local book shops, which had then been declared obscene by local Magistrates. Such cases had occurred in Manchester; in Birmingham when *The Carpet Baggers* was ruled obscene and in Swindon when *The Decameron* was condemned. After the Brighton Magistrates ruled that the books were obscene, the *Brighton Gazette* of 10 November 1967, asked:

> "Mr. Clifford Musgrave, Director of the Town's Public Library, asked . . . whether the four books adjudged obscene which were available at Church Street would be withdrawn for reconsideration. He said he would have to take advice and, looking at the list of titles, added: 'None of these mean anything to me'."[61]

J. N. Allen, Chief Librarian of Brighton Public Libraries in 1971 wrote:

> "Mr. Musgrave saved the situation by deploying a masterly inactivity. Nothing more was said and nothing else happened."[62]

Much the same thing happened in several other cases, though in Birmingham, the local Magistrates ruling was openly challenged by the Libraries Committee.

Pressure comes in different forms. In Bournemouth, two elderly ladies were reported to be compiling a 'hot list' to send to the Librarian in a bid to get the 'bad' books banned:

> "Two out of every three books they borrow seem to upset elderly Winifred Tilley and her sister Flora. . . . Grey haired Winifred said last night: 'We are great readers—you might call us book-worms—but its upsetting to read these library books. You keep coming across swear words that were once considered unprintable, and detailed sex scenes. We are both Congregationalists and we find this all so shocking'."[63]

Pressure of a different character came from the Scientology movement, after the Minister of Health, Mr. Kenneth Robinson described Scientology as a 'hollow cult who thrive on ignorance'.

> "A circular letter signed by Mr. Mark Jones, public secretary of the cult's London branch, asks members: 'Please visit your local library this week and request books and information on Scientology. You can ask for books you already have and gain some new insights from re-reading them, or ask for the books you don't have'. . . . A Ministry spokesman said yesterday: 'It is, of course, for the librarians to decide which books they should stock, although they might like to bear in mind the Minister's comments in March last year, when he told the House of Commons that the activities of this organization were potentially harmful. . . . The letter is also to

be discussed on Friday by the Association of London Chief Librarians. Their former secretary, Mr. William Maidment, chief librarian of Camden, said: 'In our library at Hampstead we have a number of Scientology books because we specialize in psychology. I will suggest to the other London librarians that if there is a sudden demand for these books, they should borrow ours rather than purchase copies for themselves'. Mr. D. D. Haslam, deputy secretary of the Library Association, added: 'Libraries in this country do not discriminate against race, religion or beliefs as far as the books they stock are concerned. But all librarians are on the watch for pressure groups who might try to create a fake demand for certain books'."[64]

The *Wiltshire Gazette and Herald* for 22nd August 1968, cited another attempt to pressurize librarians into banning a book. On this occasion the subject of the book was one which did not fall into any of the categories which commonly attract the attention of would-be censors:

"The controversial book, *The Natural Method of Dog Training,* which the RSPCA wants banned, has been withdrawn from Swindon's libraries 'for consideration', the assistant borough librarian, Mr. T. McNeil, said on Saturday. But it will still be available to branch libraries in the rest of Wiltshire, Gloucestershire and Berkshire.

The RSPCA objects in particular to certain passages in the chapter entitled Breaking Bad Habits in which the author, an American vet, advocates the use of a rat trap to discourage dogs from digging and a board studded with nails to keep them off easy chairs. 'We believe this kind of thing is not the right way to treat a dog', said an RSPCA man. 'We are suggesting to our branches that they might like to put these points to librarians. There's nothing legal we can do'.

The Wiltshire County Librarian, F. Hallworth declined to comment and the Gloucestershire County Librarian Miss E. Markwick, said: 'It hasn't come to our notice at all'. Berkshire County Council said: 'We've had the book since it's been published and we've never had any complaints. I should think our copies are almost worn out'."[65]

T. S. McNeil, who later became Chief Librarian of Swindon, wrote:

"If I remember rightly the phrase 'for consideration' was simply used to give my then Chief . . . the opportunity of examining the book and deciding on a suitable course of action. In the event, it was decided to continue issuing the book with the insertion of a notice, drawing attention to the fact that the RSPCA had criticised as cruel certain of the methods recommended in the book. In fact we still have a copy of the book in stock."[66]

Tim Hurst, of the *Havering Recorder,* interviewed Gordon Humby the Chief Librarian of Havering, on the subject of censorship and book selection after he had been surprised to find books by William

Burroughs and Jean Genet on the open shelves of Hornchurch Branch Library.

> "Were Havering's libraries so untrammeled by censorship? Mr. Humby was more explicit when he said: 'Who the hell am I to tell people what they may or may not read? Things have changed since Lady Chatterley. As a nation we demand a wider range of reading material. . . . Censorship as such does not exist in Havering's libraries. In recommending books for places on the shelves, I take into account the money I have available, potential public demand, and, in some cases, the authoritative opinion of book critics. I want to give the reader the best possible service. No librarian should see himself as a censor. It must be remembered that a librarian is a servant of his Council'.
>
> Does the library attract complaints about its wide book selection? 'We do, but not very often . . .'. About six times a year Mr. Humby finds it necessary to discuss a particular book with the chairman of his committee—before he feels satisfied in making a direct recommendation for its inclusion.
>
> Personally, I agree with Mr. Humby. Who has the right to dictate another's literary taste? But I shall continue to be surprised at the inclusion of some modern novels on our library shelves. I shall be surprised, because I was beginning to believe that as a nation we were strangling ourselves by the censorship of free expression."[67]

While some libraries have a system which identifies books which might give offence or should not be loaned to younger readers, the *Brighton and Hove Herald* of 19th September 1969 reported that J. N. Allen, then Chief Librarian of Brighton, had evolved a fore-warning system which placed the onus fairly and squarely on the reader.

John Allen's staff previously had had instructions to refer all controversial books regardless of subject matter and any complaints they generated, directly to him. All complaints were treated with respect, although with an awareness that books which offended some readers might well be of interest to others. The fore-warning system was prompted after a series of complaints about a new novel by a woman author, which in the opinion of one ninety-year-old reader, would certainly undermine the morals of the young. This reader was quoted as saying: "It's not fair that nice young things should be given the opportunity to read such filth."[68]

The fore-warning system, using a warning stamp, occurred to John Allen:

> "Whilst watching a television programme during the introduction of which a notice was flashed on the screen warning intending viewers that there may be passages disturbing to them. I thought this would be an excellent idea for translating into the world of books and chose a small stamp warning readers that there are some passages in the book which may be disturbing.

BRIGHTON PUBLIC LIBRARIES

This book must be returned on or before the last date stamped
below to avoid fines. If not reserved, it may be renewed once by post
or telephone, when the book number, your reader's number and the
last date stamped should be given. No fines are charged for overdue
books borrowed by children from the Children's Departments

Central Library   **Telephone: Brighton 62801**

> READERS ARE WARNED THAT THERE
> ARE SOME PASSAGES IN THIS BOOK
> WHICH MAY BE DISTURBING,

The stamp is placed on or adjacent to the date label of any book that I think might
cause offence to those unaware of the nature of the book. These books are now all
placed on the open shelves and of course have no exterior markings. I believe that
the idea has been successful as since the introduction of the scheme I have received
no complaints at all concerning books so stamped. Obviously if people take them
out they do so in the full knowledge of what they are likely to receive and they are
then disarmed in advance."[69]

The system has proved so effective that John Allen continues to use it
in the reorganised East Sussex County Libraries, of which he is now
County Librarian, following the local government reorganisation.[70]

1. Libraries to keep banned books. *The Times,* 2nd February 1965
2. No censorship. *Liaison,* March 1965. p.20
3. Parliamentary Debates, Commons. 1964-65, vol. 706, col. 180
4. Book ban ignored. *The Daily Telegraph,* 11th May 1965
5. Letter from A. J. Fox, Staff and Training Officer, Birmingham Public Libraries to A. H. Thompson, 26th May 1972. (Unpublished). *See also* citation 9 below
6. Library ban on Daily Worker. *Birmingham Planet,* 4th March 1965
7. X Bookmark for Birmingham. *British Books,* vol. 178, no. 4917, April 1965
8. Birmingham City Librarian's Minutes, no. 27, 1930. (Internal circulation—held by Birmingham Public Libraries.)
9. Letter from A. J. Fox, Staff and Training Officer, Birmingham Public Libraries to the author, 26th May 1972. (Unpublished)
10. Letter from a reader to D. I. Colley, City Librarian of Manchester, 20th May 1965. (Unpublished, held by Manchester Public Libraries.)

11. Letter from D. I. Colley, City Librarian of Manchester to the reader, 21st May 1965. (Unpublished, held by Manchester Public Libraries.)
12. Public reacting about books that go over mark. *Yorkshire Post,* 2nd September 1965
13. West Riding County Library. *Annual Report,* 1964-65. pp.12-13
14. Censor to end filth in books. *Liverpool Daily Post,* 15th October 1965
15. Denbighshire County Council: Annual Report of the County Librarian. 1964-65
16. Moss, Cliff. Shocked and disgusted. *Liverpool Daily Post,* 1st June 1966
17. Obscene books 'shock, disgust' Welsh Librarians. *South Wales Echo,* 3rd June 1966
18. New attack on sex in books. *Liverpool Daily Post,* 4th June 1966
19. Rees, Lesile M., editor. Report of the proceedings of the thirty-third conference of Library Authorities in Wales and Monmouthshire . . . on . . . 8th, 9th and 10th June 1966. (1967)
20. Letter from the Honorary Secretaries, the Library Association, Wales and Monmouthshire Branch, to The Publishers Association, 20th June 1966. (Unpublished, held by G. Thomas, Honorary Secretary of the Welsh Library Association).
21. Letter from Geoffrey Thomas, Honorary Secretary, Welsh Library Association to the author, 27th June 1972. (Unpublished)
22. Letter from the author to Geoffrey Thomas, 26th July 1972. (Unpublished)
23. Letter from P. C. L. Phelan, Assistant Secretary, The Publishers Association to the Honorary Secretaries, The Library Association, Wales and Monmouthshire Branch, 22nd July 1966. (Unpublished, held by G. Thomas. See citation 20 above.)
24. Letter from Col. W. C. Clissitt, Secretary, The Press Council, to the Honorary Secretaries, The Library Association, Wales and Monmouthshire Branch, 4th July 1966. (Unpublished, held by G. Thomas. See citation 20 above.)
25. Books that pander to sex, sadism. (Pontypool) *Free Press,* 22nd July 1966
26. Censorship in public libraries. *South Wales Argus,* 27th July 1966
27. Parliamentary Debates, Commons. 1966-67, vol. 732, cols. 1721-1724
28. Parliamentary Papers (House of Commons and Command). Session 18th April 1966-27th October 1967. vol. VI. p.397
29. Denbighshire County Council: Annual Report of the County Librarian. 1965-1966
30. W.I. attack pornography. *Liverpool Daily Post,* 4th November 1966
31. Censorship in library. *The Star,* 18th February 1966
32. Library 'censor' charge denied. *The Star,* 17th February 1966
33. Editorial. *The Star,* 18th February 1966
34. Enter the experts from *Last Exit. The Times,* 7th February 1967
35. *Last Exit* from Wimbledon Library. *Wimbledon News,* 26th August 1966
36. *Last Exit* conviction quashed. *Bookseller,* 3rd August 1968. p.358
37. Urgent call for return of *Last Exit to Brooklyn. Birmingham Evening Mail,* 24th November 1967
38. *Op. cit.* See note 36
39. Northern Ireland: The public library Service in Northern Ireland. Cmd. 494. 1966
40. Ministry of Education. The structure of the public library service in England and Wales. Cmnd. 660. 1959
41. *Op. cit.* See note 39

42. Parliament of Northern Ireland. Parliamentary Debates, Senate. vol. 49, no. 32. 11th October 1966. Cols. 1239-1241, 1249
43. Parliament of Northern Ireland. Parliamentary Debates, Commons. Vol. 64, no. 30. 8th November 1966. Cols. 2222-2224, 2233-2234
44. Belfast is to 'clean-up' its bookshelves. *Belfast Telegraph,* 8th September 1966
45. City Library 'clean-up' a danger, says PEN. *Belfast Telegraph,* 9th September 1966
46. Whiteman, Philip M. Libraries should not act as 'Courts of Law'. *Belfast Telegraph,* 15th September 1966
47. O'Connor, Patricia. Sense and censors. *Belfast Telegraph,* 17th September 1966
48. McKeown, Peter. Books. *Belfast Telegraph,* 17th September 1966
49. Crawley, Ivor A. Realistic approach to books. *Belfast Telegraph,* 18th September 1966
50. Letter from John R. Broom, Depute County Librarian, Caithness County Libraries, to the author, 14th August 1972. (Unpublished)
51. 'Lucian'. Ex Libris. *SLA News,* no. 75, August/September 1966. p.5
52. Bit of a bind at the library. *Scottish Daily Express,* 16th November 1966
53. Sell-out of book banned from library shelves. *Glasgow Herald,* 10th August 1967
54. Edinburgh, Town Council of. Minutes of Meeting of 7th December 1967. pp.204-205
55. "Strong meat" books to remain annexed at public libraries. *The Glasgow Herald,* 17th November 1967
56. Broom, John R. Library censorship. *The Scotsman,* 24th November 1967
57. Libraries to keep books 'annexed'. *The Times,* 8th December 1967
58. Letter from J. W. Cockburn, City Librarian and Curator, Edinburgh Public Libraries, to the author, 23rd November 1971. (Unpublished)
59. Letter from J. Alan Howe, City Librarian of Edinburgh, to the author, 9th January 1975. (Unpublished)
60. 'Obscene' books on public library shelves. *Brighton Gazette,* 10th November 1967
61. *Op. cit.* See note 60
62. Letter from John Allen, Chief Librarian of Brighton, to the author, 25th November 1971. (Unpublished)
63. Books 'hot list' by 2 sisters. *Daily Mirror,* 4th April 1968
64. Chapple, Victor. Cult chiefs launch 'ban for minds' in libraries. *Sun,* 19th June 1968
65. Book condemned by RSPCA withdrawn from libraries. *Wiltshire Gazette and Herald,* 22nd August 1968
66. Letter from T. S. McNeil, Borough Librarian and Curator, Swindon Public Libraries, to the author, 19th November 1971. (Unpublished)
67. Hurst, Tim. Shock facts. *Havering Recorder,* 4th October 1968
68. Library starts warning stamps on books. *Brighton and Hove Herald,* 19th September 1969
69. Letter from John Allen, *Op. cit.* See note 62
70. Letter from John Allen, County Librarian of East Sussex, to the author, 27th November 1974. (Unpublished)

CHAPTER 10

1970–1974

'The silly burghers of Sowerby Bridge', ran the front page headline of the *Sun* on 8th January 1970:

"Your Super Super *Sun* has been banned from the public reading room at—wait for it—Sowerby Bridge, Yorkshire.

Why? Because, apparently, it is the wrong SHAPE to suit the Librarian, Mr. Stanley Robinson. And because, according to the chairman of the Library Committee, Councillor Cecil Grenshaw, it 'places too much emphasis on sex'. . . . The ban was approved by the council after Councillor Grenshaw said: 'The practice of boosting the sex side influenced both the librarian and me. We are getting far too much of these things nowadays', the 78-year-old councillor added. . . . 'The basic reason for not taking the *Sun* is the cost. But I was asked by the librarian whether I thought it carried too much sex and, quite frankly, I had to agree'.

The council also banned the *Daily Mirror* and the *Daily Sketch* so that none of the town's population of 18,700 can read a national tabloid paper in the reading room. The *Sun,* of course, is still only 5d. But librarian Mr. Robinson said: 'Two-and-sixpence a week may not seem very much, but I can put it to good use in my annual budget'.

Mr. Robinson, who actually recommended the ban, explained: 'I showed the Committee six sample copies and they agreed with me that it is not the sort of paper they want. It is rubbish. . . . I received no complaints from the public about the contents of the *Sun*. Also, . . . the shape of tabloids is wrong. They will not fit on the special rods and they can easily be stolen'.

But they're not all silly burghers in Sowerby Bridge. Councillor Austin Benbow, a senior magistrate said: 'We should not have done this. People get pushed around too much by people in authority. The *Sun* is not my cup of tea, but my wife buys it'. Labour Councillor Leslie Godfrey said: 'I am disappointed. The paper is very forthright'."[1]

Next day, the *Sun* devoted almost three pages to the story, including two thirds of the front page. Under an unflattering photograph of

Stanley Robinson, the Librarian, the *Sun* reported that the paper might soon be back in the public library.

> "Yesterday morning two *Sun* readers marched into the library and offered to pay for the paper every day until the Council thinks it can raise the cash. John McCleery, . . . and Jim McPartling . . . made their offer to the man who first recommended the ban—Mr. Stanley Robinson, 59, and Sowerby Bridge's head book man for the past 39 years. And Mr. Robinson has decided to change his mind about the *Sun*. 'I will recommend to the next Libraries Committee meeting that we accept their offer'. . . . Some Councillors still think they should dictate what the people of Sowerby Bridge should read. Youngest of them all, 25-year-old Mrs. Wendy Sutcliffe, said: 'The Library should stock only *The Times, Financial Times* and *Yorkshire Post*. It is not up to the library to provide light reading'. Another Libraries Committee member, Councillor Frank Ogden, commented: 'We are only a small town. We can't afford all the papers'."[2]

Rigby's cartoon[3] reproduced on p. 185 sums the situation up from the *Sun's* point of view.

Robinson presented his point of view in the *Assistant Librarian,* March 1970.

> "Below is the statement which I issued to the *Sun* newspaper, among others, on 8th January, when we were invaded by a platoon of journalists from the *Sun,* including their star reporter, specially flown in from the heart of Berlin. 'For economic reasons we take neither the *Mirror* nor the *Sketch,* so it seemed logical when the *Sun* went tabloid, to drop it and save £6.10s. a year to offset the anticipated increase in the price of most newspapers. This seems to me to be good house-keeping and that's about all there is to it, so far as I am concerned. I would hardly think this is of such world shattering importance as to hit the front page of any national newspaper'.
>
> This little episode, as you will know, resulted in the *Sun* of 9th January devoting 243½ column inches to the subject. I have the greatest respect for the Editor of this newspaper. . . . I watch with interest his battle for circulation with his competitors. I had a quiet chuckle over Rigby's cartoon. He was not to know that we did away with the old-fashioned newspaper reading slopes 20 years ago, and I must mildly protest about the cob-webs. We have a first rate cleaner, and, as one customer put it the other day to one of our Councillors, this is the brightest place in Sowerby Bridge.
>
> I agree entirely with you . . . that this is the wrong sort of publicity, but can assure you that locally at any rate our image has not been tarnished but shines even more brightly."[4]

The *Daily Mirror* of 13th February 1970, reported a curious case which belongs in that miscellaneous category, which includes Wodehouse, Blyton and *The natural method of dog training:*

> "Billy Bunter, that caddish heavyweight character of schoolboy fiction, has been banished from a library's open shelves. The famous bun-stuffing adventures of the fat boy of Greyfriars School are considered unfair to tubby children. And in future

"It IS the wrong shape! It IS sexy! Nobody wants that sort of ——— YOU'RE NOT LISTENING!!" Cartoon by Rigby in the Sun, *9th January 1970*

the Bunter books will be issued only on demand at the children's section of the public library at Ipswich, Suffolk.

The decision was taken by the chief librarian, 62-year-old Miss Dorothy White. She said yesterday: 'I feel the Bunter stories are unfair to fat children. Other children tend to associate classmates with Bunter and to poke fun at them'. Miss White said that as a school girl she had read the Bessie Bunter stories about Billy's sister. 'I well remember the torment 'fatties' were subjected to . . . . Mrs. Doreen Ellis, librarian in charge of the children's section, said: 'The Bunter-style humour is not popular with children today'." [5]

Smith's *Trade News* of 21st February put the matter in perspective:

"The decision of the Ipswich Chief Librarian to take the five Billy Bunter books off the shelves of her children's library gave the national press the excuse for outcries of mock outrage. The complaints could only have been seriously justified if the books had really been banned, as all the papers said. What happened was that the Chief Librarian, Miss Dorothy White, merely had them moved. They are still as available to children (and adults) as they were before the furore, but only on demand.

According to Mrs. Doreen Ellis . . . the Bunter books go out about once a month in Ipswich. Two of them were out at the time when the stories appeared in the Press. Mrs. Ellis said half the borrowers of the books were children.

The Guardian's reporter Terry Coleman was one of the Pressmen who spoke to Miss White. She told him that she thought their style was that of 70 years ago. Was that why she had taken them from the open shelves? Coleman asked. They had *never* been on display, Miss White said. Why had she bought them in the first place, if she didn't think they were ideal children's reading? 'I wouldn't buy them normally, but we got them at the request of an elderly gentleman who read them as a boy and wanted to renew his acquaintance', she explained to Coleman." [6]

The episode gave rise to correspondence in the *Assistant Librarian,* March 1970. P. R. O. Sellers, of the Charminster Branch Library in Bournemouth, wrote:

"Journalists are quick to seize on any triviality which will show others in an unfavourable light. May I suggest that librarians do not offer themselves as a sitting target? If librarians take the notion into their heads that the works of, say, Enid Blyton, or the Billy Bunter books, are somehow corrupting their young readers, then for goodness sake let them simply cease buying these books, and allow their remaining copies to fade quietly away in the normal process of wearing out.

To make a great fanfare and performance of 'banning' them, merely makes the librarians concerned look ridiculous, and is totally unnecessary. After all, we have the cast-iron excuse that we can't possibly stock everything, and that part of our job is to make a selection from the books available. Do we talk of 'banning' every book that we don't happen to select for our stock?" [7]

Jack Dove, Borough Librarian of Hove, was moved to compose a poem on the topic:

        Yaroo!
So Billy Bunter's banished, now,
I really wonder why?
Is it because he's corpulent
Or Ipswich very shy?
I wonder where the sex books are
For there are very many.
Perhaps they too are hid away
Or Ipswich hasn't any!

A reporter of the Huddersfield *Daily Examiner* wrote in March:

"I've been investigating the reasons for the 'wooden books' in Huddersfield
Library. As users of the Library will know, certain types of book do not appear on
the shelves. Instead of the books there are wooden slabs giving the name of the
book and author, with instruction that the book may be obtained by presenting the
wood at the counter. Was there, I wondered, some sort of censorship being
operated at the Library?

I spoke to Mr. Stanley T. Dibnah, the Chief Librarian and Curator, who told me:
'The wood is merely one of three or four methods we have of informing readers of
the existence of books which are not displayed on the public shelves. They are not
displayed for a variety of reasons'. The first three reasons he gave were that there
was not enough room to display all the books the library possesses; books which are
worn, but worth keeping, are not put on public shelves and are available on request;
and books which are likely to be stolen are kept off public shelves but are available
on request. 'Finally . . . a very small number whose free circulation would probably
cause concern to a section of the public are available on request. It is not
censorship; it is restricted circulation. The books which we might be accused of
censoring are those that are likely to be stolen, and it is more from the fear of loss
that we are restricting circulation than on the grounds of defining the accepted
standard of decency, which is an impossible thing to fix. If I get equal criticism from
both extremes I feel I am achieving the correct standard for the people I'm serving.
The restricted circulation is a safeguard against those who are obviously asking for a
book for the wrong reason'.

I asked him if it were not embarrassing for people to go through the process of
striding about with a piece of wood and then handing it over at the counter. He told
me: 'There can be no embarrassment because no word need be exchanged at the
counter. Anyway the chances are that it will be a motor manual rather than a book
which might cause embarrassment—such as a book on morality'."[9]

In January 1971 a book list entitled *Sex and Marriage,* was issued by
Hertfordshire County Libraries[10] and available to readers throughout
the county. This list was the subject of a complaint by a member of the
public to the Chairman of the Hertfordshire County Libraries
Committee, Mrs. Winefride Walshe:

"An illustrated leaflet available across the counter at public libraries throughout

Sex and marriage

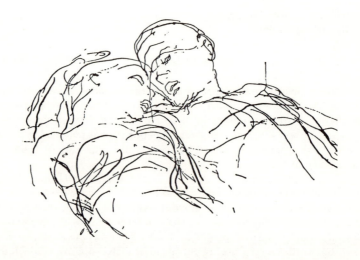

HERTFORDSHIRE COUNTY LIBRARY

Booklist issued by Hertfordshire County Libraries in 1971

Hertfordshire has caused 'raised eye-brows' among some readers. For the books listed in the leaflet deal with sex and marriage. . . . Now, County Councillor Mrs. Winefride Walshe . . . has called for a top-level investigation. She knew nothing of the books or the leaflet. . . . In it, a short description of the contents of each book is given, including sex manuals for 'younger people'. . . . Mrs. Walshe says: 'I am very grateful that this has been brought to my notice. I was not aware of this booklet and I can understand why some people would be upset. I have no objection to some of these books dealing with marriage guidance and the like being on the shelves, but there are others which, from my own Christian point of view, I disapprove of'. She explained that the choice of books to go on the library shelves was made by a 'high-powered' selection committee comprising of librarians and assistant librarians. 'The people on the selection committee are highly qualified and very experienced and we on the library committee do not feel qualified ourselves to make these choices'."[11]

Mrs. Walshe was also quoted as saying:

" 'I think the illustrations are rather unnecessary, and I would have preferred a different title. Some of the books are a bit flippant, and most seem to be written from a materialistic and hedonistic point of view. I would have preferred books by Christian writers. I was very distressed and terribly surprised that the county library staff should publish this type of booklet'.

But today Hitchin's Vicar, the Rev. Roland Meredith, said he had seen the leaflet at Hitchin Library. 'I don't think I would get upset about it . . . I trust the county officers who do this kind of selection and I see nothing to object to. How does Mrs. Walshe know that the writers are not Christian? Christians don't all have 'Reverend' in front of their name and put 'Christian' in brackets after them'.

The County Librarian Miss Lorna Paulin, said: 'The leaflet is not in any way salacious or titillating. It would be quite wrong of us to put out anything like that. I have had no complaints of any kind about the leaflet'." [12]

On 5th February, the *Hertfordshire Mercury* included two references to the matter.

"For the blue-coloured pamphlet is causing so much offence that a top level inquiry has been called for. . . . Mrs. Winefride Walshe—she is demanding the inquiry—told the *Mercury* this week that the pamphlets disturbed her and were causing concern to other members of the county council. The sex and marriage pamphlets could spark off a big storm at County Hall as chief librarians are being blamed for the leaflets appearing in public libraries . . . Mrs. Walshe . . . said: 'The pamphlets were not approved by us. I did not know they even existed until the weekend'." [13]

A letter from J. B. and V. Box of Hertford read:

"From your headline 'Blue Pamphlet on Sex' . . . one would imagine that the county librarians of Hertfordshire were going to compete with Soho and Charing Cross Road for sordid and erotic literature. Instead the books, at least the ones that we have read, contain information on sexual techniques, manners and a host of other marriage problems, presented in the style of a text-book. These books can do nothing but good to many couples and countless marriages would be brightened and even saved if couples recognised that there is more to marriage than regular meals and missionary views on sex.

Surely the public library is the proper place for such information and one would hope that those responsible for the selection of literature would be enlightened enough to make this available to all, rather than condemn those who cannot afford to buy the books to a life of ignorance and misguided views on sex." [14]

The *Welwyn Times* reported:

"The issuing of a booklist entitled *Sex and Marriage* . . . is to be the subject of an investigation by a special sub-committee of the Herts County Council library committee. . . . This week County Councillor Mrs. W. M. Walshe said she had been contacted by a number of members of the general public complaining about the booklist. 'I feel that people were startled by the drawing on the front . . . and were surprised by the title of the list. But . . . obviously people who think the booklist is a good thing have not got in touch with me'.

A spokesman for the county library said that the booklist was not being withdrawn from libraries prior to the sub-committee's investigation in March."[15]

The booklist was withdrawn from display in the libraries however, although readers who asked for it were given copies.

"A Councillor criticized the county libraries committee at a meeting of Hertfordshire County Council last week for withdrawing a leaflet produced by the County Librarian, Miss L. Paulin, listing a number of books on sexual relationships. The leaflets were withdrawn recently from public display in libraries after a number of people had complained to the committee. But they can still be obtained on request in libraries. Councillor Donald Richardson said: 'The county librarian made an honest attempt to enable people to look up a particular book they wanted and go to a shelf and take it home. Now they are placed in the embarrassing position of having to ask a librarian for the leaflet. . . . As we are now giving sex education in our schools it is silly to withdraw the leaflet. It denies older people who never had the advantage of sex education an opportunity of getting a proper book on the subject without asking for the leaflet'. The chairman of the library committee . . . said 'the leaflets were withdrawn because the synopses describing some of the books were unhappily worded and could have created an unfortunate impression in some minds'."[16]

The matter received a great deal of attention in the press and phrases such as "many readers and county councillors were shocked"[17] were used, and the Chairman of the County Libraries Committee said: "I have been contacted by quite a number of people . . . several county councillors have also expressed concern."[17] On the other hand John Jones, Deputy County Librarian, confirmed that "not one single complaint had been lodged at any of our libraries."[18]

On 18th February the Luton *Evening Post* reported:

"'An informal meeting of certain members of the library committee has been held on this matter', said the spokesman. 'If any member wishes, the subject will be discussed at the next full county council meeting on 2nd March. A report on the feelings of the informal meeting will be put before the full library committee on 15th March. I cannot say what that report will contain'."[19]

In the *Hertfordshire County Library Information,* March 1971 (the Staff Bulletin), the report of the special sub-committee of the Library Committee was given:

"i. We are right to stock the books concerned.
ii. We are right to provide printed information about them and to display it.

iii. If the list had been different in certain respects, e.g., title, illustrations, some annotations, no one would have been upset.
These views will be reported to the County Library Committee on 15th March . . . ."[20]

The next edition of *Information* (April 1971) recorded the end of the story.

"All's well that ends well. The County Library Committee on the 15th March considered criticisms of our booklist and concluded that they were not justified and so it should be displayed freely. Members expressed their determination not to yield to pressure from a very small minority, and there was a general feeling that there had been a lot of fuss about nothing."[21]

In Aberystwyth, at the Cardiganshire Joint Library Committee meeting on the 8th January 1971:

"Councillor Goronwy ap Griffiths asked how so many obscene novels came to be on the literary *(sic)* shelves. During the past year he had become increasingly aware of the number of these novels which he described as 'obscene rubbish'.
   The County Librarian, (Mr. Alun R. Edwards) replied that it was true that publishers were producing too much obscene literature, but the publishers found that these novels sold very well. Fortunately in Wales, the Welsh books bought by libraries were very good in quality, because they were safe-guarded by the Welsh Books Council. In this respect Welsh libraries were 'pioneers'. Mr. ap Griffiths was asked to retell his views at the next meeting when his opinions would be discussed further."[22]

At the next meeting Councillor ap Griffiths' remarks were discussed and:

"It was decided that the County Librarian . . . exercise his discretionary powers over the quality as well as the quantity of books acquired for the library service. Mr. Edwards would also be reviewing the books already in circulation although he said after the meeting that the number of books that could possibly be considered offensive was 'less than half a dozen'. Any books that were withdrawn would not be removed from the catalogue and would be available on request to those with a serious interest in the subject concerned."[23]

Last Exit to Brooklyn had been reinstated in most public libraries in 1968, but this was not the case in Merton where the whole affair had begun.

"After less than a month on the shelves of Merton Libraries *Last Exit to Brooklyn* has again been withdrawn following a complaint made by a solicitor representing an anonymous 'ratepayer'. The solicitor said that legal action would follow if the book continued to be available to Merton ratepayers. One Merton ratepayer is Alderman Sir Cyril Black, who was responsible for the private prosecution of the book under the Obscene Publications Act in 1966. The book was first withdrawn when Sir Cyril, then Conservative M.P. for Wimbledon, began his prosecution.

Recently, Mr. Roger Musgrave, an advertising copywriter and a Merton ratepayer wrote to the Library and Arts Committee pointing out that since it was two years since the publishers successful appeal it was time to release to the public a book which was already ratepayers' property. He backed up his request with statements he had received from more than a dozen London boroughs. Typical responses from other libraries: 'we have copies freely available' and 'unless a book has incurred penalties under the law of the land no special conditions or restrictions are ever applied'.

Merton Library Committee accepted this view and the book was put on the shelves. But less than a month later, on 28th January, the Town Clerk of Merton, Mr. Sidney Astin, wrote to Mr. Musgrave telling him that after a special meeting of the committee, following a threat of proceedings under the Obscene Publications Act, 1959, the committee resolved to rescind its previous decision. It happened that Mr. Musgrave had the book on loan and he was asked to return it. About a week ago, forty-five Conservative and Independent Councillors voted to banish *Last Exit* once again. Attempts by Labour Councillors to defer this action until the identity of the anonymous complainant was known were overruled."[24]

Interviewed by the *Wimbledon News* in February 1971, after the Council's decision had been announced, Musgrave said:

"He was absolutely astonished to learn that Merton Council had given in to an anonymous threat of legal action.

'It sets a very dangerous precedent', said Mr. Roger Musgrave . . . .' 'It means any anonymous ratepayer who disapproves of a particular book can exercise what is in fact a form of censorship by threatening legal proceedings against the council'. Mr. Musgrave . . . said it was an inexcusable situation. 'It again means that the ratepayers of Merton are being denied a book which they have paid for out of the rates'. He said he was sure that was not the last the council would hear about the book. 'But I have no further comment to make at this stage . . .'.

Mr. Leslie Hunt, the solicitor acting for the ratepayer who threatened to take the council to court if the book was not withdrawn said he had been given 'specific instructions' not to reveal the identity of his client. 'It would only be made known if the matter led to a prosecution. All I can say is he is acting for himself. He is very much a ratepayer of the borough and he has lived near the Town Hall for 30 years'.

Alderman Sir Cyril Black, who took *Last Exit to Brooklyn* to court for obscenity in a private prosecution four years ago and won his case, said he had no idea who was behind the threat of legal action 'But it was clearly a most embarrassing situation for me to be in and I am pleased commonsense prevailed and the book was withdrawn. I don't know what I would have done if the council had decided to keep lending the book—I would have had to have seriously looked at my position with the council'.

Libraries committee chairman Councillor Mrs. Iris Derriman said: 'I am surprised that a resident should take it upon himself to take action against Merton when the book has been available in about 30 London libraries without any trouble'.

When the council agreed to withdraw the book last week six copies were out being read—and 30 people were waiting to get their hands on it."[25]

However, the matter was not to rest there, for by December of the following year a number of changes had taken place in the Merton Council. On the 6th December 1972 the *London Evening Standard* reported that:

"A big row is expected tonight when Labour controlled Merton Council decides whether or not to allow the controversial novel *Last Exit to Brooklyn* back into its libraries . . . . It is a slap in the face for the father of the council, Alderman Sir Cyril Black . . . . 'I will certainly oppose lifting the ban. My attitude towards the book has not changed and I consider it to be obscene . . .' said Sir Cyril. He has the support of Councillor Joseph Watson who was one of two dissenters on the libraries committee: 'It is a filthy book and I don't think that ratepayers should have to pay for it. If people want to read such filth they can buy it themselves'. But libraries committee chairman Councillor Mrs. Vera Bonner said: 'We are not censors, or at least we shouldn't be. We are servants of the public'. Councillor Bill Brian-Smith pointed out: 'I think we should lift the ban on the book. We should not stand in moral judgment'."[26]

At the council meeting that evening thirty-nine members of the council voted to lift the ban with only six voting for its continuance.[27] The book was returned to the shelves and thus ended a unique case of library censorship.

In Wales, as in 1965/66, protests were made about obscene books in libraries.

The *Denbighshire Free Press* reported a Ruthin Rural District Councillor as saying:

"People coming across obscene passages in books on loan from the county library should refer the matter to the County Librarian, Mr. E. R. Luke, and get the books destroyed. The suggestion was made by Councillor Gordon Griffith, of Llanferres, who said he had found several such books in the library service. 'The effect on the young of this sort of thing is far greater than that of smoking', he told Monday's meeting of the council. The point arose after the chairman, Councillor John Stoddard . . . had drawn the attention of the Council to a particular book which he had borrowed from the library. It was an American book about the Vietnamese War, but he asked that the title be not disclosed. 'This book is absolutely obscene. I have read two pages of it and have put it down as not fit to read'. . . . He said he was going to ask the County Librarian to withdraw the book from the library shelves. . . . The County Librarian, Mr. E. R. Luke, told the *Free Press* this week: 'I agree it is an obscene and dirty book and I have withdrawn it from stock. It is not suitable to be on our shelves'. He said he had read enough to justify the complaint after it had been handed in on Tuesday by Councillor Stoddard. The book, he said, was ordered at the special request of a reader in the area and it had been on the shelves for more than 18 months. It had been out eight times without comment until Councillor Stoddard complained. . . . Mr. Luke said that as authors had a greater licence in the use of words, he was constantly getting complaints. He welcomed the suggestion that any member of the public with a complaint about a book should report it at once."[28]

In the *Western Mail* a month later Luke's comments were backed up by the Librarian of Bangor, William J. Jones:

"An X Certificate for 'corrupt or unhealthy' books in Britain's libraries was demanded yesterday by a Welsh Librarian who has launched a one-man campaign against permissiveness. A new code of conduct for dealing with permissive books should be drawn up for libraries and it could include a form of grading books, suggested Bangor's librarian. . . . He wants to give evidence on the issue to the national committee, set up under Lord Longford, which is investigating freedom of expression in the arts and literature. . . . Mr. Jones . . . told me last night: 'I am most certainly not against personal freedom of expression, but I want to bar amoral conscienceless authors from profiting from and spreading corrupting influences. . . . For years I have earned myself the reputation of being puritanical, but all I want is some clearly defined policy on these books which all libraries can adopt. . . . An increasing number of people throughout Britain are calling for more 'corrupt or just down right dirty' books, and librarians had to make up their own minds how to deal with the demand', said Mr. Jones. 'Librarians are in charge of buying books for their libraries, and I certainly admit there are books on my shelves which I am not happy about. . . . We, of course, choose books with our own beliefs in mind, but librarians are only employees and if their library committees want them to buy all kinds of books, then they must do so'. Mr. Jones said the Library Association also ruled that librarians should buy any books except those banned by law. 'It is quite definite that this type of stuff is growing in demand, but for us librarians it is a matter of conscience. . . . It is for us to decide whether or not this type of material should be in a public library—whether or not it is a waste of public money buying these books'. Mr. Jones report will be discussed by the full city council soon, and last night the deputy chairman of the libraries committee, Mr. W. Trevor Hughes, told me: 'We certainly agree with the remarks of our librarian'."[29]

In his annual report, Jones stated:

"Let it be clearly understood that all I have ever asked for and suggested is that there should be some clearly defined policy in regard to the arts, and, in particular, literature."[30]

The same newspaper article also quoted Eric Luke, County Librarian of Denbighshire as saying:

" 'People are getting fed up with published pornography and there is nothing left to write about as far as obscenity is concerned'. Mr. Luke has withdrawn several recent titles from the library shelves after complaints from the public. . . . 'I have withdrawn them because teenagers who believe that a public library bears the hall-mark of authority must be protected. I have refused a copy of Henry Miller's *Tropic of Cancer* which describes various sexual acts, to an English master who wanted it for a pupil. A book of that nature has no place in secondary education in my view. I would certainly not allow a teenager daughter of mine to read it'. The Chairman of Denbighshire's Library Committee, Mr. Edward Miller, said: 'If people want to read *Tropic of Cancer* they can buy it, but it is not part of our business to peddle filth, particularly to young people in their formative years'."[30]

A Bradford reader suggested in the local newspaper that 'permissive' library books should be classified:

"Regarding the corrupting influence of trashy novels; regrettably it seems that some of the new novels on the public library shelves have reached a stage of vulgarity which the discriminating borrowers find wholly repugnant. If, in this changing society, this type of fiction has the approval of the borrowers in general, it would be expedient to classify these books on the basis of permissiveness, marking the covers accordingly. This would at least avoid giving offence to borrowers who are unaccustomed to this kind of literature."[31]

P. Wilson, of Calverley, replied to this letter:

"What an admirable suggestion made by Mr. T. Grunwell. . . . A splendid idea; not only for Mr. Grunwell and people of like mind, but also for all us poor degenerates who are not in the least discriminating and who are willing, nay, eager, to be corrupted at the drop of a four letter word. When we're weary and red-eyed from desperate, furtive searches in dim corners for the really dirty ones, what a boon to have all laid bare before our lustful gaze, and with a minimum of effort. As the man said, just look for the sign. . . . But seriously, Mr. Grunwell, the best way to ensure the widest possible circulation of this type of book is to advertise its existence. I would suggest that a special classification would have precisely this effect. Hardly a consummation devoutly to be wished by either of us, I think."[32]

With the exception of those in the more rural areas of Wales, most of the cases so far reported in this chapter show signs of strong opposition to the would-be censor and in some cases, his defeat. This trend continued to show itself in most of the remaining cases to be investigated and there were examples of the outright questioning of the role of the library committee and the librarian in this area. A good example of this trend concerned the Shropshire County Libraries and the then mayor of Bridgnorth in the early months of 1972. Councillor Cyril Andrew had been shown a copy of Don Mitchell's novel *Thumb Tripping* by a Bridgnorth housewife "who was said to be embarrassed" by it. In his protest to the *Bridgnorth Journal,* the mayor urged a "clean-up of some of the country's public libraries". His protest coincided with the report *The Pollution of the Mind* by a group of conservative lawyers and presented to the Home Secretary, Reginald Maudling, calling for stronger legislation to control the display of sexual materials in shops and other public places.

> "'Mr. Maudling and his legal group may well include public libraries in the proposed probe', said the mayor, but felt that this would not be necessary if all the books were read by librarians before being put on the shelves of lending libraries for readers without depraved minds to borrow and enjoy . . . . 'Being a governor of the secondary modern school I would certainly be failing in my duty to protect the innocent minds of children if I did not make a protest. . . . It is a crude, lewd, disgusting, degrading and revolting story of dope and unnatural sexual behaviour . . . it should be banned from the shelves of any public library or bookshop. . . . It should be cast into the incinerator together with every other copy that might have reached Britain from the gutters of America'. Bridgnorth Area Librarian Mr. Tim Williams . . . had read *Thumb Tripping* and was quite surprised that it should be singled out from all the books published today. 'I certainly think it is suitable for a public library . . . and don't consider the mention of sex to be excessive compared with the general run of today's literature'."[33]

The following week the *Bridgnorth Journal* reported that the mayor had been joined in the fight by a member of the County Library's sub-committee, Councillor Jack Bowers. Councillor Bowers had read extracts from the book, and declared: "It is just unadulterated filth, anyone who can write it or read it must have a mind like a cesspit."[34] Meanwhile the County Librarian, Miss O. S. Newman had been approached by the *Journal* and had told them that the book would be studied in view of the complaint. But as all copies of the book within the County Libraries were on loan she would have to wait for a copy. It was the first complaint she had received about the book although it had been in stock for a year.

The *Journal* also contained the first letters from readers both for and against the mayor's action. John Fewtrell approved of the mayor's protest, had read the "extracts" and stated that he "would be horrified at the thought of such beastly, pornographic material getting into the hands of my wife and her friends, let alone school children."[35] More letters were to appear and they showed more clearly the number and strength of the protests against the would-be censors. Andrew James wrote:

> "I, for one, do not want my morals protected, and consider it an insult to my intelligence that someone should be asked or demand to do so for me. I reserve the right to be my own censor. Councillor Andrews bases a fair amount of his horror and disgust on the fact that this book may be 'picked up by any teenager . . . and their innocent minds would be poisoned by it'. Unless things have changed a great deal since I was sixteen, those same 'innocent' children are doing their best to

acquire a copy of this book to read . . . as I did with *Lady C* . . . all because of the publicity they were given. While I agree with Councillor Andrews right to speak his mind, may I suggest that in future he . . . stops trying to protect me from myself."[36]

The following week the *Journal* reported that the County Librarian and two members of her staff would be reading the book and would be able to comment shortly.[37] In the same issue "Youth Worker" wrote:

"Would Councillor Jack Bowers and Cyril Andrew kindly get on with the job they were elected to do instead of acting as local 'vice squad' officers. For Councillor Bowers to condemn a book after reading a few lines from it would hardly herald him as a literary critic. His horror of the thought of local teenagers being perverted by *Thumb Tripping* only makes it clear how out of touch people of his age are with the young people of today. A fourteen-year-old has a far more mature and sensible attitude to sex than the average sixty-five-year-old."[38]

On the 28th January, the *Journal* reported that the book would stay in the County Library and gave part of a statement agreed by Miss Newman and her chairman, Mrs. Daphne Gask. The statement Miss Newman issued to the press is worthy of publication in full:

"Public Libraries provide reading material for all ages and tastes. Readers must be given some degree of choice if they are to exercise their ability to judge, criticise and reject.

Reading is a private activity and involves the use of imagination, for a reader must try to understand the author's intention and to re-construct for himself the fiction a novelist has created. It was Mr. Justice Stable who once reminded a jury that it is only from contemporary novels that future generations will derive their knowledge of how people lived, thought and acted in the particular age in which they may be interested. Of an American novel he said that it was . . . 'purporting to depict the lives of people . . . and to portray the speech, the turn of phrase, and the current attitude . . .' and went on to comment . . . 'if we are going to read novels about how things go in New York, it would not be of much assistance, would it, if contrary to the fact, we were led to suppose that in New York no unmarried woman or teenager has disabused her mind of the idea that the babies are brought by storks or are sometimes found in cabbage patches or under gooseberry bushes . . .'

These comments seem relevant to Don Mitchell's *Thumb Tripping* in that the way of life described will be alien to most British readers. Newspapers and television, for several years past, have told us that many American teenagers have opted for a rootless, hitchhiking life, and an important test for this novel and others like it, is whether readers, through their imagination, can accept the characters and the background as authentic. The public library offers a wide choice for those who don't find this aspect of American life to their taste. A book can always be returned and book jackets normally give a fair indication of what a novel is about; the one on *Thumb Tripping* is reasonably explicit.

The County Library Sub-committee has always left the choice of books for the library service to the professional staff who choose with care within the money allowed and the framework of the law; the question of obscenity is decided by the courts and not by libraries."[39]

The mayor, however, was apparently not satisfied and stated that he would continue his fight and was considering what further action he could take.[40] The *Journal* devoted a good deal of space to the controversy and featured an article by Phyllis Peltor, a local clergyman's wife and school teacher. Mrs. Peltor's own view on the matter was:

> "That books, well written, even if they deal with subjects which we oldies prefer to keep private because of our notions of good taste, should be included in the Public Library. I've picked up several that I couldn't stomach—and I just did not read any further, but ditched them. We can all do just that. If they're not banned legally, let the less wealthy who are interested have their chance to read them. . . . and finally, all this sexy business won't directly touch most of us, but I'd willingly carry a banner to help cut down on all this blood and violence which IS likely to affect us whether we live in a big city, market town or remote country village."[41]

However, in a letter published the same day, Mrs. Betsy Murcott, of the Old Rectory, Bridgnorth, put forward the opposite point of view:

> "If we allow lust and perversion in our nation, then cruelty and violence follows as sure as night follows day . . . standards of decency must be maintained if we want a secure and happy future for our children. We must fight these inroads into our civilisation . . . ."[42]

There the matter rested, although Councillor Andrew, after handing over his chain of office to the new mayor in May 1972, was reported to have said that he had not given up the fight and that the matter was "still being vigorously pursued in higher circles".[43] No further action was taken, however, and the book remains freely available within the Shropshire County Libraries.

At the same time as the Shropshire protest, Councillor Harry Grant, leader of Southwark's Conservative Councillors, was leading a crusade against "filth on library shelves" and demanding that a book he found on the shelves of Dulwich Library be submitted to the Director of Public Prosecutions. "I am concerned that we are feeding filth into the minds of our people and I want action taken to prevent this."[44] He was angry because in his opinion, the council had not taken decisive action to keep "dirty books" off the shelves, although the council had issued a report on the matter. The report had stated that the library staff restricted the circulation of books which might be in doubtful taste, but continued:

> "Dealing with books that may shock is difficult and in a world of changing attitudes what may shock one section of the community or one generation will be accepted by another as perfectly natural."[44]

Questioned about Councillor Grant's crusade by the *South East London Mercury,* the librarians of nearby Greenwich and Lewisham were quite definite in their opposition to any form of censorship. Roy Rates, Lewisham's librarian said: "The public should do its own censoring. A librarian's job is not to censor books." Councillor Ian Smith, chairman of the Greenwich Library Committee said: "We leave it to our librarians. I have never had a complaint about any of our books. I am against censorship." The Deputy Borough Librarian, Harry Davis, although admitting that there were some books on restricted access and care was taken in book selection, felt that "most adults can look after themselves. I doubt if anyone is corrupted by what they read. If they are disgusted by what they read, all they have to do is to stop reading that book."[45]

In Scotland, the *Paisley Daily Express* reported that ex-magistrate James Knox was urging the town council to put stricter controls on the type of books they purchased for Paisley's libraries. He felt that the council should set up a committee to act as a "watchdog" on new books being considered for inclusion in the library's stock. Further, he called on parents, young people and educationalists to cooperate in an attempt to keep the libraries as free as possible from "pornography and 'four-letter words'."[46] He went on to suggest that, as a first step, all "possibly offensive" literature already in the library be segregated into special sections.

Ex-Bailie Knox's actions came as a result of being shocked by reading a book borrowed from the library by his seventeen-year-old son. William Foulton, chairman of the Library and Museum Committee, questioned by the newspaper's reporter on Mr. Knox's complaint stated that:

"His committee gave a mandate to the Librarian to stock the library with what she, with her professional experience, considered to be suitable reading material for all readers—with her own personal opinion not coming into consideration." He had "every confidence that she stocks the library shelves with literature acceptable to the public at large."[46]

The Librarian, Miss Alice Brown, replied to Mr. Knox's criticism the following day, the 20th January 1972. After pointing out the problems of a "watchdog committee" in keeping up with current literature, she pointed out that:

"The state of literature . . . had changed. Publishers are accepting that these four-letter words are used. These same words appear regularly in newspapers and books, and on television. The books in a library must reflect what life is about. And we have to cater for everybody in Paisley, and the very varying tastes."[47]

Mr. Knox also ran into some opposition from his son, whose book caused the protest. He felt that there were differences in attitude to censorship between the generations and could not agree with his father's proposals for a "watchdog committee" which he regarded as "too strict."

Three minor events worthy of note occurred between April and June 1973. The *Daily Telegraph* reported that:

> "A book which gives detailed do-it-yourself instructions on how to grow marijuana and use it in cookery is to be published in Britain . . . and is being bought by Public Libraries. Doctors condemned the publication . . . as 'irresponsible and dangerous', but the publishers . . . said the book had been cleared by their legal advisers."[48]

The publisher, Peter Owen, reported that over a hundred copies had been ordered by Public Libraries.

At the same time, Swansea Public Libraries Committee had turned down two requests to purchase two monthly communist newspapers for the library service. At the same time they refused to purchase more copies of the Plaid Cymru newspaper *Welsh Nation* in addition to the copy already displayed in the Central Library. However, the committee agreed to display copies of the three journals if copies were donated to the library for that purpose. There were already seven political journals including *International Socialism* purchased for the Central Library.[49]

The third event concerned Mr. David Holbrook, former Cambridge Don, a "veteran anti-pornography campaigner"[50] and a member of the Lord Longford committee. He planned to organise a conference of teachers and parents to test support for his militant campaign against what was, in his opinion, a "tide of filth." He was prepared to take an active part in the campaign which included stealing "obscene" films from cinema projection rooms, taking "dirty books" from Public Libraries and hiding them, and "raiding bookshops." Mr. Holbrook claimed these actions were justified as "many people are being driven to desperation by the refusal of the government and police to take action against pornography."[50] There appears to be no further record of the campaign or its progress.

Four reports concerning censorship in the London Borough of Richmond Public Libraries have been recorded. The first, in 1953, concerned the *Daily Worker;* but the other three concerned D. W. Cory's book *The Homosexual Outlook* in January 1954, Peter Wildblood's *Against the law* in December 1955 and lastly in 1974, *Gay News,* the homosexual periodical.

Apart from this rather curious, and, amongst the cases recorded in this book, unique coincidence of the continuing censorship of homosexual literature by one authority, the case of *Gay News* and Richmond Libraries is important for several reasons. Firstly, this is the only recorded case of the censorship of a periodical with sexual content—previously only books have been involved. Secondly, Richmond is one of the few library authorities who have produced a definite policy statement on book selection based on the Library Association's statement of 1963, and thirdly, because the actions of the Richmond Amenities Committee in 1974 appear to be a direct negation of their own Council's policy statement.

In 1965, the Richmond Council had considered the Library Association statement on censorship published two years previously and adopted the following selection policy "that 'the function of a library service is to provide, so far as resources allow, all books, periodicals, etc., other than the trivial, in which its readers claim legitimate interest. In determining what is a legitimate interest, the librarian can safely rely upon one guide only—the law of the land . . . .' The Committee agreed that all lawfully published books, other than those of a trivial nature, should be added to the library, provided there was a demand from readers, and that such books should be placed on the open shelves, except in those cases where the Librarian had good reason for believing that unrestricted circulation would be abused."[51]

A request for the Richmond Library to stock *Gay News* was first made in October 1973, when the Amenities Committee decided not to recommend it in view of the limited demand and the lack of space in the Richmond Library, which restricted the periodicals and papers taken to all but the most used.[52] When this decision became known, Derek Jones, the Borough Librarian, received several letters asking for the decision to be reconsidered, including one on behalf of the members of the Wandsworth and Richmond Branch of the Campaign for Homosexual Equality (CHE) and another from a local ratepayer who offered to take out a subscription on behalf of the Library.

As a result of this response, the Amenities Committee agreed to accept this offer in January 1974 and to display *Gay News* for a trial period of six months. The May 1974 local elections resulted in some changes in the composition of the Committee and created problems when Derek Jones reported to the September Committee the results of the six months trial. Despite the fact that the Librarian reported that *"Gay News* has brought no adverse comment from library users, it has been well used, and the Committee is asked to authorise its continued provision"[53] and without regard to the Richmond Council's previous policy statement of 1965, a decision to discontinue the periodical was taken based only on the alleged immoral influences *Gay News* could have.

"At the committee meeting, the strongest opposition came from Tory councillors. In fact, only three committee members were for *GN*'s retention—one Liberal and two Labour Councillors. Brian Bayliss, one of the Labour members, told the meeting that *GN* had only been stocked at the library by public request. 'It should continue to do so. We should not set ourselves up as censors. If this publication was one which intended to deprave and corrupt, the police would prosecute. It is not up to us to make moral judgments'. He told *Gay News* afterwards that the strongest protest had come from Tory Councillor Mrs. Nora Buckley, who had been supported by the leader of the Tory Group, Cllr. Harry Hall. Cllr. Hall, continued Mr. Bayliss, had even made a party issue of the debate, urging all Conservative members to support the recommendation."

"Mrs. Buckley told the meeting that she did not like advertisements for young male models and the 'magazine's' campaign to get the age of consent for gays reduced from 21 to 16. She objected, too, to the advertisements offering exclusive photographs and books. Explaining that she was speaking against the 'perverted sex and subversion' in *Gay News,* she continued: 'We wouldn't put down poison food for our children, and I don't think we should have poisoned literature in our libraries'. She felt that *Gay News* intended to corrupt young adolescents. 'If our council says there is a demand, we create that demand ourselves. Out of 32 other London boroughs, 29 do not have this paper. Why should Richmond feel it has to support it?' "[54]

There was a vigorous response to the Committee's decision from several quarters—from the CHE, from the Editor of the *Richmond and Twickenham Times,* and from readers of that paper, and all opposed to the decision. Ian Buist, chairman of the local group of CHE wrote to Derek Jones expressing his concern, and raised the point that "under the Public Libraries and Museums Act, 1964, the borough is required to 'provide a *comprehensive* and efficient service for *all* persons' and to cater for 'the general requirements and *any special requirements*' of the public."[55] He further pointed out that *Gay News* is the only mass circulation paper for homosexuals. Finally he requested a meeting with those councillors opposing the periodical.

The Editor of the *Richmond and Twickenham Times,* in his Editorial of 20th September 1974, wrote:

"Whenever the local politicians make one of their occasional forays into censorship of material in the public libraries, they make themselves look foolish, as they have done over their majority decision to remove . . . *Gay News*. This is a publication of no great significance or influence, that justified its place in the library, partly by the fact that it costs the Council nothing, but more by the evidence that it was looked at by a number of library users. The sensible thing would have been quietly to let it stay in the library. Mr. Derek Jones, the public librarian, apparently had no reason to believe that it was corrupting anyone, otherwise he would have told the amenities committee so, or removed it himself. In theory at least, there has been in recent years an official liberalisation in the attitude to homosexuals, but the discussion at the amenities committee last week showed the old prejudice lives on in the minds of some people who genuinely believe they are thinking and acting objectively in the interests of society in general."[56]

While accepting that politicians are dedicated people, the Editor felt that they were often out of touch with current trends and thinking. He did not believe that *Gay News* had any corrupting effects, either.

"The number of thumb marks collected by the library copy of *Gay News* is all that should have concerned the local politicians who have no qualifications to go further than that in determining the principles on which a publication should be included in the library, or excluded from it."

In his letter to the Editor on 19th September, Jonathan Compton pointed out that *Gay News* which was not an obscene publication according to the Obscene Publications Act, was placed in the library as a result of public demand and asked

"by what right therefore does Mrs. Buckley take up the role of censor against the wishes of the public? I would suggest she leaves judgment of what is obscene to the courts and would also suggest that the 'poison' she sees in these publications is in her own mind"[57]

Three other letters also registered their writer's protests, although one perhaps rather tongue in cheek 'applauded' the Committee's decision as the revenue of "this valuable publication" would now be increased by new subscribers in the Richmond area who had previously read it free in the library.[58]

Members of the Campaign for Homosexual Equality lobbied Councillors before the Council meeting on 15th October, when the Amenities Committee decision came up for consideration. The Council meeting began traditionally with a prayer—"We pray for those people this council was elected to serve. We pray for the weak and underprivileged who need our support".[59] Nonetheless the Amenities Committee decision was approved by the Council "with the minimum of fuss. But as the result of a question on the issue from Cllr. Worth, the Chairman of the amenities committee Cllr. George Kenton did state:

'There is no reason why the committee should not reconsider the provision of this publication in the future'. A rather vague assurance, and not one from which local gays can conclude that this matter *will* be reconsidered at the next committee meeting."[60]

There the matter now rests, although the local group of CHE intended to press for a reconsideration of the decision, and were taking legal advice to see if it was possible to put pressure on the Council to fulfil its obligations under the Public Libraries Act.

The final three cases bring this history to a fitting, and I believe, hopeful conclusion.

In January 1972, two Lancaster councillors told the city council that they were totally opposed to any form of censorship. Councillor W. J. Corr proposed a motion calling for an end to the policy adopted by the Lancaster Public Library, of keeping certain books which it had purchased off the library shelves. Councillor A. H. Oxtoby, who was also opposed to any form of censorship, said he thought it quite ludicrous that a public library "should withhold certain books from the shelves when paperback versions of the same book were freely available in bookshops".[61] The motion was then referred to the libraries committee where it was later considered. However, Alderman Mrs. M. J. Lovett-Horn, chairman of the Library and Arts Committee reported back to the council on the 23rd February that the City Librarian had "unqualified discretion" in deciding whether books about which he had received complaints should be removed from the open shelves. The council confirmed the committee's decision that the City Librarian should display in the library a list of all those books which he had decided not to put on the open shelves.[62]

Two months later, in March, Mrs. Susan Preston, a Newbury housewife wrote to the Newbury Borough Library Committee, protesting that a book containing "four letter words" was marked "to be kept under the counter". For Mrs. Preston objected to the practice of keeping certain books *off* the library shelves.

> "People do not have to read the books. If they don't like them they can always put them down . . . as a matter of principle. I do not think books should be kept off the shelves. These books belong to us, and no-one, no matter how pure their intentions, has the right to keep them from us on any pretext. . . . Someone is taking pains to ensure that our minds are not tainted (with what, who knows?). Do we owe thanks to these watchdogs? Can't we make up our own minds about whether we do or do not want to read a book."[63]

And finally, Councillor Mrs. Elisabeth Baker, asked the Clwyd Parliamentary and General Purpose Committee at its September 1974 meeting:

> " 'In what circumstances do Librarians remove certain books from the shelves?'.
> 'Do you mean censorship?' asked the chairman, Mr. Norman Cawley. . . . 'Some people would call it that', said Mrs. Baker. She wanted to know whether librarians removed books from the shelves at their own discretion or under direction of a committee. . . . Where had the rules come from for the librarian to take such action? The Director of Administration, Mr. Mervin Phillips, said that the Library rules and regulation which the committee were considering for the Library services in Clwyd did not seek powers of censorship. But it might be desirable in some

circumstances to arrange for some people to be able to have a book when they ask for it, rather than leave it on the open shelves.

The chairman of the Finance Committee, Mr. David Schwarz, said the Librarian and his team, who purchased the books, try to reflect the tastes of the reading public. The Librarians had their own code of conduct in these matters. Mrs. Baker: 'I am not talking about the purchase of these books, but about the books already on the shelves. Where, in these regulations, does it say a Librarian can do that sort of thing?' The Chairman thought it would be improper for the General Purposes Committee to try to take on the work of the Library Committee. The regulations they were considering gave general powers to the Librarian, but his committee would be 'chasing' the Librarian if they thought he was misusing his powers.

But Mrs. Baker fired the last shot: 'I am anxious that each individual librarian does not set himself or herself up as a censor'."[64]

1. The silly burghers of Sowerby Bridge. *Sun,* 8th January 1970
2. Those silly burghers of Sowerby Bridge (continued). *Sun,* 9th January 1970
3. "Rigby". Cartoon. *Sun,* 9th January 1970
4. Robinson, Stanley. The "Sun" and Sowerby Bridge. *Assistant Librarian,* vol. 63. March 1970. p.44
5. A library curb on Billy Bunter. *Daily Mirror,* 13th February 1970
6. The Billy Bunter 'ban'—a storm in a tea cup? *Smith's Trade News,* 21st February 1970. p.8
7. Sellers, P.R.O. Billy Bunter and Ipswich. *Assistant Librarian,* vol. 63. March 1970. p.44
8. Dove, Jack. Yaroo! *Assistant Librarian,* vol. 63. March 1970. p.44
9. Not in front of the children. *Huddersfield Daily Examiner,* 31st March 1970
10. Hertfordshire County Library. *Sex and marriage,* December 1970
11. Sex book guide causes some library frowns. *Evening News,* 27th January 1971
12. Vicar backs library sex book leaflet. *Evening Post,* 28th January 1971
13. Blue pamphlet on sex causes county library shocks. *Hertfordshire Mercury,* 5th February 1971
14. Box, J. B. *and* V. Oh Librarians! *Hertfordshire Mercury,* 5th February 1971
15. 'Sex and Marriage' booklist complaints—investigation. *Welwyn Times,* 5th February 1971
16. Library leaflet censors rapped. *Herts Advertiser,* 12th March 1971
17. Big probe into library sex shock leaflets. *Evening News,* 16th February 1971
18. Sex leaflet upsets public. *Herts Advertiser,* 15th February 1971
19. Sex leaflet goes under the counter. (Luton) *Evening Post,* 18th February 1971
20. Hertfordshire County Library. *Information.* New Series, 96. March 1971
21. Hertfordshire County Library. *Information.* New Series, 97. April 1971
22. 'Obscene rubbish' on the shelves. *Cambrian News,* 15th January 1971
23. Librarian to review offensive books. *Cambrian News,* 30th April 1971
24. People. *The Sunday Times,* 7th February 1971
25. Council rapped for book ban. *Wimbledon News,* 5th February 1971
26. Big row over move to lift Last Exit ban. *Evening Standard,* 6th December 1972

27. Letter from E. J. Adsett, Borough Librarian of Merton, to the author, 7th December 1972. (Unpublished)
28. Move to ban obscene books from library. *Denbighshire Free Press,* 14th May 1971
29. Librarian calls for 'X certificate' to be slapped on corrupt books. *Western Mail,* 16th June 1971
30. Bangor City Council. Librarians Annual Report, 1970-71
31. Grunwell, T. Classify vulgar library books. (Bradford) *Telegraph and Argus,* 18th August 1971
32. Wilson, P. Watch out for the sign of the vulgar library book. (Bradford) *Telegraph and Argus,* 25th August 1971
33. Mayor's horror at 'filthy book' on local loan. *Bridgnorth Journal,* 7th January 1972
34. Filthy library book protest. *Bridgnorth Journal,* 14th January 1972
35. Fewtrell, John. Courageous step by our leading citizen. *Bridgnorth Journal,* 14th January 1972
36. James, Andrew. Mayor's 'arrogance' in setting himself up as library's censor. *Bridgnorth Journal,* 14th January 1972
37. Library reads that 'filthy' book. *Bridgnorth Journal,* 21st January 1972
38. 'Youth Worker'. Library's 'vice-squad' officers. *Bridgnorth Journal,* 21st January 1972
39. Salop County Library. Statement to the Press regarding a controversial book. 25th January 1972
40. Mayor: I'll fight on over that 'lewd' book. *Shropshire Star,* 28th January 1972
41. Peltor, Phyllis. Parents should beware the 'We know best' line. *Bridgnorth Journal,* 28th January 1972
42. Murcott, Betsy. Make a stand on 'What is Right'. *Bridgnorth Journal,* 28th January 1972
43. Library fight goes on. *Shropshire Star,* 26th May 1972
44. The man crusading against 'filth'. *Evening Standard,* 17th January 1972
45. Censoring is not our job, says librarian. *South East London Mercury,* 16th December 1971
46. Four-letter filth in library books brings protest. *Paisley Daily Express,* 19th January 1972
47. Books must reflect life—with its four-letter words. *Paisley Daily Express,* 20th January 1972
48. 'Grow it yourself' book on marijuana bought by libraries. *Daily Telegraph,* 15th June 1973
49. Red newspapers won't be bought for library. *South Wales Evening Post,* 6th June 1973
50. Porn protesters 'may steal from libraries'. *Daily Mail,* 30th April 1973
51. Letter from Derek Jones, Borough Librarian of Richmond on Thames, to the author, 5th February 1975. (Unpublished)
52. Letter from Derek Jones, *op. cit.* See note 51
53. Letter from Derek Jones, *op. cit.* See note 51
54. Goodbye, Richmond Library . . . . *Gay News,* no. 55, 26th September-9th October 1974
55. Protests over GN ban. *Gay News,* no. 56, 10th-23rd October 1974
56. Foolishly un-gay. *Richmond and Twickenham Times,* 20th September 1974
57. Compton, Jonathan. Dull, but never obscene. *Richmond Herald,* 19th September 1974

58. Nettleton, J. V. He thinks it's good news. *Richmond and Twickenham Times,* 20th September 1974
59. Let us pray. *Gay News,* no. 57, 24th October-6th November 1974
60. Let us pray, *op. cit.* See note 59
61. Library's policy attacked. *Lancaster Guardian,* 28th January 1972
62. Call to end library censorship. *Lancaster Guardian,* 3rd March 1972
63. Library keeps 'offensive books' under the counter. *Newbury Weekly News,* 23rd March 1972
64. Why librarians remove books from shelves. *Chester Chronicle,* 27th September 1974

CHAPTER 11

Conclusion

The historical evidence shows clearly that censorship in British public libraries has been widespread during this century. Opposition to such local censorship has been considerable, providing a necessary though inadequate restraining influence. The cases recorded here represent only a proportion of those which occurred in this period. Details of many known cases have been deliberately omitted where they are similar in circumstances and arguments to those which have been described; and there must have been many further unrecorded examples.

Dr. Aitken's statement that "no librarian, no library committee can ban a book" (see p. 70), needs qualifying by the phrase "throughout the country", but the decision of a particular library authority not to take a specific book is censorship in that it imposes restrictions on the ability of many readers to gain access to it. Few readers can afford to buy every book they wish to read. With the disappearance of most subscription libraries, there are few sources, other than the public library, to which readers can turn. The decision by a library to acquire a book but not to place it on the open shelves creates a barrier—some readers may be diffident about asking for books which have been deliberately stored behind the scenes while others will simply be unaware that the book is in the library at all. Also unsatisfactory is the practice whereby a library purchases controversial material but limits access to it by acquiring *only one copy,* the waiting list of readers wishing to see it ensuring that it does not reach the open shelves for a long time. Books have been discarded or subjected to controlled access on the basis of a single complaint and it was not unknown in the 1930s and 1940s for the librarian to decide by interview, whether a prospective borrower should be allowed a particular book.

It is clear that a librarian, motivated by himself or others, can make very difficult for a reader to obtain certain books. This situation reflects both aspects of the *Oxford English Dictionary* definition of a censor: "One who exercises . . . officious supervision over morals and conduct" in that the control is exercised mainly to protect the reader from the book, and in some instances to protect the book from the reader.

There are indeed books which need to be protected from readers: expensive art books, photographic books, motor-car manuals, radio and T.V. repair manuals and so on; theft and defacement are so common that restrictions on access and use are necessary. Such controls are "censorship" by the Oxford English Dictionary definition, but they are absolutely essential for the protection of public property, and maintenance of a good public service. 'Controversial' books are not normally in this category though they are sometimes forced into it where copies have been defaced.

Demands for censorship in the library can come from any of four main sources: individual readers; organised groups; council and committee members; and librarians. Among those who are shocked by what they read, some are content to exercise self-censorship only, while others set out to try to protect other people by denying them the right to decide for themselves. It has been noted that for every reader who complains about a controversial book, there are others who make no comment—whether they are not offended or merely apathetic is a matter for conjecture. Some readers who complain show signs of being publicity seekers or "professional complainers".

Organisations from which pressure can arise are generally speaking those which set out to "do good". It is natural enough that such organisations should attack controversial books in the public library, to protect the young and those who in the opinion of these bodies, are not competent to make their own decisions. Such an approach is something of a hangover from the puritan tradition—but can be guaranteed to gain public attention through the mass media and a significant measure of public support.

Where council members are concerned, attempts at censorship are sometimes politically motivated. A council member is elected by the people to represent them and he likes to be seen to be doing so. He may act in response to representation by individuals or organised groups, or on his own behalf. He may see himself as being in a position of responsibility and authority and consider it part of his duty to protect those whom he represents, whether or not his constituents request him to do so. In some cases, motives are transparently political. A councillor may perhaps propose a controversial motion a few months before he is due to stand for re-election in order to gain publicity for himself. Library books with a sexual content are excellent raw material for this kind of publicity. There is of course, genuine concern among some councillors regarding the young and the possible effect of unsuitable library books upon them, but it has been noted that many councillors do not subscribe to any restriction on intellectual freedom and are prepared to fight attempts to impose restrictions.

Librarians for their part, have been seen to impose their own tastes and opinions under the guise of "book selection". In recent years, a few of them have felt so sure of the rightness of their policies that they have admitted publicly that they practice censorship. These librarians serve predominantly rural areas where local circumstances have contributed to a continuance of the belief that the librarian is a guardian of public morals. Many librarians have no general policy regarding the acquisition of controversial material and they tend to judge each case on its own merits. Some librarians who are in this position may tend to avoid all controversial books, others acquire some while a minority tend to buy more or less all such books. Certain librarians have stated publicly that there is no censorship in their library systems—these systems include Brighton (now East Sussex), Glasgow, Manchester, Nottinghamshire and Shropshire. However, only in three of those mentioned will nearly every book published in the United Kingdom be purchased, and an element of book selection or rejection must exist.

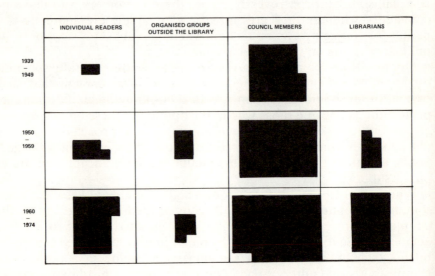

Sources of Pressure, 1939-1974

Examination of many cases of local censorship has made it possible to establish roughly in quantitative terms, the extent to which *direct pressure* on the library, for restriction of access to books, has come from (1) individual readers; (2) organised groups; (3) council members; and

(4) librarians. In some cases of course, pressure by councillors resulted from complaints to them by individual readers. The diagram on page 210 indicates the total number of cases investigated in each category for the period 1939-1974. This period was selected because there was little done before this date to document evidence of censorship in any form.

It is very far from being the case that all censorship in libraries is related to books with sexual content. Censorship of many kinds of books has been noted, the four main categories being: political literature; religious literature; literature with sexual content; and "miscellaneous" literature.

The "miscellaneous" group is necessary to take in the extraordinary assortment of books which cannot be placed in any of the other three categories: the works of P. G. Wodehouse, Enid Blyton, W. E Johns, Richmal Crompton and Frank Richards, books which are inoffensive by most standards. The category also includes a book on dog training, one about the Duke of Windsor, *Picture Post* and *The Sun*. Together the publications in the "miscellaneous" group have received far more attention than has religious literature though there have been cases of censorship of certain religious periodicals and a ban on a novel for reasons involving religion in Caithness County. Religious literature has otherwise caused few problems.

Political literature on the other hand has caused much more controversy than either the "miscellaneous" group or religious literature both as regards books and periodicals but predominantly the latter. The book *The New Unhappy Lords* was rejected by libraries in Wallasey in 1966, while periodicals from Communist countries, political newspapers published by Communist and Fascist groups as well as the more moderate political newspapers have been the focus of demands for local censorship.

Sexual content is the basis of the majority of cases of local censorship noted. In almost every case, only books have been involved—there was no record of attempts to censor periodicals with sexual content, such as *Evergreen Review* taken by some libraries, until 1974, when a case involving *Gay News* occurred in Richmond, Surrey. Perhaps this is because there are very few periodicals of this type which a librarian would be likely to select for his library.

The graphs on p. 213 show the number of cases of censorship ("successful" or otherwise) noted for the period 1939-1974 in terms of the four categories referred to. Some interesting trends are revealed by relating the graph to the account of events:
1. The large number of cases in the "miscellaneous" category during 1939-1941 was primarily due to reactions against the works of Adolf Hitler and in 1941 only, those of P. G. Wodehouse. While these cases had political overtones, they do not easily fit into the political category

and they have therefore, been treated as "miscellaneous".

2. The passing of the Obscene Publications Act, 1959, was followed by a considerable increase in the number of attempts to censor controversial books, partly because of the increased freedom of literary expression which resulted from the *Lady Chatterley* acquittal, and partly, perhaps, because some people did not approve of the intention or some of the effects of the Act.

3. Fears of Communism explain the significant increase in attempts at political censorship during the early 1950s.

4. Some levelling off is apparent in recent years—indeed 1969 and 1970 showed a considerable decrease over previous years. Whether this trend will continue remains to be seen.

There are perhaps implications for democracy in the fact that the vast majority of cases of attempted censorship result from the actions of council members. Although these cases include some in which councillors have acted on behalf of individual readers or organised groups the vast majority show the motivation for censorship as deriving from the personal opinions and tastes of individual councillors. It is fairly clear that some councillors feel that their position as elected members of the library authority gives them the right to exercise their own judgement in matters of taste and morals—in particular, in respect of what their constituents may be safely permitted to read. There are those, for example, who believe that if a book:

"Was considered sufficiently filthy and obscene to warrant it being banned for children, it was sufficiently so for adults. Dirt, or mud or filth is certainly going to leave a trail of trouble behind it . . . no matter whether it is read by adults or children". (See p. 116.)

Equally disturbing is the fact that a number of librarians admitted to being the source of censorship, despite the fact that their professional association opposes all attempts to deny access to books unless to do otherwise would be contrary to law. At the same time it must be admitted that lacking specific statutory protection (the Public Libraries and Museums Act 1964 makes no reference to censorship) the public librarian is in a difficult position by reason of his being the officer of his authority and subject to its direction.

Examination of the many cases of local censorship gives rise to several distinct impressions. In the first place those who engage in censorship are always apparently altruistic—they invariably claim to be acting for the benefit of others. They never appear to show any of the signs of corruption and depravity which they claim are the results of exposure to the material they seek to restrict. Both councillors and librarians are apparently not corrupted by reading controversial books

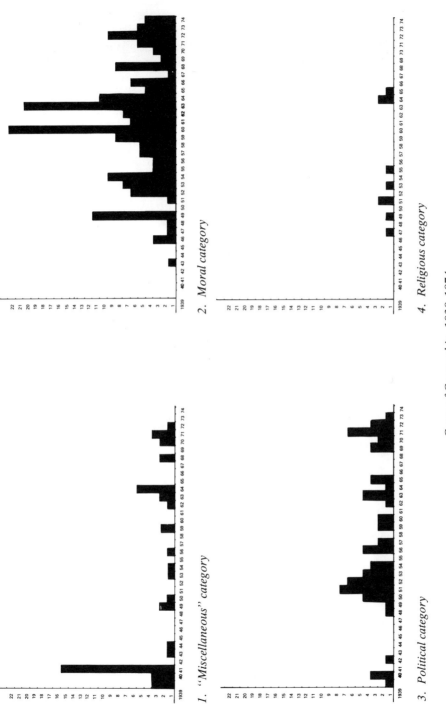

1. "Miscellaneous" category

2. Moral category

3. Political category

4. Religious category

Cases of Censorship, 1939-1974

as part of their duties. Indeed, one report stated that councillors were known to manoeuvre for places on the sub-committee in their eagerness to serve! Censorship carried out by council members and librarians is undertaken in the sure knowledge that those who are affected by such actions can in practice do little or nothing about it. Yet councillors are elected to represent the community and librarians are employed to serve it. The right to make judgements on the community's behalf on matters of taste and opinion are nowhere written in the Public Libraries Act or indeed into any other acts concerned with local government services.

Secondly, all local censorship may be regarded as contrary to the intentions of the Obscene Publications Act 1959. The State, either by not taking action against a book under the Act, or by allowing it to circulate freely after it has been cleared by a court of law, gives tacit approval to the book. Action against a book other than through the Courts, thus means that the self-appointed censors do not approve of the State's inaction. They therefore take matters into their own hands—councillors are in a good position to do so. Inevitably those readers most adversely affected by local censorship are the lower and middle classes. If a controversial book is published in hardback form at a high price or has its controversial passages printed in a foreign language, as in some early editions of the Decameron, nothing is said, but if a book is published in the vernacular at a reasonable price and thus available to a wider audience, it may then be the subject of local censorship.

Thirdly, one of the problems posed by controversial novels is the elusive nature of the line of demarcation between *erotica* and *pornography*. In the opinion of the author the terms *pornography* and *obscenity* have been misapplied by local censors who clearly believe that to be sexually aroused by any art form is wrong. An attempt to distinguish between *pornography* and *erotica* was made by Mary Miles in an article published in *The Observer* in 1972:

> "The word 'pornography' . . . has come to mean 'the treatment of obscene subjects in literature. The definition of obscene in the Oxford English Dictionary is simply 'repulsive, filthy, loathesome, indecent, lewd'. Erotica is defined as that which pertains to sexual love.
>
> This last word, 'love', marks, I think, the essential difference between pornography and erotica. The first treats of sexual practice divorced from any tender consideration for one's partner. Erotica deals with the pleasure and art of sexuality, but always in terms of a positive emotional relationship, whether transitory or lasting."[1]

Alec Craig, in his book *The Banned Books of England,* also attempted to define these terms. Concerning pornography, he wrote:

"There is a large volume of writing devoted to sexual subject matter which makes no pretence to be a contribution to literature and which claims no scientific or artistic merit. Its publication meets no intellectual or social interest except perhaps that of the psychiatrist. . . . The titles of pornographic books frequently advertised the nature of their contents: e.g., *Lustful stories, The new lady's tickler* or the adventures of *Lady Love-sport* . . . . The distinguishing feature of this type of publication is that its sole aim is entertainment by sexual stimulation. Its authors are either strangers to artistic integrity and moral responsibility or have taken temporary leave of those controlling influences. . . . Pornography is in fact no more than a species of a much larger genus of sub-literature which aims solely at entertainment divorced from the higher aims of literature and indifferent to moral and social responsibility. The line between this sub-literature and true literature is not sharply discernible and the better sort of pornography is often classed as literature and the worst literature, if it has a sexual content, is often condemned as pornography. Furthermore, the term 'pornography' and 'pornographic' are often applied to genuine literary and scientific works by people who disapprove of their content or style.

In a recent study (Eberhard and Phyllis Kronhausen, Pornography and the Law. New York, 1959) the authors have attempted a more exact definition of pornography than can result from following the common usage of the word as above. They distinguish between 'erotic realism' and 'hard-core obscenity' and only stigmatise the latter with the perjorative designation 'pornography'. The essence of erotic realism, they say, is the truthful description of the basic realities of life as the author experiences it. So far as sexual stimulation is concerned, such descriptions (by reason of revulsion, absence of appreciation of humour, or other responses on the part of the reader) may have a decidedly anti-erotic effect. On the other hand, it is perfectly proper for the reader to respond erotically to such writings.

Erotic realism, by the author's classification, embraces the erotic works of the oriental and classical worlds, the erotic writing of . . . Rabelais, Casanova, . . . Zola and Henry Miller. . . . Frank Harris's *My Life and Loves* and Vladimar Nabokov's *Lolita* are also included, while D. H. Lawrence's *Lady Chatterley's Lover* and Edmund Wilson's *Hecate County* are instanced as outstanding examples of erotic realism that has been mistaken for pornography.

From an examination of numerous examples of 'hard-core obscenity' or pornography, the Kronhausens conclude that this class of writing can be distinguished by a typical general structure or make-up. A book which is designed to act as a sexual stimulant must present to the reader's mind a succession of erotic scenes which rise in a crescendo of intensity until they culminate in an orgiastic climax. Besides conformity to this general structure, pornographic books may be recognised by the recurrence of unrealistic situations which provide fantastic wish-fulfilment for their readers. . . . the authors insist on the paucity of evidence regarding the emotional and social effect of pornography, and venture the opinion, based on psychiatric clinical experience, that instead of being the cause of delinquent conduct it may more often than not act as a safety valve for anti-social tendencies."[2]

Failure to appreciate the distinctions between these terms is characteristic of many of the attitudes revealed by this study of censorship in public libraries. It is significant that *none* of the official and unofficial reports on pornography published in the U.K. and abroad, including that of the Longford Committee[3], has taken a stand against *erotica,* into which category these controversial novels almost invariably fall. The report of the Church of England's Board of Social Responsibility on Obscene Publications, 1970, while insisting as might be expected, on very high standards, stated that the erotic may be "positively good where the personal relationship and proper intimacy is beautiful".[4] Similarly in the Kronhausens' view, erotic realism reflects a basically healthy and therapeutic attitude to life, and its effects on the average person are generally beneficial.[5]

There are several other aspects of censorship in public libraries, for example, the considerable difference between what librarians and the Press consider to be censorship. Many librarians, questioned about cases involving their libraries, stressed that they did not consider the incidents concerned involved censorship at all. In each case the Press did so consider and generally used the term 'censorship' in its reports. The Press and many readers appear to regard any incident in which a book or a periodical is not bought or borrowed, or in which it is kept in a controlled situation, as a form of censorship. The financial and administrative difficulties facing a librarian, attempting to run an efficient service on a limited amount of money, are often not obvious to Press or readers. It is now widely recognised that book selection is central to the work of the qualified librarian, and that it is not a job for a committee of elected councillors because these do not have the expertise to carry out such a task, although in the earlier years of the century, some committees exercised considerable control over book selection. One of the main tasks of a librarian is to select from the considerable range of new (and older) books and other publications that become available each year, a reasonably comprehensive range of good quality material to meet the needs of his readership. This is termed "book selection" by the librarian, and is governed by two main factors:

(a) The money made available to him by his local authority for book purchase. (This, incidentally, is usually the only variable figure in a librarian's budget. It is liable to suffer considerable reduction in times of economic difficulty *and* is rarely sufficient to meet the needs of the community).

(b) The demands of the readers he is employed to serve. With the exception of the largest authorities which may set out to acquire a copy of nearly everything published in the United Kingdom, the theory of book-selection must start with the basic premise that some books must be chosen and others rejected—even the largest libraries must *select* where foreign publications are concerned.

The distinction between book selection and censorship is not easy to define. If however, the librarian attempts to build up a reasonably comprehensive collection of books on all subjects and of all types likely to be of interest to his readers, and his selection is non-political, non-sectarian and representative of all shades of opinion so that his readers may feel assured that any book of reasonable literary or other quality will be represented in the stock or will be borrowed for him from elsewhere, then the librarian can be said to be engaged in *book selection*. If, however, it is apparent that he is not selecting books of particular types or on particular subjects, then he can justifiably be accused of *censorship*.

The possibility of a librarian who follows a liberal book selection policy, being prosecuted under the Obscene Publications Acts 1959 and 1964 is more or less non-existent. No public librarian has ever been prosecuted for circulating 'obscene books', although one library authority was threatened and gave way (Merton in 1972), and at least three subscription lending libraries were prosecuted before the 1959 Act.[6,7,8] At least two library authorities, Swindon and Birmingham, defied local magistrates; Birmingham even inviting the authorities to prosecute. The Obscene Publications Acts 1959 and 1964 aimed:

> "To provide for the protection of literature; and to strengthen the law concerning pornography."[9]

Although a librarian is, in principle, no more immune from prosecution than anyone else, in that "for the purpose of this Act a person publishes an article who—distributes, circulates . . . or lends it . . .",[10] the Act also states:

> "A person shall not be convicted in an offence . . . if he proves that he had not examined the article in respect of which he is charged and had no reasonable cause to suspect that it was such that his publication of it would make him liable to be convicted of an offence . . . ."[11]

Thus it is highly unlikely that a librarian would be prosecuted for circulating any book which he had acquired through the normal process of book selection and purchase and which had not previously been declared by the Courts to be obscene.

A problem which some people consider arises in the context of progressive book selection policies is that of the potential exposure of young readers to a comprehensive range of adult literature. It is argued that the exposure of a child to a controversial book or a book on sex education for instance, before he is really ready for it, may do the child considerable harm. There is no proof on the point, one way or the other. It is desirable that a child's development should dictate the stage at which his changeover from the children's to the adult collection takes place. He should be aided in the process by flexible arrangements regarding use whereby there is no fixed age at which a child may use the adult library. Freedom to move from one collection to the other and back again will enable him to find the books he can cope with. Such an approach takes into account the fact that one does not suddenly cease to be a child and become an adult. It is unlikely that a child will begin to tackle a subject like sex until he is ready to begin to find out for himself with some understanding and at this stage he should be allowed free access to appropriate good quality material. The fact that there is nothing to stop a child wandering around the shelves of a public library if he so wishes and browsing where he will and indeed, borrowing books from them, remains a matter of concern to some people. For the librarian concerned by this problem, the East Sussex system of forewarning, or the Birmingham "star" system have some value, as the young reader (say of under 16) can be prevented from taking out a book carrying a warning sign until he has obtained his parent's permission. Such an arrangement is similar to the system used to control the admission of children to the cinema.

In contrast to the view that children and young people need protecting from adult material, is the attitude of a prominent Danish public librarian interviewed in September 1972. In his library, no attempt is made to keep literature with sexual content away from younger readers. Indeed, books containing illustrations of a sexual nature are displayed openly in the library where they can be seen by children who are quite free to borrow them if they so choose. The librarian has had *occasional* complaints from parents about books which their children had taken home, but his reply had been that as a librarian he had to stock in his library books on every subject and it was up to parents to exercise control over their children's reading if they so wished. It was not for him to limit any reader's access to these books. This attitude is common to many Scandinavian public librarians.

Study of the many cases of local censorship in the public library field leads to the view that both local authority members and librarians are implicated. The profession of librarianship in the United Kingdom is less committed to the ideal of intellectual freedom than its counterparts in the United States, Canada, Scandinavia and latterly Australia.[12] British librarians need a fresh commitment to this ideal for it is at the very basis of their claim to professional status. The Library Association could well contribute a fuller and even more positive statement than that of 1963. The Library Association and *all* those concerned with intellectual freedom should press for an amendment to the Public Libraries and Museums Act 1964, which would eliminate all forms of censorship.

Such provision is already made in Ministerial Regulations under the Danish Public Libraries Act of 1964[13,14]. According to Danish librarians consulted this has proved to be so effective that censorship in the public libraries of Denmark is non-existent. The Danish Act requires that book stocks shall be selected on the basis of two criteria—quality and complete objectivity. This latter point means that all opinions, however controversial, shall be represented and the reader left to form his own views. The exclusion of books which are controversial but of good quality, whether the controversial element is political, religious or moral, is considered to be a breach of the law and in certain cases can lead to action by the Danish State Inspectorate of Public Libraries. Similar legislation is urgently needed in Britain. Until such time as legislation is passed to prevent local censorship, the Arts and Libraries Branch of the Department of Education and Science might well investigate any cases reported either to it or to the Press. Such investigations would appear to be possible without any change in the law, for the Public Libraries and Museums Act, 1964, places public library services in England and Wales "under the supervision of the Secretary of State".

Finally a scheme of forewarning for adult readers regarding the controversial nature of certain books has many advantages and could be usefully adopted by those librarians who feel that local circumstances require it. There will always be some readers who are shocked by controversial books, whether these appear on the open shelves or not and a small minority of these will attempt to protect others by pressing for censorship. These people have a right to be warned of the controversial nature of certain books—they then have the option of exercising their right of self-censorship. When a book has been selected for the library however, it should be freely available on the open shelves, unless there is good reason to think that theft or mutilation would result. The scheme used by East Sussex County Libraries, whereby a warning stamp appears on the date label of a book considered to be controversial (see p. 180), ensures tnat susceptible readers are forewarned but does not restrict access. A criticism of this method is that it will encourage *some* readers to search out the books bearing the warning stamp, but they too have the right to decide for themselves and it is not for councillors or librarians to question their motives.

It is too soon to tell if the extent of local censorship has decreased as a result of local government re-organisation. There are now far fewer library authorities, and larger library systems than previously. This situation, together with changing concepts in the field of local authority management should tend to lessen committee control, and place more executive power in the hands of officers. Pressure by individuals and groups will no doubt continue to occur, but librarians should find it easier to resist. Problems and inconsistencies will arise, however, until there is a firm commitment to intellectual freedom by all librarians and until legislation makes it clear beyond doubt that censorship by library authority edict is contrary not only to the public library ideal but also to the law.

1. Miles, Mary. The basis of perversion. *The Observer* (Review), 9th April 1972
2. Craig, Alec. *The Banned Books of England.* London, George Allen and Unwin, 1962. pp.211-213
3. Longford Committee on Pornography. *Pornography—the Longford Report.* London, Coronet Books, 1972
4. Church Board of Social Responsibility. *Obscene publications: law and practice.* London, Church Board of Social Responsibility, 1970
5. Kronhausen, Eberhard and Phyllis. *Pornography and the law.* New York, Ballantine, 1959
6. "Suggestive" novel. *Daily Dispatch,* 21st March 1935
7. Changed views of obscene books. *The Times,* 19th September 1953
8. Library banned for obscene book. *The Times,* 13th March 1954
9. Obscene Publications Act, 1959. 7 & 8 Eliz. 2. Ch. 66. p.1
10. Obscene Publications Act 1959. *Op. cit.* 1 (3)
11. Obscene Publications Act 1959. *Op. cit.* 2 (5)
12. Statement on freedom to read. *Library Services of Western Australia Newsletter,* March, 1974
13. The Danish Standards for Bookstocks and Accessions. I. *Scandinavian Public Libraries Quarterly,* 1969, no. 2, p.67
14. Denmark. *Public Libraries Act,* 1965

Index

The index is arranged in four sequences: SUBJECTS, TITLES, PERSONS and PLACES. Entries in *italics* refer to cases of censorship; entries in roman type indicate reports, comments and criticism on censorship. All references cited in the bibliographies at the end of each chapter have been indexed but where a source is not named in the text, the index refers to the relevant page with the citation number given in parentheses. Names of individual members of local authorities involved in cases or censorship have been omitted except when they are cited in the bibliographies.

Index of Titles

Entries in italics are titles censored;
entries in roman are titles reporting
censorship

Index of Persons

Index of Places